T0342101

PSYCHOANALYSIS AND THE GLOBAL

**Cultural Geographies
+ Rewriting the Earth**

Series Editors
Paul Kingsbury, Simon Fraser University
Arun Saldanha, University of Minnesota

PSYCHOANALYSIS AND THE GLOBAL

Edited and with an introduction by Ilan Kapoor

University of Nebraska Press | Lincoln & London

Library of Congress
Cataloging-in-Publication Data
Names: Kapoor, Ilan, editor.
Title: Psychoanalysis and the global / edited
and with an introduction by Ilan Kapoor.
Description: Lincoln; London: University of
Nebraska Press, [2018] | Series: Cultural
geographies + Rewriting the Earth
Identifiers: LCCN 2017049908
ISBN 9781496206800 (cloth: alk. paper)
ISBN 9781496207326 (pbk: alk. paper)
ISBN 9781496208590 (epub)
ISBN 9781496208606 (mobi)
ISBN 9781496208613 (web)
Subjects: LCSH: Finance—
Psychological aspects. | Psychoanalysis.
Classification: LCC HG173 .P78 2018 |
DDC 306—dc23 LC record available at
https://lccn.loc.gov/2017049908

Designed and set in Minion Pro by L. Auten.

Contents

Illustrations

Chapter Summaries

Introduction: Ilan Kapoor: "Psychoanalysis and the GlObal": An introduction to the key concepts that frame this book (the unconscious, the Real, enjoyment, ideological fantasy). It reflects, first, on why the question of unconscious desire is crucial to a contemporary critique of globalization ideology and, second, on the extent to which psychoanalysis can be universalized.

Keywords: psychoanalysis, the unconscious, the Real, *jouissance*, ideology, globalization, political economy, culture, the city, Freud, Lacan, Žižek.

Chapter 1: Dan Bousfield: "Faith, Fantasy, and Crisis: Racialized Financial Discipline in Europe": This chapter critically assesses the racialized hierarchies underpinning European responses to debt and financial crises. It begins by exploring the social and cultural identities that underpin contemporary understandings of capitalism and economic decision making. Bousfield argues that the coherence of European capitalism reflects a Lacanian sense of fantasy that denies the racialized hierarchies that frame European responses to the crisis. Specifically, belief in capital and the European project was used by the European Central Bank (ECB) and the Court of Justice of the European Union (CJEU) to justify imposing market discipline and responsibility on new European members through extralegal decision making. Technocratic responses to crisis deploy a supposed "necessity" and "objectivity" to bypass democratic, legal, and constitutional limits but rest on a vision of capitalism that denies the subjective and fantasmatic nature of this authority. As these "policies of faith" are propagated via European debt and restructuring, Bousfield sees it is necessary to expose their cultural and political assumptions about capital, capitalism, and expertise.

Keywords: European crisis, capital, Lacanian fantasy, European Stability Mechanism (ESM), Outright Monetary Transactions (OMTs).

Chapter 2: Maureen Sioh: "The Logic of Humiliation in Financial Conquest": Financial crises, far from being watershed moments of extraordinary financial danger, are now a common part of life in the era of globalization. This chapter focuses on the Western response to the 1997–98 East Asian financial crisis. In a crisis that saw national currencies lose 75 percent of their value and stock markets wiped out, the international focus instead became an antagonistic and racialized referendum on identity in the form of Asian values. Building on psychoanalytic frameworks used to study narcissistic injury, anger, and psychopathology, Sioh argues that the referendum on Asian values can be understood as contests over the changing place of the East Asian states within the global hierarchy. In addition, Sioh claims that while humiliation is a key factor in enforcing discipline in economic globalization, the West's desire to humiliate was also an unconscious acting out of anxieties as a reaction to the perception of economically and geopolitically ceding its premier international position. Western anxieties of retaliation by former colonial subjects and now erstwhile competitors in globalization erupted in the very aggressive public discourse that highlighted the long-denied racialized dimension of the global economic order.

Keywords: East Asia, emerging economy, financial crisis, humiliation, racism, narcissistic injury and rage, psychopathology.

Chapter 3: Robert Fletcher: "Beyond the End of the World: Breaking Attachment to a Dying Planet": Increasingly, contemporary environmental governance reflects Fredric Jameson's well-known dictum that "it is easier to imagine the end of the world than the end of capitalism." There is growing promotion of capitalist market mechanisms despite widespread claims that in fact this same capitalist system is responsible for many of the ecological and social problems it is now called on to address. Fletcher suggests that Lacanian psychoanalytic theory can help illuminate this dynamic, demonstrating the deep-seated attachments subjects may develop even to situations they perceive as negative and claim to want to leave. He applies a psychoanalytic perspective to arguably the most urgent environmental challenge facing the planet today: anthropogenic climate change. He suggests that, more than a lack of practicable alternatives, it may be our unconscious attachment to the contemporary capitalist order, despite our expressed desire to transcend it, that helps hold it in place. To break this attachment, Lacanian theory suggests that what is needed is the development of a more powerful attachment to a valued alternative, generating the desire needed to face the pain required to sever the hold of the status quo. In short, as Žižek asserts, "freedom hurts" and requires coming to terms with the fact that many of us may not be nearly as willing to make the dramatic changes necessary to develop a just and sustainable world as we would like to believe.

Keywords: psychoanalysis, environment, capitalism, climate change, oil, fantasy, ideology, enjoyment, disavowal, drive, the Real.

Chapter 4: Eleanor MacDonald: "Integrative and Responsive Desires: Resources for an Alternative Political Economy": This chapter argues that, while there are three modalities of desire depicted in psychoanalytic theory, Freudian theory tends only to accord serious consideration to one of these: the "anaclitic" mode. MacDonald posits that the advantageous position accorded to anaclitic desire in the dominant paradigms of psychoanalytic thought is consonant with a particular imagined relationship between self and Other—that of acquisition. In this sense, psychoanalytic theory dissembles Western culture's desacralization of self-Other relationships, while naturalizing capitalism's market ethos. MacDonald suggests that an alternative political economy must not merely criticize the acquisitive and instrumentalist propensities of our culture; it needs also to draw on the emotional resonance of other modalities of desire. These alternative desires are derisively designated by the dominant forms of psychoanalytic theory as narcissism and passivity. MacDonald argues that these latter modalities should be more neutrally and more accurately characterized as integrative and responsive, offering important affective resources to engender counter-cultural responses and an alternative environmentalist political economy.

Keywords: desire, capitalism, political economy, narcissism, consumerism, environmentalism.

Chapter 5: Anna J. Secor: "'I Love Death': War in Syria and the Anxiety of the Other": This chapter examines how the war in Syria props up global circuits of anxiety and enjoyment. Secor argues that the affective geopolitics of the conflict has called forth a masochistic register in which what is sought is the Other's anxiety on the global stage. She shows how the photograph of the dead Syrian child, Alan Kurdi, washed up on the Turkish beach in September 2015, becomes a support for an eroto-politics in which anxiety is the affective experience of the lethal side of *jouissance.* Further, she argues that the eroto-politics of the Syrian war is masochistic; in the debasement of the body as object, its blind aim is the anxiety of the Other—that is, of God. She further elaborates this point through an analysis of a music video, "I Love Death" (2014) by the Syrian performance artist (and refugee) Batool Mohamed. She argues that this YouTube video makes explicit the position of Syrian bodies as the support for an obscene enjoyment, not only within the orbit of the immediate violence, but in the global field.

Keywords: anxiety, affect, geopolitics, Syria, masochism, images, refugees.

Chapter 6: Chizu Sato: "Empowering Women: A Symptom of Development?": Over the last two decades, empowering women has become a popular scenario in the social fantasy of development. While technologies for empowerment shift, today's "smart economics" continues to see women as potentially rational entrepreneurs able to multiply investments through their contributions to their own familial, communal, and national well-being. Mirroring the evolving technologies used for women's empowerment, critical feminist academics elaborate analytic tools that capture these technologies' nature. Yet the tendency of their analyses to remain at the level of unthreatening critique bears investigation. This chapter draws on Lacanian psychoanalytic insights to extend transnational feminist critiques of women's empowerment in development. Sato sees the constantly evolving invention of new technologies of women's empowerment, as well as concomitant critiques, as a symptom of development, that is, as an effect of an intersubjective dialectics of desire constituting women as subjects/objects of empowerment. Through a practice of transnational feminist literacy that attends to the dynamics of negativity, Sato helps expose our relationships with such changing technologies as well as their critiques and offers a possibility for a different articulation of women's empowerment, attempting to move beyond the mutually constitutive practices of those who empower, those who are (to be) empowered, and those who critique.

Keywords: women's empowerment, development, smart economics, transnational feminist literacy practices, Lacanian psychoanalysis, the Real, negativity, enjoyment.

Chapter 7: Lucas Pohl: "Architectural Enjoyment: Lefebvre and Lacan": In a recently published manuscript, Henri Lefebvre develops the notion of an "architecture of enjoyment" (*l'architecture de la jouissance*). Surprisingly, he does not mention Jacques Lacan, although it was Lacan who originally introduced the term *jouissance* to academic discourse. This chapter uses this previously unknown manuscript of Lefebvre as a unique starting point to exemplify a different reading of Lefebvre and Lacan. Pohl discusses the basics of their notions of enjoyment, while giving special attention to the latter's political implications and ways to grasp architecture in its relation to the production of space. Finally, Pohl's chapter seeks to outline the possibilities of an architectural enjoyment. By focusing on vertical architectures, particularly Ballard's novel *High-Rise* and a 2014 Frankfurt building detonation, Pohl's claim is that a discussion of Lefebvre and Lacan can assist in grasping architectural enjoyment to better understand the utopian fantasies and the constitutive lacking structure that haunts a building.

Keywords: enjoyment, architecture, the Real, spatial theory, Frankfurt, Lefebvre, Lacan, J. G. Ballard.

Chapter 8: Japhy Wilson: "Anamorphosis of Capital: Black Holes, Gothic Monsters, and the Will of God": This chapter draws on Marxian value theory and the psychoanalytic critique of ideology in developing a theory of the Real of Capital, which Wilson approaches through an exploration of three of its sociocultural symptoms: black holes, gothic monsters, and divine providence. Viewed "from awry," these anamorphic stains in the symbolic universe of late capitalism reveal specific dimensions of the Real of Capital—as immaterial but objective, as an abstract form of domination, and as the hidden subject of capitalism itself.

Keywords: anamorphosis, the Real, global capitalism, drive, enjoyment, cosmology, popular culture, evangelism, Žižek.

Chapter 9: Nathan F. Bullock: "A Feminist Psychoanalytic Perspective on Glass Architecture in Singapore": The goal of this chapter is to expand the emerging field of psychoanalytic geographies by using a feminist perspective that includes visual analysis to critique the glass architecture of contemporary Singapore. Bullock considers four major glass buildings in Singapore: Marina Bay Sands, Marina Bay Financial Centre, the Esplanade Theatres by the Bay, and the Singapore Flyer. Given that these buildings are largely composed of glass—the defining feature of their façades and construction—and are prominently placed in highly visible locations surrounding Marina Bay—the architectural center of the city—the buildings function as the iconic architecture of Singapore. In their role as icons, the buildings perpetuate the spectacle of the city—its "landscape of consumption" targeted at the transnational capitalist class. Bullock's feminist psychoanalytic perspective characterizes this architectural spectacle as a drag performance.

Keywords: Singapore, iconic architecture, urban spectacle, mirror stage, drag, masculinity.

Chapter 10: Adam Okulicz-Kozaryn and Rubia R. Valente: "City Life: Glorification, Desire, and the Unconscious Size Fetish": Social scientists have spilled much ink trying to understand what cities do to humans. This chapter argues that an unconscious size fetish plays a key role in luring people to the city. Although the city provides many freedoms to urbanites, Okulicz-Kozaryn and Valente claim that it also entraps city dwellers in dreams and illusions. For the authors, urbanization has tended to be depicted as an overly positive phenomenon, especially by economists; there is, therefore, a need to highlight its shortcomings and problems and to understand why people prefer living in cities regardless. Okulicz-Kozaryn and Valente argue that cities have much in common with capitalism and that likely both do more harm than good.

Keywords: urbanization, cities, size fetish, desire, disavowal, capitalism.

Chapter 11: Pieter de Vries: "Corruption, Left Castration, and the Decay of an Urban Popular Movement in Brazil: A Melancholy Story": In this chapter, de Vries reflects on the current situation of disarray within the Brazilian Left, what he calls "Left melancholy," by analyzing, first, the discourse of corruption in Brazil and, second, the history of the decay of a popular urban social movement in Recife. The chapter rests on two arguments. First, Left melancholy is a narcissistic sentiment resulting from a feeling of loss the subject experiences when compromising her desire. The loss of the object of desire (that of radical transformation) generates feelings of guilt and disorientation that are sublimated by a never-ending drive to get things done, as manifested in the enjoyment of corruption and engagement in a multitude of dispersed developmental activities. In psychoanalytic terms, de Vries claims this is a shift from desire to drive: while in desire the object of desire is always fleeting, in drive loss itself becomes the object. De Vries's second argument is that the disavowal of Left desire in Brazil expresses itself biopolitically, taking on the structure of drive and emerging as a by-product of the clash between popular participation and neoliberal market forces. The result of this (failed) encounter, according to de Vries, is the hollowing out of popular sovereignty.

Keywords: biopolitics, desire, drive, enjoyment, melancholy, castration, Left politics, Brazil.

Chapter 12: Ilan Kapoor: "The Pervert versus the Hysteric: Politics at Tahrir Square": The pervert in Lacanian psychoanalytic thought is one who appears to be violating the Law but is in fact simply being incited by it: what looks like a challenge to the status quo is, in this sense, merely a guilt-ridden yet pleasurable acting out of it. The hysteric, on the other hand, is one who is much more deviant and out of joint: she/he gets off on doubting and questioning the prevailing hegemony, thereby posing a threat to it. This chapter examines the recent politics at Tahrir Square in this light: the politics of the perverts (the Muslim Brotherhood, standing for a communitarian religious fundamentalism, and the Egyptian army, upholding a secular authoritarianism that entails further integration into global capitalism) versus the politics of the hysterics (engaged citizens demanding democracy and economic justice). Kapoor also reflects on the broader psychoanalytic potentialities and pitfalls of popular uprisings, including the danger that a politics of hysteria can all too easily morph into a politics of perversion.

Keywords: politics of perversion, politics of hysteria, enjoyment, obscene superegoic supplement, popular protest, 2011 Egyptian revolution, Freud, Lacan, Žižek.

Epilogue: Ilan Kapoor: "Affect and the Global Rise of Populism": The epilogue offers a brief reflection on the recent rise of populist politics (e.g., Trump, Brexit, Modi, Erdogan, Duterte) and its ties to both the unconscious and global political economy. The advent of neo-populism, Kapoor suggests, is further evidence of the need for psychoanalysis in understanding the glObal.

Keywords: populism, the unconscious, global capitalism, demagoguery, loss, fantasy, enjoyment, ideology critique, Laclau, Žižek.

Acknowledgments

Many thanks to all the contributors in this book, whose insights, professionalism, and friendship have made my task as editor all the more pleasurable. Bridget Barry and the production team at UNP have been invaluable to this project, as have the series editors, Paul Kingsbury and Arun Saldanha. I must thank Paul especially—for his continuing warm support throughout and his perceptive feedback on the manuscript. The contributors and I are delighted that our book helps inaugurate Paul and Arun's new UNP series; we wish it much success. On a more personal note, let me express my gratitude to my family, friends, and colleagues (you know who you are), and especially to my partner, Kent, who somehow manages to be unconditionally caring and supportive, while at the same time humorously disarming: a true-life art!

Ilan Kapoor

Introduction
Psychoanalysis and the GlObal

Ilan Kapoor

This book is about the *hole* at the heart of the glObal: it deploys psycho-analysis to expose the unconscious desires, excesses, and antagonisms that accompany the world of economic flows, cultural circulation, and sociopolitical change. In contrast to the mainstream discourse of global-ization, which most often assumes unencumbered and smooth movement across borders, the point here is to uncover what Jacques Lacan calls "the Real" of the glObal—its rifts, gaps, exceptions, and contradictions. So, for example, rather than celebrate the prospect of greater capital accumulation, cultural hybridity, or environmental cooperation brought about by our interconnected world, the book's contributors adopt a psychoanalytic lens to highlight the unconscious circuits of enjoyment, racism, and anxiety that trouble, if not undermine, globalization's economic, cultural, and environmental goals and gains.

The use of the concept of "the global," a term that fortuitously bears a void at its center (glObal), is meant to take account of these chasms and inconsistencies. It is an admittedly awkward term—a notably abstract, adjectival noun—yet thereby helps convey the notion of instability and indecipherability (i.e., the Real) that lies at the hub of globalization. Thus, to put it formulaically, the GlObal = Globalization + the Real.

The contributors to this book, accordingly, psychoanalyze the glObal, attempting to uncover its *unconscious*, which, as implied earlier and elab-orated further later, is mostly synonymous with, or at least proximate to, the Real. They interrogate how unconscious desires and drives are externalized in our increasingly globalizing world: the ways in which traumas and emotional conflicts are integral to the disjunctures, homogeneities, and contingencies of global interactions; the ways social passions are manifested and materialized in political economy and urban architecture, as much as climate change, refugee and gender politics, or the growth of neo-populism (Brexit, Donald Trump, Recep Tayyip Erdogan, etc.); and the ways the unconscious serves as a basis for the rise and breakdown of popular movements against authoritarianism and neoliberal globalization.

Psychoanalysis, the Unconscious, and the Real

If Sigmund Freud (1976) is the one who discovered the unconscious, seeing it as the realm of the repressed (i.e., the domain of primal fantasies, fears, and forbidden desires), Lacan is the one who revealed it to be "structured like a language" (1998a, 11), that is, a site with a logic and grammar where desire *speaks out*. As a result, psychoanalysis is about deciphering the unconscious, listening to and prodding the deadlocks of desire when and where they manifest themselves. Such is certainly the task of this edited volume, and its authors draw on both Freudian and Lacanian psychoanalytic theory (although mainly on the latter) to tease out these deadlocks.

Now because of this goal of interpreting the unconscious as a signifier, the Lacanian variant of psychoanalysis, likely more than the Freudian one, easily lends itself to a cultural practice: one is able read and decode not just texts but, perhaps more important, socio-institutional politics as well, so as to uncover their unconscious desires. Treating the unconscious linguistically, as Lacan does, denaturalizes and de-psychologizes it, wresting it from notions of an inner condition or individual mind. The unconscious is thus constructed as transindividual, so that it becomes part of our subjectivity without residing inside us. Moreover, as Slavoj Žižek underlines, "the unconscious is outside" (1991, 69): since it exists only in relation to the symbolic order, it is always extrinsic and Other (Lacan 1966, 265; see also Kingsbury 2007, 245–46; Kingsbury and Pile 2014, 5). This is why the essays in this collection see unconscious desire (e.g., anxieties, fetishes, enjoyment, perversion) as externalized and materialized in such varying

Ilan Kapoor

social practices and institutions as capitalism, financial policymaking, media representations, gender empowerment projects, social movement politics, or city planning and architecture.

Just as the unconscious exists as the limit to consciousness, so the Real exists as the limit to our symbolic world. "The real is . . . the mystery of the unconscious," writes Lacan (1998b, 118; see also Soler 2014, 19, 57), proceeding to underline the enigma and trauma at the core of the speaking subject. In fact, this idea of the traumatic Real is typically Lacanian, although important traces of it can also be found in Freud (1976), who sees trauma as fundamental to subjectivity. In the Freudian scheme, real or imagined childhood traumatic encounters have lasting impact on the subject's life, including the prospect of yielding to self-destructive behavior. But it is Lacan (especially the late Lacan) who makes the Real so central to the psychoanalytic endeavor (1988, 66ff.; 1978, 49ff.). According to him, the Real is one of three registers that structure our psychical lives: the Symbolic is the world of language, customs, laws; the Imaginary is the sphere of consciousness that provides us with the illusion of stability and wholeness; and the Real is that elusive point of eruption in "reality" that indubitably fissures the Symbolic and the Imaginary.

For Lacan, the Real stands for the gap(s) within the symbolic order, that is, what human animals get cut off from when they become sociolinguistic beings. The Real has no positive consistency: it "resists symbolization," existing only to the extent that language fails (Lacan 1988, 66; see also Kay 2003, 3–6, 168–69; Eyers 2012). Our sociolinguistic reality, then, is haunted by an ineliminable internal void, an always present/absent dimension of lack, excess, or antagonism. And this is why, psychoanalytically speaking, it can be argued that the glObal is ruptured by an abyss: the Real threatens every attempt at establishing a stable global economic order, a unified national or cosmopolitan identity, or a gentrified urban aesthetic.

Importantly, the register of the Real is closely linked with *jouissance* (enjoyment), which refers not simply to pleasure but (unconscious) excessive enjoyment. Accordingly, *jouissance* is treacherous and disruptive: it overwhelms the subject to the point of irrationality, for example, in the way that the extreme skydiver jumps not despite but because of danger (i.e., she/he "gets off" on the peril) or the way that nationalists so enjoy their nation that they end up scapegoating "outsiders" (e.g., migrants, refugees, people of color). Thus, in chapter 6 Chizu Sato elucidates the enjoyment derived by the development establishment in its perpetually inadequate attempts at empowering Third World women (i.e., *jouissance* lies not in success but in repeated failure); and in chapters 7 and 9, respectively, Lucas Pohl and Nathan Bullock underline how enjoyment is central not just to urban gentrification and aesthetics but at the same time to urban degeneration and destruction (i.e., enjoyment in urban growth and renewal goes hand-in-hand with enjoyment in urban pauperization and decline).

The Hole in the GlObal

The Real refers, then, to the dirty underside of the glObal—its holes and excesses—and it is psychoanalysis that helps discern the contours of such ruptures and negativity. So we may well stand wondrous at the "outer" natural beauty and technological achievements of our planet, but the psychoanalytic Real is quick to spoil the party by pointing to our own complicity in globalization's accompanying environmental decay and socio-technological intemperance. The glObal, in this sense, is never fluid or unfettered; it is always discontinuous, contradictory, and unstable.

Such an unsettling view contrasts sharply with what Radhakrishnan calls a certain triumphalism in the mainstream discourse of globalization "as though the very essence of reality were global" (2001, 315). "Hyperglobalist theory" (e.g., Ohmae 1990, 1995; Guéhenno 1995) is notable precisely for its celebration of a borderless world, facilitated by new communications technologies and an integrated global economy. Here, the market is taken as the ultimate horizon of globalization, as transnational corporations span the globe and economic and information flows intensify. Neoliberalism is increasingly naturalized as the ideology of this economic globalization, with its promotion of capital mobility, free trade, and market mechanisms as a cure-all for socio-environmental problems.

There is much to reckon with here: despite the contention that globalization is not just about economic flows, it is difficult to deny that the market drives much of what is commonly accepted as other forms of globalization (e.g., cultural or migratory flows). Thus, Néstor Canclini (1995) may well applaud the cultural hybridity and production of newness brought about by globalization, but as David Harvey (1989, 147) is quick to remind us, newness and product differentiation are synonymous with flexible accumulation. In this sense, capitalism establishes the horizon for globalization, and a Lacanian psychoanalysis would push the point further by suggesting that capitalism is, in fact, central to the construction of our present-day symbolic order as well (see Žižek 1999, 222, 276; Tomšič 2015). This is indeed the import of Japhy Wilson's piece (chapter 8), which develops a theory of the Real of Capital exploring three of its contemporary cultural symptoms (black holes, gothic monsters, and divine providence). This is also the argument of Adam Okulicz-Kozaryn and Rubia Valente (chapter 10), who underline how the fetish for big cities and architecture is closely bound up with the development of global capitalism.

Unconscious desire has much to do with both the establishment and sustenance of such a capitalist global order. As Eleanor MacDonald maintains in chapter 4, "anaclitic" or acquisitive desire is central to explaining the materialistic and instrumentalist propensities of our capitalistic cultures. Rob Fletcher concurs (in chapter 3), stressing that it is our unconscious attachment to, and enjoyment (*jouissance*) of, contemporary capitalism that helps hold it in place. In fact, late capitalism successfully exploits such desire/enjoyment, always ready to offer up new products, which are cheerfully consumed yet never quite satisfy; what is on offer is always lacking in some way, with the result that we continually desire more and better products. And such infinite lack is precisely what keeps capitalism going, enabling it to become vampire-like, in the way that Wilson describes it in chapter 8 (see also Stavrakakis 2006; Kapoor 2015).

Yet, even if market-driven globalization is so dominant today, its gaps, inconsistencies, and excesses (the Real) are never far away. The hyperglobalist celebration of an integrated, borderless world can be seen, in fact, as an attempt to cover over these gaps. The tendency to refrain from problematizing unencumbered capital mobility fits too neatly into the neoliberal mythology of a frictionless world. This is certainly what the globalization "skeptics" (Hirst and Thompson 1996) and "transformationalists" (Hay and Marsh 2000; Held and McGrew 1993; Held et al. 1999) suggest, although of course their argument is not a psychoanalytic one. They accentuate a much more complex and differentiated process of globalization that is punctured by discontinuity, inequality, and unevenness (what we are calling the Real).[1]

An important dimension of globalization that is often ignored is its history, particularly its colonial history (Dirlik 2002). Hyperglobalists tend to assume that globalization began in the 1990s or, at most, that it is a logical or natural unfolding of history (see this critique in Hirst and Thompson 1996, 19ff, 256ff). They thus disavow that colonial plunder was a key stage in the development of capitalist globalization, which ensured the global economic integration of former colonies. It is precisely such disavowal that enables present-day Western triumphalism, perpetuating the (developmental) myths of a level playing field and the survival of the fittest, with Third World countries cast as laggards, always having to imitate the Western model of growth yet always playing catch-up: "globality shores up dominance and continues the anthropological fantasy of maintaining the other in intimate yet exotic relationship" (Radhakrishnan 2001, 318). It is such dominance that lays the background for Maureen Sioh's piece (chapter 2), which contends that humiliation of East Asian countries is a key factor in enforcing discipline in economic globalization. In the same vein, Dan Bousfield highlights (in chapter 1) the racialized hierarchies underpinning the recent European debt and financial crises, as a result of which southern European countries are subalternized.

Seen in this light, the discourse of globalization is a kind of rebranding of imperialism (Halliday 2002, 77), attempting to obscure its many symptomatic ills (the Real), ranging from inequality and environmental destruction to "illegal" migration and cultural deracination (or, to riff on the "vulgar" sexual overtones of "hole," globalization discourse is a bid to disavow capital's unceasing penetration [invagination?] and buggery of the glObe). As Žižek (2008, 102) points out, increasingly we have greater mobility of capital but declining movement of people, with the construction of physical and politico-legal barriers to better and more strictly regulate the flow of people (e.g., "fortress Europe," walls between Israel and Palestine and the United States and Mexico, gated communities, slum cities). The human dimension of globalization is thus greater immobility. To ensure its smooth functioning, global capitalism requires a logic of social apartheid, positioning people as either "inside" or "outside" the formal social economy. It is this other side of globalization—its fissures, gaps, and exclusions—that several chapters in this book make it a point to examine: the "disempow-ered" women of the global South (chapter 6); the favelas in Recife, Brazil (chapter 11); the dispossessed and unemployed in Egypt who rise up against authoritarianism and austerity (chapter 12); and the enraged white working classes that elect Trump or vote for Brexit (epilogue).

But if globalization is often a code word for economic discipline and social apartheid, it is also a cover for hostility and war. The never-ending "war on terrorism" is just a recent manifestation of this, but there are countless other conflicts (e.g., the invasions of Iraq and Afghanistan, the toppling of the Allende regime in Chile, perhaps even the First World War—if Lenin [1917] is to be believed) that are also the product of the violence, inequality, and imperialism that lie at the core of globalization. In this regard, in chapter 5, Anna Secor focuses on the war in Syria and its production of human suffering and refugees. She reflects on the affec-tive dimensions of conflict and migration—their circuits of anxiety and obscene enjoyment—underlining once again the libidinal underpinnings of the Real of globalization. Her intervention strikes a cautionary note for those who too easily rejoice at the greater exchange, communication, and border crossing enabled by globalization: despite human suffering and need, the Other—the neighbor, the refugee, the migrant—is not necessarily a welcome friend. Psychoanalytically speaking, the Other can in fact be a traumatic intruder, whose sociocultural differences trouble or threaten us (see Žižek 2006). As a consequence, the closeness of the Other brought about by global flows, far from being a cause for celebration, can instead yield to anxiety, fear, resentment, or even envy (see the epilogue).

Psychoanalysis, in the way that it is deployed in this book, therefore, is a way of doing an ideology critique of globalization. To the extent that the discourse of globalization constructs an ideological fantasy—"the spread of capitalism yields prosperity," "free trade is beneficial to all," "globalization brings about greater mobility and mutual understanding"—the role of psychoanalysis is to help uncover the Real (excess, anxiety, hostility) that such a fantasy disavows. Following Žižek (1989), the contributors of this book argue, in fact, that ideology can no longer be prosecuted only through ideas; it increasingly requires identifying the kernel of enjoyment on which ideology is founded. In a world where critique is easily blunted or co-opted (e.g., green- and pink-washing, the granting of minority civil rights as opposed to broader socioeconomic or land rights), ideology critique must happen not just at the level of the intellect—identifying its blind spots or exclusions—but, more important, at the level of affects—reckoning with its production, maintenance, and circulation of (unconscious) desire. And here, only psychoanalysis can offer us insights.

Finally, a note about the potential for change associated with such a psychoanalytic perspective: because the Real at the core of the global is so destabilizing, this very destabilization can be grounds for a transformative politics. Unconscious desire or enjoyment may well bind us to (capitalist) globalization, but its excess and unpredictability may also open up spaces for liberation. This is the import of Fletcher's and MacDonald's contributions (chapters 3 and 4, respectively), each arguing for the need to reorient desire toward an alternative global political economy. If our unconscious attachments to the contemporary global order are what help hold it in place, then drawing on other modalities of desire or struggling to turn our *jouissance* to alternative ideological practices may be our only way out. In chapters 11 and 12, Pieter de Vries and I agree with the need for such a reorientation, but we each warn of the perils of so doing: in the context of the local politics of Recife, de Vries pins the disarray of the Left on its having compromised its desire for change in the face of neoliberal

Ilan Kapoor

market forces, and similarly, in the context of Egypt's 2011 revolution, I analyze how a radical "hysterical" political movement is seduced by the comfort and stability of the status quo. Thus, a politics of the Real rooted in the difficult struggle to reorient our unconscious desires is promising but never guaranteed; it can all too easily be diverted by the hegemony of the glObal.

The Universalizability of Psychoanalysis

Before moving to a brief outline of the book, an important consideration is whether psychoanalysis *can* be universalized: is it legitimate to apply a psychoanalytic lens to the sheer diversity of the global? I want to suggest that it is, and the reason is surely tied to the question of the Real (see Kapoor 2014).

Fanon is one of the first to raise the question of the universalizability of psychoanalysis. His work certainly draws on psychoanalysis but nonetheless interrogates its premises. Of particular concern to him is the relevance of the Oedipus complex to the colonized world: he argues that, for the black child, it is not entry into the family but the white world that is traumatic (1967, 151–54). It is the process of racialization, through which the child discovers the social stigma of blackness, that is crucial to subject formation. This suggests the limited universalizability of the Oedipal model of subjecthood.

Several postcolonial critics take their cue from Fanon to make a broader critique by underlining the colonial backdrop to the development of the discipline of psychoanalysis. Indeed, some of Freud's work pathologizes colonial subjects, characterizing them as "savages" and "primitive peoples" in order to distinguish them from their European counterparts (e.g., Freud 1989, 3). In this regard, Ranjana Khanna (2003, 6) states that Europe's national-colonial self "situated itself, with fascination, in opposition to its repressed, concealed, and mysterious 'dark continents': colonial Africa, women, and the primitive." Freud's psychoanalytic perspective thus grows out of a particular time and place (i.e., early twentieth-century Europe) but is constructed as universal. As Mary Ann Doane puts it, psychoanalysis becomes a kind of "ethnography," a "writing of the ethnicity of the white western psyche" (1991, 11; see also Nast 2000, 2014).

There is undoubtedly danger in applying Freud indiscriminately, and those contributors in this volume who do draw on his work are well aware of the previously mentioned postcolonial concerns. Eleanor MacDonald's piece (chapter 4), for instance, is not only sensitive to these worries but centers on the search for other (cross-cultural) modalities of desire than the mainstream Freudian one (i.e., "anaclitic" or acquisitive desire). But in any case, almost all the contributions in this book rely not on Freud but on Lacan, who as we know averts Freud's biological essentialism by reinterpreting his work linguistically. For Lacan, trauma is constructed around symbolic processes, not biological drives or anatomy. Yet, even if Lacan averts essentialism through a linguistic model, there is still the thorny issue of upholding this very linguistic model as universal.

Let me tackle the problem in two ways. First, I want to suggest that, for all intents and purposes, the Western symbolic order has become the de facto global symbolic order. As suggested earlier, through processes of globalization and (neo)colonialism, the West's dominant representational and knowledge systems are all-pervasive (although not unchallenged). Ashis Nandy (1983, xi) contends in this regard that "colonialism colonizes minds in addition to bodies and it releases forces within the colonized societies to alter their cultural priorities once and for all. . . . The West is now everywhere, within the West and outside; in structures and in minds." Psychoanalysis is thus applicable in non-Western cultures, not because of universal categories of mind but because of the history of globalization/colonialism, which has ended up imposing a Western(ized), and increasingly capitalistic, symbolic order.

And second, even putting aside this historically constructed universalism, the Lacanian viewpoint is notable for what can be called a negative universalism, which is represented by the Real. The idea here is that every symbolic order—Western or non-Western, contemporary or historical—is undone by the Real. As Eisenstein and McGowan put it, "There are no transcendent principles that every society shares, but there is a constitutive failure that marks every society" (2012, 69). In the same vein, Žižek writes, "What all epochs share is not some trans-epochal constant feature; it is, rather, that they are all answers to the same deadlock" (Žižek and Daly 2004, 76). The Real is, therefore, a contextualized antagonism: it is not some unchanging and transcendental substance but immanent to every social order, reflecting any such order's inability to fully constitute itself.

This is why Lacanian psychoanalysis can be seen as negatively (or contingently) universal, and hence universalizable.[2] It is sensitive to sociohistorical specificities (e.g., to the different manifestations of patriarchy or perversion across the world or to the predominance of racial over patriarchic law in some contexts, or vice versa), while pointing out the internal self-division of every social order (e.g., capitalist globalization and the glObal; urban landscapes in Singapore, Frankfurt, and Dallas; or popular protest movements in Brazil and Egypt).

Outline of the Book

An important implication of all this is that the traumatic Real that psychoanalysis aims to uncover is not simply destabilizing but productive and creative. That is, as Žižek intimates, social reality is constructed precisely as a response to trauma; it comprises multiple repeated attempts at answering a deadlock (see also Blum and Secor 2014). This is why psychoanalysis maintains that subjecthood would be impossible without trauma. And it is also why it can be argued in this book that the glObal is meaningless without reference to the Real or unconscious (hence the formula, the GlObal = Globalization + the Real). As the contributors contend, diverse global phenomena—from capitalist accumulation and gender programs to climate change, urbanization, and social uprisings—are specific responses to a constitutive loss or lack. So the ideology of mainstream globalization may well be averse to its inherent castration, denying the lack at its core, but our goal in this volume is nonetheless to expose such disavowal, probing a range of unconscious desires and deadlocks. The glObal, in this sense, is an indicator of trauma, and the book's contributors aim at revealing its unconscious underpinnings.

The book is divided into three main sections, each composed of four essays, all aimed at revealing the unconscious grounds of the Real of the glObal. The first section on "Libidinal Economy and Political Economy" interrogates how unconscious desires and drives trouble, and are externalized in, global political economy. The point is to underline that the unconscious is integral to political economy, which is to say that the realm of the market is never purely economic; it always disregards and deviates from its own rules by resorting to unconscious desire. Authors ask what psychic mechanisms (e.g., fantasy, racism, humiliation) support financial crises, structural adjustment, and debt (chapters 1 and 2). They also consider modalities of desire and enjoyment that might help bring about an alternative, postcapitalist global political economy or ecology (chapters 3 and 4).

The second section on "Cultural Anxieties" focuses on how unconscious desire and excess manifest in the global cultural arena. The Symbolic, after all, is the sociocultural order that frames human life and identity, and since it is always replete with gaps and holes, it makes for often anxious and uneasy human exchange and interaction. Contributors in this section examine the eroto-politics (e.g., anxiety, masochism, enjoyment) embedded in a range of global cultural phenomena, ranging from representations of war (chapter 5) and feminist literacy practices (chapter 6) to architecture (chapter 7) and black holes (chapter 8). The question of the Real and its associated circuits of enjoyment are front and center here, pointing to the disturbance and excess at the heart of cultural flows.

The final section on "The GlObal in the Local: Desire, Resistance, and the City" investigates not just how, in today's world, the global is localized foremost in the city but, more important, how the hole(s) in the glObal (i.e., the unconscious, the Real) also manifest in the local. Desire is, in this sense, central to the life and politics of the city, as are the antagonisms of desire, which may open up (or close down) new forms of resistance to globalization. Authors examine the libidinal dimensions of architecture and urban development (chapters 9 and 10), as well as the psychic-political limits and potentialities of popular movements and uprisings (chapters 11 and 12), in specific places ranging from Singapore and Dallas to Recife and Cairo.

Of course, the division of the book into these three sections is neither sufficient nor definitive: the contributors simply wish to highlight some key psychoanalytic dimensions of contemporary global socioeconomic and cultural problems, without thereby proposing to be comprehensive about either psychoanalysis or the glObal. Moreover, the boundaries between each of the sections are porous, for example, with the question of political economy integral to all three sections (as is perhaps made most plain in Wilson's piece on the sociocultural symptoms of the Real of Capital) and with several chapters demonstrating overlapping concerns (Pohl's chapter on architectural enjoyment in relation to Frankfurt, for instance, could easily fit in the last section on the global in the local). Nonetheless, the organization of the book is not arbitrary; it does help illuminate the problems of the Real or unconscious in three important contemporary global realms— material relations (political economy), the symbolic order (culture), and the universal/particular conjuncture (the global in the local)—highlighting the surfeits and ruptures in each.

Notes

1. There is overlap but difference between a Marxist approach (e.g., Massey 2007; Harvey 2003; Smith 2014) and a psychoanalytic approach to capitalist globalization. While both are critical of a neoliberal, frictionless view of the global and both point to the antagonisms, unevenness, and inequalities wrought by the global capitalist order, what psychoanalysis adds to political economy is the dimension of the Real—the unconscious desires that are constitutive of socioeconomic relations and whose excess yields to the inherent crises of capitalism (see Tomšič 2015; Feldner, Vighi, and Žižek 2014; Kapoor 2015).

2. Žižek's work, on which many of this book's contributors draw, can be seen precisely as an attempt at universalizing psychoanalysis. As Badiou points out, "Žižek offers us something like a general psychoanalysis, a psychoanalysis that exceeds the question of clinics and becomes an absolutely general psychoanalysis. This is the first time that anyone has proposed to psychoanalyze our whole world" (Badiou and Miller 2005, 41). I thank Lucas Pohl for alerting me to this quote.

Works Cited

Badiou, Alain, and Alain S. Miller. 2005. "An Interview with Alain Badiou 'Universal Truths and the Question of Religion.'" *Journal of Philosophy and Scripture* 3 (1): 38–42.

Blum, Virginia L., and Anna J. Secor. 2014. "Mapping Trauma: Topography to Topology." In *Psychoanalytic Geographies*, edited by Paul Kingsbury and Steve Pile. Burlington VT: Ashgate.

Canclini, Néstor G. 1995. *Hybrid Cultures: Strategies for Entering and Leaving Modernity.* Minneapolis: University of Minnesota Press.

Dirlik, Arif. 2002. "Rethinking Colonialism: Globalization, Postcolonialism, and the Nation." *Interventions* 4 (3): 428–48.

Doane, Mary Ann. 1991. *Femmes Fatales: Feminism, Film Theory, Psychoanalysis.* London: Routledge.

Eisenstein, Paul, and Todd McGowan. 2012. *Rupture: On the Emergence of the Political.* Evanston IL: Northwestern University Press.

Eyers, Tom. 2012. *Lacan and the Concept of the "Real."* Basingstoke, UK: Palgrave Macmillan.

Fanon, Frantz. 1967. *Black Skin, White Masks.* Translated by Charles Markmann. New York: Grove Press.

Feldner, Heiko, Fabio Vighi, and Slavoj Žižek. 2014. *States of Crisis and Post-Capitalist Scenarios.* Farnham, UK: Ashgate.

Freud, Sigmund. 1976. *The Interpretation of Dreams.* Translated by James Strachey. Hammondsworth: Penguin.

———. 1989. *Totem and Taboo.* Translated by James Strachey. New York: Norton.

Guéhenno, Jean-Marie. 1995. *The End of the Nation State.* Minneapolis: University of Minnesota Press.

Halliday, Fred. 2002. "The Pertinence of Imperialism." In *Historical Materialism and Globalization: Essays in Continuity and Change*, edited by M. Rupert and H. Smith, 75–89. London: Routledge.

Harvey, David. 1989. *The Condition of Postmodernity: An Enquiry into the Origins of Cultural Change.* Oxford: Blackwell.

———. 2003. *The New Imperialism.* Oxford: Oxford University Press.

Hay, Colin, and David Marsh, eds. 2000. *Demystifying Globalization.* Basingstoke, UK: Palgrave.

Held, David, and Anthony McGrew. 1993. "Globalization and the Liberal Democratic State." *Government and Opposition* 28 (2): 261–88.

Held, David, Anthony McGrew, David Goldblatt, and Jonathan Perraton. 1999. *Global Transformations.* Stanford CA: Stanford University Press.

Ilan Kapoor

Hirst, Paul, and Grahame Thompson. 1996. *Globalization in Question*. Cambridge, UK: Polity.

Kapoor, Ilan. 2014. "Psychoanalysis and Development: Contributions, Examples, Limits." *Third World Quarterly* 35 (7): 1120–43.

———. 2015. "What 'Drives' Capitalist Development?" *Human Geography* 8 (3): 66–78.

Kay, Sarah 2003. *Žižek: A Critical Introduction*. Cambridge, UK: Polity.

Khanna, Ranjana. 2003. *Dark Continents: Psychoanalysis and Colonialism*. Durham NC: Duke University Press.

Kingsbury, Paul. 2007. "The Extimacy of Space." *Social and Cultural Geography* 8 (2): 235–58. DOI: 10.1080/14649360701360196.

Kingsbury, Paul, and Steve Pile, eds. 2014. *Psychoanalytic Geographies*. Farnham, UK: Ashgate.

Lacan, Jacques. 1966. *Écrits*. Paris: Seuil.

———. 1978. *The Four Fundamental Concepts of Psycho-analysis*. Edited by Jacques-Alain Miller. Translated by A. Sheridan. New York: Norton.

———. 1988. *The Seminar, Book I: Freud's Papers on Technique, 1953–54*. Edited by Jacques-Alain Miller. Translated by J. Forrester. New York: Norton.

———. 1998a. *The Seminar, Book XIV: The Logic of Fantasy, 1966–67*. Edited by Jacques-Alain Miller. Translated by C. Gallagher. New York: Norton.

———. 1998b. *The Seminar, Book XX: Encore: On Feminine Sexuality, the Limits of Love and Knowledge, 1972–73*. Edited by Jacques-Alain Miller. Translated by Bruce Fink. New York: Norton.

Lenin, Vladimir I. 1917. *Imperialism, the Highest Stage of Capitalism: A Popular Outline*. New York: International Publishers.

Massey, Doreen. 2007. *World City*. Cambridge, UK: Polity.

Nandy, Ashis. 1983. *The Intimate Enemy: Loss and Recovery of Self under Colonialism*. New Delhi: Oxford University Press.

Nast, Heidi J. 2000. "Mapping the 'Unconscious': Racism and the Oedipal Family." *Annals of the Association of American Geographers* 90 (2): 215–55. DOI:10.1111/0004-5608.00194.

———. 2014. "'Race,' Imperializing Geographies of the Machine, and Psychoanalysis." In *Psychoanalytic Geographies*, edited by Paul Kingsbury and Steve Pile. Farnham, UK: Ashgate.

Ohmae, Kenichi. 1990. *Borderless World*. London: HarperCollins.

———. 1995. *The End of the Nation State*. New York: Free Press.

Radhakrishnan, R. 2001. "Globalization, Desire, and the Politics of Representation." *Comparative Literature* 53 (4): 315–32.

Smith, Neil. 2014. *The Endgame of Globalization*. London: Routledge.

Soler, Colette. 2014. *Lacan: The Unconscious Reinvented*. Translated by Esther Faye and Susan Schwartz. London: Karnac Books.

Stavrakakis, Yannis. 2006. "Objects of Consumption, Causes of Desire: Consumerism and Advertising in Societies of Commanded Enjoyment." *Gramma* 14, 83–105.

Tomšič, Samo. 2015. *The Capitalist Unconscious: Marx and Lacan*. London: Verso.

Žižek, Slavoj. 1989. *The Sublime Object of Ideology*. London: Verso.

———. 1991. *Looking Awry: An Introduction to Jacques Lacan through Popular Culture*. Cambridge MA: MIT Press.

———. 1999. *The Ticklish Subject: The Absent Centre of Political Ontology*. London: Verso.

———. 2006. "The Antinomies of Tolerant Reason: A Blood-Dimmed Tide Is Loosed." Lacan.com. http://www.lacan.com/zizantinomies.htm.

———. 2008. *Violence: Six Sideways Reflections*. New York: Picador.

Žižek, Slavoj, and Glyn Daly. 2004. *Conversations with Žižek*. Cambridge: Polity.

Ilan Kapoor

PSYCHOANALYSIS AND THE GLOBAL

PART 1   Libidinal Economy and Political Economy

1 Faith, Fantasy, and Crisis
Racialized Financial Discipline in Europe

Dan Bousfield

In fact, some of the most basic details, including the $700 billion figure Treasury would use to buy up bad debt, are fuzzy. "It's not based on any particular data point," a Treasury spokeswoman told Forbes.com Tuesday. "We just wanted to choose a really large number."

B. WINGFIELD and J. ZUMBRUN, "Bad News for the Bailout"

Macroeconomics textbooks discuss "capital" as if it were a well defined concept—which it is not, except in a very special one-capital-good world (or under other unrealistically restrictive conditions).

H. D. KURZ, *Critical Essays on Piero Saffra's Legacy in Economics*

This chapter explores the relationships among capitalism, fantasy, and the global economic crisis. I begin by exploring the absent center at the core of our current capitalist system exemplified by the Cambridge controversy in economics—or the ways in which faith is central to the functioning of capitalism. I continue by framing responses to the crisis as political and racialized interventions seeking to overcome structural myths that underpin the notions of Europe and the ideology of capitalism. I argue that the Lacanian notion of fantasy is necessary to reconcile the necessarily subjective (and ideological) core of capital with the objective economic practices of global stimulus and austerity in crisis management practices.

Thus, to politicize the ideological processes of the economic crisis, we need to understand the importance of the geospatial construction of racialized identities and the way they are supported by underlying psychoanalytic structures of fantasy.

What Is Capital?

As Marieke de Goede has argued, one of the central questions of political economy today is: What is capital? Her response to this question echoes those who have been wrestling to bring critical analyses to bear on the complex array of institutions, practices, norms, and materials that compose the spatial construction of the international political economy. De Goede's work has foregrounded the way in which currency, finance, and risk are underpinned by cultural and normative assumptions that have emerged through political and social struggles in their formation (de Goede 2005, 2006). However, the political character of this struggle has been largely erased from memory through practices that act as if the struggle never existed. As de Goede argues, "Modern finance, perhaps more than any other area of politics, has acquired a logic of calculability and an appearance of scientific objectivity that places its fundamental assumptions—such as its indicators of performance—beyond discussion and debate" (2005, 3). Critical efforts must attempt to recover the historical practices and fundamental assumptions that constitute contemporary understandings of financial capital and capitalist practices and to politicize the seemingly scientific and professional efforts to manage the economy. This is to challenge the abstracted and totalizing agency granted to this thing called "capital" that utilizes a geospatial imaginary of the center of a system to expand and replicate in ways that are supposed to "fix" systemic problems. David Harvey's (2003) rearticulation of Marx has been premised on these spatiotemporal fixes, premised on the notion that capitalist contradictions trigger these responses. However, as I will discuss later, this chapter argues that the roles of ideology and faith are more strongly linked to identities and social difference than a strictly capitalist focus will allow. In other words, we need to concretize the often abstract and tightly theorized spaces of professional and critical writings

Dan Bousfield

on capitalism that can tend to reify "capital as a unitary sovereign and (all-) powerful agent (or system) [that] does little to clarify the precise ways in which value and entitlements are created and distributed in modern capitalist practice" (de Goede 2003, 82). Situating capital in a geographic and historical context is important in countering the tendency toward overly abstract and structural perspectives on capital in Harvey and others' work (e.g., Frank 1998; Wallerstein 2004; and other world systems perspectives). Indeed, de Goede's efforts to develop the discursive and textual elements of capital draw her closer to the long-standing postmodern engagement between economics and literature and the ways in which culture informs our framing of capitalism (McCloskey 1998).

Inescapable in a discussion of capital is Karl Marx's seminal thesis on the very subject. While I will continually return to his insights throughout this chapter, Marx's interest in the social relations that allow for the emergence of commodity fetishism are of particular importance here. The process of "primitive accumulation" represents Marx's efforts to deal with the translation of capital from one social context to another and the deepening processes of commodification. As Tim Di Muzio (2007) has argued, primitive accumulation foregrounds the inherent social property relations of capitalism in a geopolitical context and the ways in which the abstracted values of capital are imposed through spatial strategies of accumulation. This means that if socio-spatial growth is a marker of primitive accumulation, these processes should be understood as ongoing and continuous, facilitated by efforts to resolve social and capitalist crises as they emerge. And while Marx's insights into the commodity form are of particular relevance to an understanding of capital, in Marxism the definition of capital as "determination of the magnitude of value by labour time" has presented a persistent and recurring problem (Marx 1977). The Marxist definition of capital as the difference between exchange and use value (or the amount of embedded labor in a commodity) does not explain the link between labor and prices, also known as the transformation problem. This transformation problem results in a theory that cannot provide a basis for determining the specificity of capital—its value or price at any given time under capitalism (for a discussion of this debate, see Kliman 2011). Marx's recognition of the social character of capital's value (in the difference between use value and exchange value) limits the extent to which the contingency of social values inform and dictate the specificity of capital. As I will argue later, the central problem of political economy stemming from the question, What is capital?, is the denial of faith and ideology that underpins the abstracted principles of economic planning and crisis responses.

The social underpinning of the question of capital allows for a better geospatial and racialized construction of the dynamics of contemporary capitalism. In their recent works, John M. Hobson and Srdjan Vucetic outline how racialized history of international relations introduces tacit and explicit Eurocentric values into the institutions and structures that govern the international realm. As Hobson argues, the legacies of imperialism are manifest in new efforts to "actively impose cultural conversion of non-Western states to a Western civilizational standard" but utilize policy tools to continue the legacies of imperial policy and to co-opt anti-imperial practices of resistance (2012, 27). Just as the whitewashing of the underlying premise of Eurocentric institutionalism removes the cultural characteristics of Eurozone expansion, the "failed" economies of European peripheral states become the target of good governance and disciplinary practices (Hobson 2012, 325). This is what Slavoj Žižek characterizes as multicultural racism, or the way in which cultural and ethnic characteristics are projected onto the other as a form of patronizing disrespect (2011, 46; see also chapter 2 in this volume). In the context of the European debt crisis, this hierarchy of racialized identity places responsibility for the crisis on the practices and values of weaker and ethnicized states and regards similar characteristics in decision-making states as sources of superiority and expertise. Faith in the European project and the superior values of core states underpins the debt crisis through hierarchal and racialized responses. As Costas Douzinas explains, "The populist Western press describes the Greeks with epithets used in the past against groups considered ethnically inferior. Calling Greeks cheats or lazy is an ideological statement with racist undertones, turning them into the contemporary colonial subjects" (2013, 41). This is similar to Vucetic's (2011) analysis of Anglosphere countries that rely on the legacies of colonial and imperialist mechanisms of international coordination and control, while denying the role of race and imperialism in a system of sovereign states. Consequently, the cultural underpinnings of political and economic coordination are disavowed in times of crisis through the civilizational and historical lenses of identity.

Challenging the Technocratic Vision of Capital

The central importance of the Cambridge controversy in economics lies in the psychoanalytic core of its notion of capital, that is, the way in which it includes issues of faith and fantasy in arguments that are often dominated by dense economic and mathematical expertise. The debate (between economists in Cambridge, England, and Cambridge, Massachusetts) stems from the ability to count "capital" as a thing (machinery or inputs in the production process) and the heterogeneous nature of capital that necessitates its valuation through prices (tractors and apples can be related through their market price). The debate demonstrates that the "quantity" of capital is dependent on the rate of profit, producing a tautological argument over the ability to "count" capital as a material input like labor and land. As Steve Keen has explains:

> The concept of capital as a homogeneous substance is an illusion, and that [which] is capital intensive depends on the rate of profit. If the rate of profit is low, then the labour embodied in an ancient wine barrel is of little consequence, and the process of aging wine might appear to be labour-intensive. But if the rate of profit is high, then compounding this high rate of profit makes the ancient wine barrel of great value—and the process could be described as capital intensive. Rather than the rate of profit being dependent on the quantity of capital, the quantity of capital (in terms of its value measured by embodied labour value) depends on the rate of profit. (2001, 146–47)

As a consequence, the rate of profit is not simply dependent on factors of production but reflects the relative power to control production and the ability to accumulate faster than other sectors in society. The central concern of the Cambridge controversy is the tautological quantification of capital in terms of capital (tractors in terms of apples and vice versa) and the way this creates fundamental problems for the core tenets of the market system (including supply/demand and equilibrium, which is the central organizing principle of a market-based system). As Jonathan Nitzan explains, the inability to define what capital is without resorting to tautology exposes a problem at the core of capitalism: "With the 'quantity of capital' undefined, there is no production function, no supply function and no equilibrium. And with these gone, economics fails its two celebrated tasks of explaining prices and quantities" (1998, 171). The extent of this problem is so potentially devastating that it challenges the explanatory and predictive abilities of economics in general. The truth of this discovery is not that the system is based on a lie, but rather that the system continues to function quite well with this gaping hole at the center of its edifice. People's participation in a system without a core could only be described as an issue of faith. Thus, "the neo-classicists conceded there was a problem, offering to treat Clark's quantitative definition of capital not literally, but as a 'parable' (Samuelson 1962). Some, like Ferguson (1969), even went so far as admitting that neo-classical theory was a 'matter of faith.' . . . While the shell called 'capital' may or may not consist of individual physical inputs, its existence and pivotal social significance are hardly in doubt" (Nitzan 1998, 171). The parable of equilibrium, supply and demand, and the system of market exchange rests on a foundation of faith, which is far removed from daily business reports, the stock market, and global financial speculation. And yet we hear reiterated daily the necessity of this system as the only viable political-economic system for policymakers today. The expansive edifice of economic laws, rules, suppositions, and assertions of contemporary economics rests on their ability to explain the truth that is already known: capitalism functions.

The central ideological issue of the Cambridge controversy returns to overly simplistic arguments that are echoed throughout contemporary discussions on capitalism, namely, there is a social benefit or ethical basis for profit, and the continued functioning of capitalism must mean that it "objectively" works. In the context of the European crisis, the premise of the European Central Bank (ECB) was that, by treaty, it was a limited and restricted mechanism concerned only with the narrow conception of monetary policy disembedded from the economic and cultural concerns of member countries. This technocratic view of central banking is clear and well known, as it insulates the ECB from the partisan policies of government and elections. However, as Alicia Hinarejos has argued, unlike central banks, which operate alongside democratic institutions and national political processes, the ECB operates in something of a "political vacuum," reinforcing the objectivity and supposed impartiality of the bank (2015, 18). Thus, as I argue in this chapter, when the crisis demanded a political response beyond the legal capabilities of the ECB, faith in the "European project" was inserted necessarily (and in a sense, illegally) to sustain the Eurozone area from collapse. As will be discussed later, Germany's legal challenge to the ECB's project of debt relief through Outright Monetary Transactions (OMTs) violated the premise of the ECB to remain apolitical. Consequently, the establishment of the European Stability Mechanism (ESM) was a way to socially stabilize European capitalism by reinjecting a racialized faith into the core of the European project. This racialization of responsibility reflects the social and political power that underpins the technocratic functioning of European capitalist markets.

The desire to develop an objective foundation for policy under capitalism is by no means new and itself betrays the very thing such efforts are attempting to eliminate—an inherently subjective and therefore politically vested foundation for economic development. We should reject the idea that capitalism is based on objective criteria of growth and development, replacing it instead with the insight that capitalism, like religion and the state, has an inherently subjective element, which I will now foreground through the Lacanian notion of fantasy (see chapters 3 and 8). In Lacanian terms, it is the supplement of subjectivity that provides the very consistency and apparent "objectivity" of the world, such that meaning is always ascertained through the cognitive and genetic differences that are unique to each person at a specific time in a certain place. As Žižek argues, if we did not mediate the constant torrent of information bombarding our senses through selective (and therefore subjective) positions, the very concept of "self" would be meaningless (1997, 81). A Lacanian notion of fantasy is important because it helps to explain how the desire for objectivity itself emerges from the processes of identity formation, as truth emerges through the intersubjective formation of the self. Fantasy is the subjective consistency that creates the perception of an immutable other, the imagined place uncompromised by the fallibility and weakness of the self. As Žižek argues, the fantasy "resides in the fact that it subverts the standard opposition between 'subjective' and 'objective.' Of course, fantasy is by definition not 'objective' (in the naïve sense of 'existing' independently of the subject's perceptions); however, it is also not 'subjective' (in the sense of being reducible to the subject's consciously experienced intuitions). Fantasy rather belongs to the bizarre category of the objectively subjective—the way things actually, objectively seem to you even if they do not seem that way to you" (2005, 113).

Thus, while there is a certain sense in tying together the monolithic power of capital in order to attempt to explain and regulate its certainty (its "objectivity"), to characterize that as beyond the subjectivities of the participants is to occlude and reinforce the social character of power. Despite all efforts to the contrary by the so-called troika of the ECB, the European Commission (EC), and the International Monetary Fund (IMF), I want to suggest that they could not overcome the tension between the fantasy of Europe and the racialization of responses to the crisis. Recall that the doubt about the ability of Ireland, Portugal, and Greece to repay their debts was one of the primary triggers of the crisis in Europe, magnified by the misrepresentation of Greece's economy during its joining of the euro. The debt holders—Spain, Italy, and eventually Portugal—were pulled into the crisis, raising the specter of greater defaults across the region, foregrounding the tension with "better off" countries and their refusal to fund growing debt problems. As Hinarejos argues, the abandonment of monetary policy tools as a condition for entry into the euro was not enough to overcome the

Dan Bousfield

asymmetry at the heart of the Economic and Monetary Union (EMU)—the fantasy of Europe was at the core of the crisis (2015, 12). The expansion of the European project was limited by the core countries refusing to allow their new members fully into the European project, a subjective issue that contributed to and expanded the crisis's scale and scope.

The problem of fantasy was exemplified in July 2015, when the IMF began openly criticizing the ECB and the efforts by Germany to pursue policies for its creditors without a clear program to deal with a mounting debt crisis in Greece. As the IMF (2015) memo argued, "Greece's debt can now only be made sustainable through debt relief measures that go far beyond what Europe has been willing to consider so far." In part, this was because the OMT mechanisms used by the ECB utilized market discipline to impose political constraints without debt forgiveness: requiring participation in the ESM, accepting the role of international law in disciplinary measures through a memorandum of understanding (MOU), and avoiding traditional quantitative easing through use of private lending markets (ECB 2012). Each of these efforts was undertaken in a way that pushed well beyond the monetary constitutional limits of the ECB and utilized markets to discipline the aggrieved countries, effectively bypassing traditional forms of fiscal policy (e.g., taxation, spending). Such efforts follow long-standing practices of what has been characterized as "new constitutionalism," that is, "locking in" mechanisms designed to reinforce disciplinary governance by international markets, while restricting available government policies and embedding market principles through flexible legal standards (Gill and Cutler 2014, 7). The response to the crisis is both ideological and geospatially racialized: bad lending practices by core EU states are "responsibilized" onto new EU members who are restricted from access to core EMU mechanisms, while forced to undertake austerity, reform, and discipline through extralegal mechanisms. The July 2015 IMF memo rebuked the ECB and Germany's efforts as nonsensical, using projections of debt that were verifiably wrong, proposing bailout amounts that were not based on evidence, and refusing to adequately finance their own proposals. The public intervention by the IMF highlighted the extent to which crisis mechanisms protected creditors in core European states and failed to address basic underlying structural problems because they could refuse to do so.

The ideological triumphalism of capitalism is well documented, from Fukuyama's "end of history" to Thatcher's "there is no alternative" (Žižek 2014, 8). The underlying issue of determining what capital "is" is thus caught between the subjective experience of capitalism (the necessary decisions by which we constitute ourselves) and our belief in principles, which seem to govern the system and appear to be objective. To the extent that capitalism appears to us as a set of abstract rules and objective laws, we have effectively adopted the position of the (nonexistent) ideal capitalist, one who sees past the social constraints, resistance, and limits in order to come to terms with the ever-increasing deepening hold of the capitalist system. When this occurs, capital has become an issue of faith—a belief beyond reason, a choice made without logic—enacted in our day-to-day lives as something we effectively believe because we are so deeply embedded in the practices and logics of the capitalist system. Thus, we can understand from a subjective position that the effective coherence provided by the absent figures of both "the state" and "capital" or even "God" comes from the accompanying rules, institutions, codes, and conducts by which we effectively show our faith. Imparted by law, order, tradition, and sovereign control, these absent symbols effectively assert their quasi-material status through our implicit and explicit recognition of their importance. The key question becomes not whether God, capital, or the state exists; it is rather, How do we act in ways that affirm our belief in their existence? In ideological terms, this distinction is the difference between the reality of our practices and the "Real" core of capital: "'Reality' is the social reality of the actual people involved in interaction, and in the productive process; while the Real is the inexorable "abstract" spectral logic of Capital which determines what goes on in social reality. This gap is palpable in the way the modern economic situation of a country is considered to be good and stable by international financial experts, even when the great majority of its people have a lower standard of living than they did before—reality does not matter, what matters is the situation of Capital" (Žižek 2001, 15–16).

The depoliticization of belief thus comes not only from the assertion of market principles, but also from the active supposition that there is no viable resistance and no viable alternatives to the central tenets of contemporary capitalism (see chapters 3 and 8). Moreover, these absent symbols mutually reinforce one another, as the logics of order, rule, law, and normalcy are upheld by the sovereign power at the center of the nation-state, beyond the specific and contingent actions of any specific actors or groups. In the case of Greece, the inability of the promises of capitalism to materialize through euro participation is projected as failure of the country rather than the system. As the former Greek prime minister George Papandreou characterized it, "It is wrong to assume that a small country like Greece—which represents just 2 percent of Europe's GDP—could be responsible for 'undoing the confidence of a unified Europe.' The recent crisis in Greece is part of a broader sovereign debt crisis in Europe that, it is true, also reflects a deeper institutional and identity crisis" (quoted in Rajan 2010, 21).

The crisis of Europe should not be thought of in terms of its objectivity, or systemic nature, apart from the participation and belief of its participants. The sovereign vision of capital always relies on an implicit recognition that the subjective interests of its participants are aligned with the supposed system of social order (i.e., subjective decisions in some way conform with the interests of capitalism). In this regard, the hold of ideology and the absurdity of faith in the European project were exemplified in the July 5, 2015, Greek referendum on the ECB bailout/austerity measures. When the populace overwhelmingly voted no to greater austerity, the ECB and the Greek prime minister simply imposed the opposite, a deal that included greater austerity than the one rejected by the referendum. The ideological character of these politics was not lost on the Greek finance minister during the negotiations. He explained:

[The] view was "I'm not discussing the programme—this was accepted by the previous government and we can't possibly allow an election to change anything. Because we have elections all the time, there are 19 of us, if every time there was an election and something changed, the contracts between us wouldn't mean anything. So at that point I had to get up and say 'Well perhaps we should simply not hold elections anymore for indebted countries,' and there was no answer. The only interpretation I can give [of their view] is 'Yes, that would be a good idea, but it would be difficult to do. So you either sign on the dotted line or you are out.'" (Lambert 2015)

Capital here functions in a frame of faith: an indisputable belief, one that overrides principles of democracy, notions of justice, and purported political equality of the European project because the situation of capital is beyond debate. The ideological function of faith is one that grounds an immutable necessity in the available options, foreclosing even the possibility of alternatives. And foregrounding the socially disputed character of capital is a way of exposing economic necessity as theological.

Capital and Power

The dynamic of faith functions ideologically to mask the power relations that underpin, sustain, and benefit from historical and racialized experiences. This has been characterized by Stephen Gill as the common sense of neoliberal "market civilization," or the way in which struggles manifest institutional power that reflects the history of colonization and imperialism. The power dynamics of capitalism necessarily retain a legacy of settler colonialism, the dispossession of the peasantry, and the establishment of property relations over other social values embedded in the processes of primitive accumulation (Gill and Cutler 2014, 30–31). As Gill argues, at the core of these efforts are "processes through which people are dispossessed of their means of livelihood, generating the compulsion on the market for subsistence and survival" (Gill and Cutler 2014, 32). The economic crisis in Europe has seen austerity imposed across countries often in violation of the EU fiscal rules and constitution. Some of those results have included a quarter of the Greek population unemployed, tax reform efforts to change "the culture" of tax evasion in Italy, Portugal chastised for passing noncompliant budgets, and budget cuts in Ireland while the country retains its status as a corporate tax haven (Kondilis et al. 2013, 973; Bordignon, Giannini, and Panteghini 2001; *Economist* 2016; Gravelle 2009). Consequently, the tension between the rights of European citizens and the austerity policies has been highlighted at each step of the crisis. Two dynamics have foregrounded the tension between capital and justice, namely, the constitutional legality of crisis responses and the viability of policies in the context of the European Courts of Human Rights. The first was dealt with by the *Pringle* decision by the Court of Justice of the European Union (CJEU). The EU charter included a "no-bailout clause" (article 125 of the Treaty on the Functioning of the European Union [TFEU]) that prohibited the union from being responsible for a member government's debt. The CJEU ruled that the reason for this clause was to maintain economic and financial security and that the EMU itself existed for that purpose, therefore "discovering" that bailouts were permissible even though the constitution said exactly the opposite (Hine-jaros 2015, 125–26). Second, in the *Gauweiler* case Germany questioned the constitutionality of the OMT program's use of market discipline as a way to bypass the ECB's inability to impose fiscal policy austerity. To simplify, the *Gauweiler* decision asserted that because the ECB acted publicly and has an obligation to purse price "stability" (despite an absence of law or explicit treaty), the decision was lawful. Essentially, the ECB's reasoning was that it is legal because it is authoritative and authoritative because it worked (Hofmann 2015). (It is important to recall here Lacan's [2007] comment in "The Purloined Letter" about the structural logic of signification, where the contingent result appears to be the product of foresight.) The power of faith is reaffirmed through the law and deference to authority. So taken together, the ECB decisions reinforce both the economic reality behind the law and the disciplinary power of markets to enforce market principles on states over explicit treaty and legal authority.

Returning to Gill's characterization of market civilization, this is the creation of a form of private government, whereby the interest in property supersedes or supplants democratic, public, or human principles establishing the supremacy of market relations over all other forms of governance (Gill and Cutler 2014, 7). Gill argues that the consequences of these actions are that the market is the foundation of three dimensions of this new constitutionalism: first, to serve as the source of measures to reconfigure state apparatuses; second, to both construct and extend capitalist markets; and third, to allow measures to deal with dislocations and contradictions from these transformations (Gill and Cutler 2014, 38–41). Austerity is the consequence of power reaffirmed by law and the inevitability of capital.

Misplaced Faith

The problem of responses to the crisis in Europe is a misrepresentation of the question of capital and the role of social struggle in the dynamics of accumulation. This is to challenge Harvey's framing of a socio-spatial fix in defense of capital as an abstract ahistorical process and instead propose the notion that capital is also the object of social struggle. This is the idea in Nitzan and Bichler's work on a "differential accumulation" theory of value that argues corporate control of accumulation manipulates and represents a social claim over future income, one that can change the "quantity" of capital today (Nitzan and Bichler 2009). In other words, a company like Facebook can profit through traditional production processes such as investing in new resources and technology (e.g., Greenfield investment), but it can also profit by purchasing a competitor (amalgamation), reducing expenditure through internal cost cutting, or "sabotaging" production while controlling prices (triggering stagflation)—all actions increase its profitability relative to its market competitors and still increase its claim over future profits. Thus, differential accumulation explains the importance of the power to control and expand the role of markets over social production and the way this leads some actors to accumulate faster than other capitalists and sectors. The greater the level of differential accumulation, the greater breadth and depth of accumulation are both possible and *required* in order to continue to "beat the average." The concept of differential accumulation effectively politicizes the most abstract financial processes of contemporary arbitrage and renders them as a social struggle for control over production in order to control the future flow of profit. Political power, historical trends, and market expectations affect both the perception and the capabilities of the future viability of economic activity. This is why Germany's public debt can be at levels near or above that of Greece, Italy, or Ireland but considered manageable; yet Germany is at the same time linked to the repayment of those same countries' loans (Giugliano 2015). In terms of the European economic crisis, we can see how the aggressive tactics of certain sectors of social accumulation (such as the German banks) can benefit from the statutes and institutions that support their central role in the European economy. These firms (German public banks are the largest component of nongovernment German debt) can exert pressure on other countries because of their historical and racialized notions of expertise, experience, and future viability. Moreover, recall that the trigger of the current crisis in the American housing market came from too shortsighted practices by a sector of the economy that forestalled future profitability by encouraging increased spending and credit in the present (in subprime mortgages). Indeed, much of the success of these strategies resulted from the ability to politically influence the practices of regulatory and government oversight (i.e., Fannie Mae and Freddie Mac) in order to allow and encourage such practices (Cristie, Jickling, and Weiss 2007). Governance and regulation in "market civilization" are effective strategies of differential accumulation for major market players.

Thus, the concept of differential accumulation supports the notion that the capital of capitalism in itself is a struggle over societal strategies of accumulation. In other words, any income stream becomes a potential source of profitability (and of risk, which is discounted in share price), utilizing all forms of socialization to invest, gamble, and benefit from human endeavors. As Nitzan and Bichler explain, "Capitalists routinely discount human life including its genetic code and social habits; they discount organized institutions from education and entertainment to religion and law; they discount voluntary social networks; they discount urban violence; civil war and international conflict; they even discount the environmental future of humanity. Nothing seems to escape the piercing eye of capitalization: if it generates earning expectations it must have a price, and the algorithm that gives future earnings a price is capitalization" (2009, 158). Thus, capitalization is a way of accumulating based on projected future income streams that stem from all forms of human life. As a theory of capital, such an approach encompasses all forms of social undertaking from the minute (i.e., individual choices) to the massive (i.e., debt repayment of peripheral countries). Everything becomes a path of accumulation. In this way, capitalism can be seen as the new form of all social organization, since capital both dictates the path of human development and benefits from the wagering on these paths, differentially accumulating into bigger and bigger masses of wealth through the immortal legal entities of corporations. Unlike neoclassical or Marxist approaches, this framing explains prices as a mechanism of social struggle and social capacity, not tied to the laboring bodies of workers or the desire to explain the social need for profit.

The Myth of Control

The problem of capital as a unitary force is the substitute of faith for an understanding of the historical and geopolitical trajectory of societal relations. The concept of Europe is more than an issue of identity; it is a source of accumulation, profitability, and exclusion. It helps to define just practice, legality, and the terrain of political and social possibility. This stems from an equation of capital as a unitary object with sovereign order, a top-down perspective of control whereby the goal of all power and counterpower consists of people having a unitary identity. Indeed, this understanding of power is tainted by the issue of faith—that the ability to impose order itself is inevitably subjective. As Žižek explains, "Sovereignty always . . . involves the logic of the universal and its constitutive exception: the universal and unconditional rule of Law can be sustained only by a sovereign power which reserves for itself the right to proclaim a state of exception, that is, to suspend the rule of law(s) on behalf of the Law itself—if we deprive the Law of the excess that sustains it, we lose the (rule of) Law itself" (2006, 373).

From the Lacanian perspective, fantasy is significant because its existence sustains the semblance of law, sociality, and order (see chapter 3). This is typified in the concept of Europe, an identity that both justifies and retroactively legitimates decisions made in its defense. Order is maintained by drawing on institutional and contingent power by presenting that power as inevitable and inescapable. Social order is maintained by the transgressions and excesses that are inherent to sustaining order. This is a necessarily *irrational and subjective* condition of capitalism, which stems from the structural foundation of the state's authority and introduces a deeply political and contested core to any assertion of capitalist power. Order is never simply fully constituted, no more than it is apolitical or ahistorical.

More to the point, Marx's notion of primitive accumulation addresses this problem directly and continues to argue that struggle is inherent in the most universalized forms of capitalization. As he argues:

> Direct extra-economic force is still of course used, but only in exceptional cases. In the ordinary run of things, the worker can be left to the "natural laws of production," i.e. it is possible to rely on his dependence on capital, which springs from the conditions of production themselves, and is guaranteed in perpetuity by them. It is otherwise during the historical genesis of capitalist production. The rising bourgeoisie needs the power of the state, and uses it to "regulate" wages, i.e. to force them into the limits suitable for making a profit, to lengthen the working day, and to keep the worker himself at his normal level of dependence. This is an essential aspect of so-called primitive accumulation. (1977, 799–800)

The experience in common between developed capitalist workers and communities facing forms of primitive accumulation is the use of *partisan* political force to ensure the expansion and deepening of capitalist commodification. This means that all power is inherently fantastic: it involves configurations and contingent conjunctures (i.e., the Real) of subjective events that are defined by their inherent subjectivity rather than their moments of abstract similarity. Identification with order as objective represents an effort to avoid the complicated and contested political practices that defy oversimplifications of reason and predictability. Fantasy is important because it undermines claims of objectivity and exposes the desire to sublimate subjectivity. As an extension of this power, politics needs to be seen as inherently fantastic, in that it is capable of projecting a vision of the world that is greater than that which exists. The supplemental belief of society's members is what renders politics possible; there is a seeming cohesiveness, which is split by their participation in processes of accumulation through which the benefits are distributed by partisan, not abstract, processes. Lacanian fantasy provides a foundation for challenging the myth of a universal capital while thoroughly politicizing the nonrational and psychoanalytic foundations of the contemporary capitalist system. However, unlike Jean-François Lyotard's (1993) efforts to develop a libidinal economy, here fantasy provides clear insights into both the politicization and the need for counter-politicization of struggles over capital. Psychoanalysis has not been able to develop a libidinal (nonrational) foundation for economic analysis precisely because it has assumed a totally subjectivized response to the objectifying processes of capitalism (with the body as the starting point). Such an approach misses the way in which *capital itself* is necessarily subjective and therefore politicized from the outset.

There are thus three key aspects of the European response to the crisis and its relationship to faith and fantasy:

1. *Analysis of the problem*: While responses to the crisis persistently refer to systemic collapse, there is little direct consideration of the systemic issues involved in the crisis. Unlike in the New Deal or even after the 1997 East Asian financial crisis, little effort has been made to change the fundamental practices that led to the problem, and the ECB responses only further deepened the role of the market in Europe. Analysis of the crisis could be said to follow Naomi Klein's (2007) shock doctrine thesis in that it compartmentalized any larger analysis or possible connections with other political issues (such as the failure to establish adequate funding for European migration in these same regions). It also follows Klein's thesis that the crisis has led to a deepening of neoliberal privatization efforts and that this response reflects historical and racialized notions of responsibility. When economic crises emerge, existing hierarchies of power are able to hoist responsibility on ethnicized others, so Greek,

Spanish, and Portuguese debtors are scrutinized for cultural deficiencies, whereas French and German creditors demand "reasonable" solutions.

2. *The role of fantasy*: The extent to which the economic crisis was driven by a belief that debt would result in economic failure in new eurozone members sustains a fantasy imposed by core ECB actors. Debt ratios and the need for economic austerity are as much a product of the vision of Europe as they are about underlying economic fundamentals.

3. *The role of faith*: Despite the early and persistent argument about public interest in ECB discussions on the goals of the intervention, the constitutional separation of the ECB and fiscal policy mechanisms is a persistent and ongoing matter of dogma. The notion of fantasy is important here for the way in which it both remakes the glObal through faith, while simultaneously occluding the truth of the mechanisms that expand and contribute to market civilization. The ability to impose mechanisms with no legal or constitutional basis and yet accept limited responsibility for bearing the costs of austerity is a project of historical and geopolitical power. Greek and even IMF objections to the ECB's plan were framed as hysterical and unreasonable. The language of mastery in economic policy occludes the lack of an "objectivity" from any actor in the context of the crisis. As Lacan argues, the hysterical subject is one that acts out against the certainty provided by order (what he calls the "Name of the Father"), trying to occupy the position of authority but without the means to do so (see chapter 12). The geopolitical core of the European project utilizes the margins as the place of failure to impose "good governance." The goal of a (psycho)analysis of capital is to question the core assumptions of the current economic system and to provide an alternative framework of interpretation of these events.

Conclusion

This chapter has argued for the importance of articulating the inherently subjective core of capitalism and its absent center called capital. The Cambridge controversy in economics is a useful way to reassert the ways in which faith is integral to capital "itself" and is apparent in the current economic stimulus efforts. The role of faith and the differential character of capitalist accumulation challenges the ideas that expertise is apolitical governance, which is to say that the subjective and racialized nature of the responses reflect deeper problems in the idea of Europe and European identity. The Lacanian notion of fantasy allows us to develop a response to the crisis framed almost exclusively in the language of expertise. Just as the benefits of economic success are politically manipulated and dispro-portionately distributed, so too are the responses. Capitalism must then be framed in terms of cultural and psychosocial relations, in which the fundamental fantasy of depoliticized economics is disrupted and opposed and in which political struggle is recognized, instead of the apolitical asser-tion of expertise in the face of crisis.

Works Cited

Bordignon, Massimo, Silvia Giannini, and Paolo Panteghini. 2001. "Reforming Business Taxation: Lessons from Italy?" *International Tax and Public Finance* 8 (2): 191–210.

Cristie, James R., Mark Jickling, and Eric Weiss. 2007. *Fannie Mae and Freddie Mac: Scandal in U.S. Housing.* New York: Novinka Books.

De Goede, Marieke. 2003. "Beyond Economism in International Political Economy." *Review of International Studies* 29 (1): 79–97.

———. 2005. *Virtue, Fortune, and Faith: A Genealogy of Finance.* Minneapolis: University of Minnesota Press.

———. 2006. *International Political Economy and Poststructural Politics.* New York: Palgrave Macmillan.

Di Muzio, Tim. 2007. "The 'Art' of Colonisation: Capitalising Sovereign Power and the Ongoing Nature of Primitive Accumulation." *New Political Economy* 12 (4): 517–39.

Douzinas, Costas. 2013. *Philosophy and Resistance in the Crisis: Greece and the Future of Europe.* Cambridge: Polity.

Economist. 2016. "Fudging the Revolution." February 20. http://www.economist.com /news/europe/21693250-italy-and-portugal-are-leading-revolt-against-eu-austerity -sort-fudging-revolution.

European Central Bank. 2012. "Technical Features of Outright Monetary Transactions." Press release, September 6. http://www.ecb.europa.eu/press/pr/date/2012/html /pr120906_1.en.html.

Ferguson, Charles E. 1969. *The Neoclassical Theory of Production and Distribution.* Cam-bridge: Cambridge University Press.

Frank, Andre Gunder. 1998. *ReOrient: Global Economy in the Asian Age*. Berkeley: University of California Press.

Gill, Stephen, and A. Claire Cutler, eds. 2014. *New Constitutionalism and World Order*. Cambridge: Cambridge University Press.

Giugliano, Ferdinando. 2015. "Does Germany Have a Bigger Public Debt Problem than Greece?" *The World* (blog), *Financial Times*. February 11. http://blogs.ft.com/the-world /2015/02/does-germany-have-a-bigger-public-debt-problem-than-greece/.

Gravelle, Jane. G. 2009. "Tax Havens: International Tax Avoidance and Evasion." *National Tax Journal* 62 (4): 727–53.

Harvey, David. 2003. *The New Imperialism*. Oxford: Oxford University Press.

Hinarejos, Alicia. 2015. *The Euro Area Crisis in Constitutional Perspective*. Oxford: Oxford University Press.

Hobson, John M. 2012. *The Eurocentric Conception of World Politics: Western International Theory, 1760–2010*. Cambridge: Cambridge University Press.

Hofmann, Herwig. 2015. "Gauweiler and OMT: Lessons for EU Public Law and the European Economic and Monetary Union." Research paper, Universite du Luxembourg. SSRN (2621933). https://ssrn.com/abstract=2621933.

International Monetary Fund. 2015. "Greece." IMF Country Report No. 15/186, July 14. http://www.imf.org/external/pubs/ft/scr/2015/cr15186.pdf.

Keen, Steve. 2001. *Debunking Economics: The Naked Emperor of the Social Sciences*. London: Zed Books.

Klein, Naomi. 2007. *The Shock Doctrine: The Rise of Disaster Capitalism*. London: Macmillan.

Kliman, Andrew. 2011. "Values and Crisis: Bichler and Nitzan versus Marx." *Journal of Critical Globalization Studies* 1 (4): 61–92.

Kondilis, Elias, Stathis Giannakopoulos, Magda Gavana, Ioanna Ierodiakonou, Howard Waitzkin, and Alexis Benos. 2013. "Economic Crisis, Restrictive Policies, and the Population's Health and Health Care: The Greek Case." *American Journal of Public Health* 103 (6): 973–80.

Kurz, Heinz D., ed. 2000. *Critical Essays on Piero Saffra's Legacy in Economics*. Cambridge: Cambridge University Press.

Lacan, Jacques. 2007. *Écrits: The First Complete Edition in English*. Translated by Bruce Fink. New York: Norton.

Lambert, Harry. 2015. "Yanis Varoufakis Full Transcript: Our Battle to Save Greece." *New Statesman*. July 13. http://www.newstatesman.com/world-affairs/2015/07/yanis-varoufakis -full-transcript-our-battle-save-greece.

Lyotard, Jean-François. 1993. *Libidinal Economy*. London: Athlone Press.

Marx, Karl. 1977. *Capital: A Critique of Political Economy*. Introduction by Ernest Mandel. London: Penguin Books.

McCloskey, Deirdre N. 1998. *The Rhetoric of Economics (Rhetoric of the Human Sciences)*. 2nd ed. Madison: University of Wisconsin Press.

Nitzan, Jonathan. 1998. "Differential Accumulation: Towards a New Political Economy of Capital." *Review of International Political Economy* 5 (2): 169–216.

Nitzan, Jonathan, and Shimshon Bichler. 2009. *Capital as Power: A Study of Order and Creorder*. London: Routledge.

Rajan, Rahguram G. 2010. "Rebalancing the Global Economy." *New Perspectives Quarterly* 27 (4): 7–9.

Samuelson, Paul A. 1962. "Parable and Realism in Capital Theory: The Surrogate Production Function." *Review of Economic Studies* 29 (3), 193–206.

Vucetic, Srdjan. 2011. *The Anglosphere: A Genealogy of a Racialized Identity in International Relations*. Stanford CA: Stanford University Press.

Wallerstein, Immanuel M. 2004. *World-Systems Analysis: An Introduction*. Durham NC: Duke University Press.

Wingfield, Brian, and Josh Zumbrun. 2008. "Bad News for the Bailout." *Forbes*, September 23. http://www.forbes.com/2008/09/23/bailout-paulson-congress-biz-beltway-cx_jz_bw_0923bailout.html.

Žižek, Slavoj. 1997. *The Plague of Fantasies*. London: Verso.

———. 2001. *The Fragile Absolute: Or, Why Is the Christian Legacy Worth Fighting for?* New York: Verso.

———. 2005. *Interrogating the Real*. Edited by Rex Butler and Scott Stephens. New York: Continuum.

———. 2006. *The Parallax View*. Cambridge MA: MIT Press.

———. 2011. *Living in the End Times*. New York: Verso.

———. 2014. *Trouble in Paradise: From the End of History to the End of Capitalism*. London: Penguin UK.

Dan Bousfield

2 The Logic of Humiliation in Financial Conquest

Maureen Sioh

Their neighbour for them is not only a potential helper or
sexual object, but also someone who tempts them to satisfy
their aggressiveness on him, to exploit his capacity for work
without compensation, to use him sexually without his con-
sent, to seize his possessions, to humiliate him, to cause him
pain, to torture and to kill him.

FREUD, *Civilization and Its Discontents*

This chapter focuses on the Western response to the Malaysian government's controversial decision to defy the international financial community by implementing currency controls during the 1997–98 East Asian financial crisis. In the chapter, "Western" refers mainly to Anglo-American commentators as well as representatives of global institutions such as the International Monetary Fund (IMF) and World Bank. Financial crises, far from being watershed moments of extraordinary financial danger, are now a common part of life in the era of globalization. The coverage of the current Greek crisis is notable, among other things, for the preponderance of the use of the word "humiliation" to describe the negotiations between the troika (comprising the European Central Bank, the European Commission, and the IMF) and Greece on the Greek repayment schedule (Matteo Renzi, quoted in Halimi 2015, 2; Nougayréde 2015; Smith 2015). Former Greek finance minister Yanis Varoufakis has described the €86 billion bailout deal agreed to by Prime Minister Alexis Tsipras as "a new Versailles Treaty" and as "the politics of humiliation" (McClintock 2015).

For East Asian observers, the coverage of the Greek crisis may seem like "dreaming a never-ending nightmare over again" (Shin 2015, 76). Paul Krugman describes global governance institutions such as the troika as "learning nothing from experience" (2015, para. 7), implying repetitive neurotic behavior that does not succeed in achieving its stated aims. Joseph Stiglitz (2001, xiv; 2006; 2015) has long noted that the Asian financial crisis was the forerunner of the modern financial crisis and the subsequent international response, particularly in the concerted attempts to roll back the sovereignty of the state.

I revisit the 1997–98 East Asian financial crisis to examine the psychoanalytic mechanisms underpinning the externally imposed punitive political and economic restructuring in the affected countries. The East Asian crisis saw national currencies lose 75 percent of their value and stock markets wiped out, and it became an antagonistic and racialized referendum on "Asian values" between certain Asian governments and their Western critics. Asian values is a concept vaunted by several East Asian governments in reference to Asian societies' prioritizing the role of community and family over the individual, order and harmony over personal freedom, while also upholding such social values as thriftiness, hard work, and respect for authority (Mahbubani 2002, 31). I argue that the debate over Asian values can be understood as contests over the changing place of the East Asian emerging economies within the global hierarchy. These contests reflected the psychoanalytic challenge and defense of the conventional hierarchy of international relations that followed its symbolic disruption due to the success of regional Asian economies before the crisis. Until the financial crisis, East Asian countries were perceived as models of the promised land of development theory (Ghesquire 2007, ix). While the World Bank (Birdsall et al. 1993) attributed their success to their embrace of free-market export-oriented production, East Asian governments equally attributed their success to state intervention, in the form of the developmental state and Asian values. The developmental state is one in which the political elites influence the direction and pace of economic development by directly intervening in the development process through policy activism (Beeson

Maureen Sioh

2004, 30). The developmental state was already considered a challenge to free-market economic principles, but even more controversially, it came to be associated with Asian values by both its proponents and its critics. While the East Asian governments invoked Asian values as the cultural basis of their success (Mahathir and Shintaro 1995; Mahbubani 2002), their critics invoked Asian values as a linguistic code to conjure images of corruption, greed, and general dishonesty (see essays in Goodman, Kwon, and White 1998; Bell 2000; Barr 2002).

My question is not whether a discernible set of Asian values exists, but rather, what is the geopolitical significance of the deployment of the concept of Asian values by its proponents and critics? During the crisis, the IMF-imposed financial restructuring (more commonly known as austerity and deregulation programs) occurred in tandem with a humiliating, racially pejorative commentary. Economic choices are seen as belonging to the domain of rationality, yet in the case of the East Asian financial crisis, the public discourse consistently transformed economic decisions into cultural and, more significantly, emotional battlegrounds. I argue that the emotional force surrounding these decisions on the side of their proponents and detractors can only be explained by examining the contests and negotiations that take place in the parallel narratives that foreground issues of race and identity. Group conceptions such as race may be cultural constructs, but they are important because development has come to be viewed as the potential of a group or region to progress (Kasese-Hara 2004, 545). And development is still commonly equated with economic growth. Finance, race, and human worth are yoked together in a relationship of logical equivalence. This raises the stakes for economic growth.

The chapter uses a psychoanalytic framework to examine the unofficial discourses that parallel the economic debates on the region's monetary policy to elicit the real, politically charged responses. I work with Heinz Kohut's (1973) framework of narcissistic injury and anger and Christopher Bollas's (2011) framework of psychopathology to analyze financial crises as the outcome of displacements of the libidinal economy in globalization. In particular, I analyze the use of humiliation to enforce discipline in economic globalization. When I began this research, I set out to argue that humiliation, even more than material austerity, is the key factor in inducing the psychic regression that leaves the targeted countries open to an identity compliant with the neoliberal aims of economic restructuring. But this opens up the question, who was supposed to be implementing the strategy? And did Western pundits and representatives of global governance institutions have anything in common to allow them to coordinate such a strategy? After all, there is a distinction between official IMF figures (e.g., Michel Camdessus and Stanley Fischer) and Western media pundits. Yet the surprising issue was how much the discourse of humiliation is repeated and deployed among all these figures. Perhaps what is often overlooked is that these figures have a cultural and geopolitical location as much as a professional location. Moreover, coordination implies a conscious effort, which presupposes a mastery of a situation. Instead, as we shall see, every attribute of narcissistic injury and anger appeared present in the behavior of the perpetrators of the humiliation. This is not to say that the humiliation did not anger the East Asians governments, or for that matter, the general population, but that the desire to humiliate was an act of aggression by the West that needed explaining. I want to suggest that the strategy to humiliate was not a covertly conscious attempt at economic discipline but rather an unconscious acting out of anxieties by the West, a reaction to the perception of economically and geopolitically ceding its premier international position (see chapter 1). These anxieties resulted from the changes that began the move to a postindustrial economy in the 1970s in the West as part of what David Harvey (1989) calls the "spatial fix" of globalization to ensure continuing profits for Western capital. Harvey (1982) uses the term "spatial fix" to describe the tendency of Western capital, when confronted with declining profits in the West, to seek a solution through expanding operations geographically to exploit new resources and investment opportunities. But Western anxieties of retaliation by former colonial subjects and now erstwhile competitors in globalization erupted in the aggressive public discourse that followed in the wake of the Asian financial crisis, highlighting the long denied racialized dimension of the glObal economic order.

Maureen Sioh

The Logic of Humiliation

Development theory highlights the material dimension of inequality while postcolonial theory highlights the links among issues of identity and culture, representation and agency (Kapoor 2008). What has never been explained is why East Asian economic decisions have turned into such vitriolic cultural battlegrounds internationally. During the East Asian financial crisis, the Asian values discourse included both criticism and defense of monetary policy in the region at large and, specifically, of currency controls in Malaysia. This section provides a theoretical framework for analyzing how economic success becomes a means of identity construction so that economic challenges, in turn, become threats to identity. After his studies on narcissism, Sigmund Freud was preoccupied with how individuals come to identify with a larger entity (Rose 2004, 14). For a group to exist, the fate of the group must become part of the individual's fate. But for this to happen, its members must understand what the group stands for and who qualifies for membership (Freud 1959, 24–25, 72, 86). Hence the appeal of race and ethnicity, so that members are easily identifiable. The libido attaches itself to the people who have a common share in its needs; therefore, the libidinal tie is narcissistic (Freud 1959, 44; see also chapter 4 in this volume). The tie that binds is the experience of being loved in compensation for group devotion.

In his early theorization of the libidinal tie that gave members of a group a common identity, Freud (1959, 1962) focused on the leader as the tie, but he later went on to argue the significance of an idea as the libidinal tie in constructing a common identity. However, if in identifying as part of a group, the individual becomes less vulnerable, he or she also takes on new anxieties based on group identity. Perceived injuries against one's group become a personal injury even as competition with other groups actually solidifies identity (Freud 2004, 23, 48). However, if the acquisition of distinct group identity requires sublimation or renunciation of individual instincts, the aggression must be redirected outside; to be part of a group is to project everything hated onto an external object (Rose 2004, xii). In this sense, the phenomena of racism and colonialism gave historic substance to the language used in the Asian values discourse because both Western and Asian commentators recognized the morally condemnatory stereotypes of Asians being invoked (see introduction and chapter 1). Finally, Freud (1962, 23–27) argues that competition not only solidifies identity through perceived external threats but that we also derive intense enjoyment from contrast. Emerging as winners in economic competitions becomes a means of satisfying this impulse for contrast and exerting superiority. Paradoxically, if groups need competitors to fashion their identity, they also require their competitors to recognize, acknowledge, and desire them to maintain their ideal self-image.

Capitalism is a way of servicing an ideal version of the self. East Asian countries' adoption of the export-oriented manufacturing model of development made them the ideal junior participants in a racialized capitalist narrative that featured the West as the dominant subject. But the slow decline of Western manufacturing from the 1970s and the rise of its capitalist protégés as competitors trampled on the self-image of the omnipotent West. The latter's approval of East Asian countries, an expedient relationship contingent on an anticommunist alliance during the Cold War, was unlikely to survive the challenge to the West's self-image. And when a people's self-love is threatened, they resort to narcissistic self-defense (Freud 1959, 37).

AGGRESSION

Freud (1962, 39) suggests that people will repress their aggression and anxiety sufficiently to bind themselves to some people, as long as there are others left to be the recipients of their aggression. Just as the fear of others binds a group, complicity in inflicting aggression onto an external scapegoat binds the perpetrators together. Freud (1962, 23) suggested that the oppression of others is a precondition of a group's satisfaction and that the acceptable form of aggression through mastery of others in competition and ranking is pleasurable. Aggression is a means to achieving both security and pleasure. Peter Gay (1994, 4–5) describes aggression as ranging from

Maureen Sioh

confident self-advertisement to sadistic torture. Verbal aggression is less fatal but still unmistakably aggressive, as is flaunting one's possessions, overcoming a rival in love, making social comparisons, and winning competitions or prizes in sports, politics, trade, art, and literature. Gay (1994, 6) notes that the kind of aggressiveness a culture rewards depends on the times and circumstances, but the point is everyone recognizes aggression because it leaves casualties in its wake. In our time, the obvious acceptable place for aggression and the ultimate assertion of superiority lies in the financial arena. An act of aggression is transactive (Gay 1994, 6–7). It must be recognized by both sides in order for the effect to register, and so must have culturally commensurable meaning. Economic globalization has meant that signals of economic contests are now widely culturally commensurable.

Freud postulated that aggression was a "drive to mastery" (1962, 8) and therefore linked to libido, but he also thought that aggression was subsumed within the death instinct. Gay suggests that aggression rises out of a "capacity to be aggressive which works itself out in a wide variety of circumstances. It is mobilized by whatever is experienced as unpleasurable, whether external pressures or internal impulses" (1994, 536). For my purposes, I argue that earlier historical manifestations of colonial or imperial aggression are now acceptably channeled into finance. Ironically, for postcolonial states in globalization, economic space is the safe space that they try to create. When Freud (1959, 18, 27) suggests that prestige is a sort of domination exercised over us by an individual but is lost in the event of failure or, similarly, by a competitor's success, it is easy to understand why the proposition of Asian values as a cultural basis for their economic success came to be experienced as a narcissistic injury by the West. Within the hegemonic framework of global capitalism and its antecedents in colonialism, the East Asian assertion of an indigenous basis for success was culturally commensurable as a challenge to the old order.

NARCISSISTIC INJURY AND RAGE

Understanding the Asian values discourse in the wake of the financial crisis requires an understanding of why it evoked such an emotional response.

Much of the contemporary scholarly work applying psychoanalysis to the role of group identity in international aggression focuses solely on nationalism and military conflicts (see Rachjman 1995; Rose 2004, 2005, 2007). Yet the most common contemporary deployment of aggression in the international arena lies in finance. Old patterns of hegemonic identity are being superseded by those that are finance-oriented because that is where the stakes are highest. I argue that because the prestige of a group's identity is so closely associated with its economic status, a change in that status is experienced as a narcissistic injury. This section expands on the related concepts of narcissistic injury and rage developed by Heinz Kohut (1973) to explain how the antagonistic Asian values debate was played out.

Kohut (1973) reconceptualizes narcissism using the term "selfobject" to refer to any narcissistic experience in which the other is in the service of the self, the latter being defined as a structure that is required for an individual's sense of psychic coherence and well-being. He sees a selfobject as inseparable from the self so that the other person's functions are related to the self (Kohut 1973, 637–38). The selfobject offers support for the vulnerable self through an approving mirroring response, which Kohut (1973, 628) envisions as forming the basis for realistic self-esteem. But he argues that if the subject's prior experience has not allowed for transformation of the narcissistic cathexis with the grandiose self into a healthy self-esteem, then deprived of an "approving mirroring response" (Kohut 1973, 628) from the selfobject, the self will experience a narcissistic injury and respond with extreme rage. In this chapter, I extend the concepts of self and selfobjects to encompass groups.

Bollas (2011, 81) suggests that under intense emotional pressure such as envy or anxiety, an individual or group's negative traits will be projected externally to coalesce into allegories or stereotypes of other groups. Likewise, Kohut proposes that defensive responses, of which narcissistic rage is an extreme version, are activated because the recalcitrant selfobject is not seen as an autonomous source but as a *"flaw in a narcissistically perceived reality"* (1973, 644; emphasis in original), over which the narcissistically vulnerable self had expected to exercise control. Thus, the selfobject's inde-

Maureen Sioh

pendence or difference is experienced as offensive. This is the crux of Western behavior to challenges, real or perceived, to its authority under globalization. Given that Kohut (1973, 643–45) posits that a narcissist must exert absolute control over his or her environment and demand unconditional availability of the approving mirroring for the maintenance of self-esteem, the narcissist must grind down the opponent who dares to outshine him or her because this contradicts the self-image of the grandiose self. Global economic competitions create intense anxiety even among the winners, and envy among those who perceive themselves as losers, even if this loss is only relative (see introduction and chapter 5). When the only identity that counts is an economic one, and this is coupled with a sense of historically based racial entitlement, then by the above logic, the success of rivals becomes a defeat of the self and is experienced as narcissistic injury. The success of the East Asian emerging economies destroyed the sense of unconditional approval of Western social organization, especially when the East Asian states put forth a cultural and racial basis (Asian values) for their economic success. Their subsequent stumbling and weakness during the financial crisis then seemed to invite the moralistic punitiveness of the IMF and Western commentators. It is in this context that I argue that the vaunting of Asian values as the cultural or racial basis of East Asian economic success became a flashpoint for the economically punitive austerity programs that were imposed on East Asian countries, as well as for gloating by Western pundits in the wake of the financial crisis.

HUMILIATION

Kohut (1973, 642) argues that we can recognize that narcissistic rage is involved when an individual is excessively preoccupied with a situation involving other people, which he attributes to the narcissistic individual's inability to recognize others as independent subjects. We see this in the West's response to the Asian financial crisis, which focused on denigrating the cultural basis for East Asian success. Kohut (1973, 637–38) suggests that narcissistic rage occupies a specific position in the spectrum defined by an obsession for revenge because of an archaic fixation. I suggest Kohut is making the point that narcissistic rage is as much a reaction to a past relation rather than the one ostensibly at hand, and in the case of the Asian values discourse, the rage was a function of a historic sense of Western entitlement. Bollas (2011, 176) goes on to hypothesize that extreme reactions occur as part of an unconscious restructuring of past trauma in which the subject puts others through an equivalent, if different, trauma. In this logic, aggressive narcissists identify only with those aspects of their identity that provide them with admiration and a sense of superiority (Bollas 2011, 82). Western contempt and ridicule of Asian values is a reflection of narcissistic rage at the economic challenge, but it could also be a function of the West projecting its own anxieties of the social dislocation inherent in the rising inequality in their home countries that accompanied the transition from a manufacturing to service economy from the 1970s onward. And while both Western and East Asian responses during the crisis originate in defensiveness, the West is defensive and outraged at the perception that its culturally privileged position has been assailed, whereas East Asian outrage is driven by fear or anxiety at their relative lack of power in economic globalization. In any case, the East Asian response to the humiliating economic policies imposed on them in the aftermath of the financial crisis was tempered by their inability to retaliate.

For Bollas (2011, 83–87), the shame of narcissistic injury must be projected elsewhere in the "circuit of depersonalization" (87) in which a psychopathic subject dehumanizes his or her victims in the name of a militant ideology. Here, it is the ideology of neoliberalism that asserts its higher purpose to create a prosperous world through its proponents' intellectual superiority. Bollas (2011, 168–71) describes a militant ideology as an active process involving seduction, the promise of a false safe space, and the development of a dependent relationship so that the subsequent shock of betrayal becomes even more traumatic. The goal is to cause the victim to lose perspective and induce a traumatic experience, leaving the victim more likely to comply with further victimization (Bollas 2011, 171–73). This process makes sense when it is applied to the promises of financial deregulation in globalization. In globalization, Western financial institutions

Maureen Sioh

present freedom for capital to developing countries as the solution to their poverty. In the event of asset bubbles, and subsequent unsustainable debt leading to capital flight and a liquidity crisis, the false hope of prosperity is replaced by the imposition of shock therapy in the form of austerity by the very institutions that once promoted the asset bubbles. In tandem with the material betrayal, the trauma is reinforced through a parallel humiliating discourse that dehumanizes the victims. This form of the narcissistic injury is inflicted through the following practices: stereotyping through aggregate group identity, distorting the victims' views so that they appear less intelligent, and belittling and caricaturing the victims, which can include character assassination of specific individuals (Bollas 2011, 88–89). All of these practices were present in the Asian values discourse during the financial crisis in 1997–98 as we shall see later.

Insurgent East Asia

Anxiety about the West, as represented by the United States being "defeated" by an economically insurgent East Asia, was on display in the 2016 American presidential election, most prominently in Donald Trump's "Make America Great Again" campaign slogan. But anxieties about the West's position of preeminence have been voiced less bombastically with regard to East Asia (Panitch 2014; Hutton 2013; Cox 2012; Jacques 2009). These anxieties have pivoted around economic gains, because in the contemporary world the ultimate assertion of superiority lies in the financial arena. Financial prestige, long the privilege of the West, was now threatened by the competitor's success. Hutton (2013) asserts that even an emergent East Asia is the creation of Western values so that emergent East Asia is conceptualized as an extension of the West. Recalling Kohut's (1973, 637–38) description of the selfobject as inseparable from the self, we can say that East Asia is perceived as the selfobject of the West. Therefore, even East Asian success could be considered an approving mirror of the West. While much of contemporary Western anxiety has to do with the rise of China, it has roots in the fears of Japanese competition in the 1980s and the bloc of Asian countries—South Korea, Taiwan, Singapore, Hong Kong, and to a

lesser extent Malaysia, Indonesia, and Thailand—in the 1990s. The significance of East Asian financial success lay in two factors: it proved that Japan
was not a racial aberration in economic development, and it represented
an indigenous development model acceptable to the West, as opposed
to the socialist-inflected Latin American import-substitution model. In
the early 1990s, the World Bank described the East Asian economies as a
miracle (Birdsall et al. 1993). Until the 1997–98 financial crisis, they were
the poster children, to invoke Bollas, for the "militant ideology" (2011, 168)
of the neoliberal policies promoted by the IMF and World Bank that were
supposed to create a safe and prosperous future.

So why was a financial crisis tacitly reframed in the international, and
largely Western, media within the cultural and psychological parameters
of a debate on Asian values? While Western opprobrium targeted all the
governments affected by the crisis, Malaysia was especially singled out
for its defiance of the IMF in imposing currency controls. Originally a
controversial decision, it is now accepted that the move stabilized the
Malaysian economy (Kaplan and Rodrik 2001; IMF 2012). But even in
1998 it was accepted that Malaysia's ability to defy the international financial community rested on its healthy reserve-to-debt ratio (Jomo 2001,
41). This would have long-term consequences in the buildup of foreign
reserves by all East Asian states. In January 2016 the figure for the affected
East Asian states, as well as Japan and China, came up to over $5.9 trillion
(Trading Economics 2017). In the immediate aftermath of the crisis, an
IMF-led Western intervention forced countries that appealed for external
help to restructure their economies, resulting in massive local social unrest.
Instead, by overlooking the material hardship and social upheaval, I argue
that the Western media reframed the financial crisis as a referendum on
Asian values. Finance, race, and human worth became yoked together in
a relationship of logical equivalence (see chapter 1).

Before the financial crisis in 1997, poverty in Malaysia was down to 8
percent from 60 percent in 1970 (Jayasankaran and Hiebert 1997). By the
mid-1990s GDP growth was averaging 9 percent a year (Fox 1998, 100). The
Financial Post described the Malaysian model of privatization as one of the

Maureen Sioh

most successful in the world (Wheeler 1995, 29). On the left of the political spectrum, Mahmood Mamdani (2008) held up Malaysian development to African countries as a model of the material benefits and dignity that development could deliver. Globalization as the savior of the developing world was primarily a trope referring to East Asian countries. Their success offered hope to the rest of world that exiting poverty was possible through their own agency (Sheridan 1997, xiii; Ghesquire 2007). Malaysia, like the other East Asian economies, was admired for its pro-capital, pro-West policies (Khanna 2008, 267). But even before the crisis, Malaysia and the other East Asian economies were rebelling against the model student image of one who has succeeded by simply copying the West (Inoue 1999, 39). This rebellion manifested itself in the promotion of the developmental state, itself implying a socialistic turn toward state intervention. More subtly, the conflation of race and nation-state, a legacy of colonialism, meant that the promotion of the role of the state set the stage for arguing that culture and race played a role in success. This indirect appeal became overt through the promotion of Asian values. Freud (1959, 1962, 2004) would have noted the significance of race as the libidinal tie that was strengthened through competition with the West in globalization.

Malaysia became a focal point for Western critics because of its combative prime minister at the time, Mahathir Mohammad. As the *Guardian* described him, "Nobody has symbolized East Asia's confidence in itself and its ability to take on the world single-handedly more than the [now former] Malaysian Prime Minister, Mahathir Mohammad" (Brummer 1997, 19). What exactly was Mahathir taking on? Development, after all, as Kasese-Hara (2004, 547) notes, is construed as an indicator of racial potential for progress. In asserting that the economic improvement of East Asian national economies was a product of controversial Asian values, proponents implicitly argued that race and culture, the traits that condemned East Asians to official and unofficial colonization, were now the basis of Asian success. A number of Asian commentators observed that Western unease over this Asian success is rooted in Western anxiety over the region's rise from former colonies to competitors (Lim, Ho, and Yee

1998; Inoue 1999; Mahbubani 2002). Admittedly, the position of East Asia in the colony role precludes official colonized status—colony is used here to indicate a differential power relationship. If in Kohut's (1973, 637–38, 644) framework, the former colonies are selfobjects meant to provide an approving mirror to the West, then the success of the East Asians is now construed as an offense to the West. Mahathir's pronouncements convey the new confidence that emerged in the region at the time of record-breaking economic growth. The Asian values controversy signaled a psychic shift that got underway in the 1980s with Japan and was continued by the other East Asian countries and now China.

THE ASIAN FINANCIAL CRISIS

The 1997–98 financial crisis began with the slide of the Thai baht in May 1997 (Lee 1998; Radelet and Sachs 1998; Berg 1999; Jomo 2001). By July 1997 currency traders were short-selling other Asian currencies resulting in currency depreciation, lowered share prices, and a trade deficit in those countries. The spillover effects of market uncertainty in the region frightened off potential investors while existing investors began to sell their securities. In August 1997 Thailand abandoned its currency peg and defaulted on its debts, turning to the IMF for help. It was followed by Indonesia in October and South Korea in November. In return for IMF aid, those countries had to abide by IMF conditions to raise domestic interest rates, lower social spending, open domestic markets, and deregulate foreign ownership of local assets, policies that would have long-term consequences for opening up those countries to foreign control (Berthier 2000). Given that only a short time ago they were held up by the IMF and the World Bank as examples of what market freedom could deliver, this was a sharp reversal of fortune; it reminds us of Bollas's (2011, 168–73) suggestion that it is the shock of the sudden betrayal by a former mentor that disorients the victim and causes it to lose perspective beyond that of its victimizer. Through economic contagion, Singapore, Taiwan, and Hong Kong all suffered currency depreciations but were spared the worst because they had no external debt and healthy reserves. Singapore and Taiwan also successfully managed exchange rates, which reduced the threat of currency speculation. And Malaysia avoided IMF intervention as its debts were held by the private sector and the government possessed a positive reserves-to-debt ratio, avoiding a liquidity shortfall (Jomo 2001).

Nevertheless, by July 1997 the Malaysian ringgit was depreciating steadily and share prices began to fall, in turn causing the debt-holding banks to experience liquidity difficulties. The Malaysian government also faced revenue shortfalls as businesses were unable to pay taxes and purchasing power fell by about 50 percent (Jomo 2001). Initially, Malaysia voluntarily adopted IMF-type policies to cut government spending, increase reserves, and defer government projects, but it soon found these austerity measures exacerbated the financial crisis (Jayasankaran 1997). The ringgit continued to depreciate, at one time almost reaching five ringgit to one U.S. dollar, increasing the cost of debt servicing (today the value is approximately four ringgit to one U.S. dollar, because of current political turmoil). As the crisis worsened, Prime Minister Mahathir made the controversial decision to suspend currency trading and place a one-year moratorium on the outflow of foreign portfolio capital in October 1998, to reduce reserve requirement to increase liquidity, and to lower interest rates to stimulate investment and consumption (Hiebert 1999). The ringgit was fixed at 3.80 to the U.S. dollar, ending ringgit speculation. The government announced it would guarantee bank deposits and a special agency would restructure corporate debt and recapitalize financial institutions. State-owned firms also bought shares to halt the slide on the bourse. Finally, also in defiance of IMF wisdom, the government maintained price controls on essential consumer items and boosted government spending, thus triggering a Keynesian reflation of the economy (Meesook et al. 2001).

HUMILIATION AND FINANCIAL CONQUEST

Unfortunately, Mahathir's judicious policy activism was overshadowed by his intemperate and anti-Semitic comments blaming George Soros for the Asian financial crisis (Soros 1997). This served to deflect attention from the Western commentators who interpreted the economic crisis as the death of the Asian values debate (Milner 2000). But in the "us" against "them" pressure of economic globalization, we also see the truth of Bollas's (2011, 81) assertion that an individual's or group's negative traits projected externally coalesce into allegories of Asian versus Western values. The economic crisis was a manifestation of Freud's (1959, 18, 27) point that the failure of a competitor can reestablish the prestige of the narcissistic subject, in this case the West. The role of the economy in the real contest over racial and cultural superiority was important because the parameters of economic success were understood and accepted by both sides. As Gay (1994, 6–7) reminds us, because aggression is transactive, the aggressive act must be culturally commensurable. One commentator even boasted that "American values . . . have much to offer for the financial stability in the global economy" (Hoagland 1997b).

East Asia's economic challenge transformed its role from the provider of the "approving mirroring response" (Kohut 1973, 628) to the competitor, which Western commentators experienced as a narcissistic injury and to which they responded with rage. This took the form of practices of erasure through humiliation (Bollas 2011, 82, 88–89, 176), given the imposition of austerity programs. The humiliating discourse included aggregating Asians into derogatory stereotypes. Asian leaders were at best "amoral" and "opportunist" and at worst "drug traffickers and gangsters" (Mallet 1999, 16). Wealth was given the gloss of vulgarity so that the Thais and the Singaporeans were "nouveaux riches" and Indonesians "witless," while Mahathir was singled out as a blackmailer of the West and a "menace to his country" (Hoagland 1997a).

I have argued that finance, race, and human worth became yoked together in a relationship of logical equivalence. The *US News and World Report* claimed that "Asian values have become Asian liabilities" (Zuckerman 1998, 77). The *Washington Post*'s Jim Hoagland similarly equated ringgit and baht depreciations with racial devaluation: "Just as sharply devalued are the political hubris and racial conceit [of] 'Asian values'" (1997a). Elsewhere, Francis Fukuyama wrote that the crisis would "puncture the idea of Asian exceptionalism" (1998, 27). For his part, Walter Russell Mead (1998) titled his article on the topic, "The Real Asian Miracle; Asia Devalued." And Victor Mallet (1999, 45) claimed that Westerners had been too diffident in criticizing Asian governments. The gloating over the Asian crisis appeared to span the ideological spectrum in the Western media. *The Independent's* Diane Coyle concluded that the crisis will "finally lay to rest this unquestioning worship of Asian values" (1997). The *New Statesman's* Jonathan Mirsky sarcastically labeled Asian values "a fabulous notion" only good for "crushing dissent and fending off criticism from democrats" (1998, 26), and strangely, for crashing planes. However, perhaps Sebastian Mallaby got to the heart of the matter: "Asia is vulnerable. . . . The IMF's progress through Asia over the past year recalls the long-ago voyage of Commodore Perry" (1998, 2). Highly critical of the concept of Asian values himself, Amartya Sen (1999, 96–97) questioned whether underlying Western criticism was an anxiety about the threat posed to the West by the combination of economic success and nationalist confidence. Sen's views echo Kohut's (1973), so that while Western elites play on racial and cultural anxieties to perpetuate the global political and economic status quo, the appropriation of the same tools by others provokes narcissistic rage among Western politicians and media commentators.

Conclusion

As we look back on the recent financial bailout in the United States as a necessary action to resuscitate the American economy, it bears remembering Western criticism of the Malaysian government's bailouts in the late 1990s as "crony capitalism" (Summers, quoted in Bello 2000, 182). Similar negative moral aspersions have been cast on the Greeks, implying that their financial crisis is a consequence of their version of crony capitalism (Zingales 2012). Malaysia survived the crisis, although credit for its survival remains contested, variously attributed to its policies, selective reflation, the worldwide electronics boom, or inevitable regional recovery (Khor 2008). But the acrimonious rhetoric, not to mention the punitive measures imposed on indebted countries by the IMF, ironically led to much farther-reaching financial policymaking: in the late 1990s, Malaysia was able to defy the IMF because its foreign debt did not exceed reserves and, moreover, was concentrated in three partly privatized companies, as opposed to held by government (Jomo 2001). Its example triggered the subsequent regional trend of high reserves, which today continues to finance the American deficit even as East Asian currency devaluations in the aftermath of the crisis created an export boom and facilitated the U.S. trade deficit. Subsequently, other East Asian countries took note of what had saved Malaysia. And at the start of 2016, the East Asian countries, including China, held $5.9 trillion in reserves (Trading Economics 2017).

Malaysia's danger has always been that it might be seen as an example by other Asian states of defiance to the United States. The other significant lesson noted by the East Asian countries concerned the U.S. and IMF objection to Japan's proposal during the crisis for an Asian monetary fund that would tide members over future financial emergencies (Golub 2016, 99). Recognizing that access to credit during the Asian crisis was firmly in Western control, in 2015 China created the New Development Bank (commonly referred to as the BRICS Bank) as a source of investment and as lender of last resort to provide an alternative to the World Bank. I have argued that the debate over Asian values can be understood as contests over the changing place of the East Asian emerging economies within the glObal hierarchy. These contests reflect the psychic challenge to, and defense of, the conventional hierarchy of international relations, in the wake of the East Asian miracle, followed by the crisis in 1997–98. The emotional force underpinning the economic policy decisions during the crisis can only be explained by examining the parallel narrative on Asian values, in which Western commentators sought to humiliate East Asian states through their public rhetoric. But using the psychoanalytic framework of narcissistic injury and rage, I have tried to show that public humiliation may have been an unconscious acting out of anxieties by the West, a reaction to its perception of a slow economic and geopolitical decline. In my argument, Western anxieties are projected onto its perceived competitors and erstwhile protégés in East Asia, resulting in the very aggressive public discourse that brought out the long denied racialized dimension of the glObal economic order.

But we must be careful in choosing to stand by in such emotionally vicious conflicts: "It cuts all common bonds between the contending peoples and threatens to leave a legacy of embitterment that will make any renewal of those bonds impossible for a long time to come" (Freud 1915, 5). Freud was writing about the long-term psychic consequences of a military conflict (the First World War), but his words could just as easily be applied to our contemporary economic conflicts. Our vulnerability has been turned into a weapon of mass destruction and trained on ourselves. We are in such a time now, and there will be no return.

Works Cited

Barr, Michael. 2002. *Cultural Politics and Asian Values: The Tepid War*. London: Routledge.

Beeson, Mark. 2004. "The Rise and Fall (?) of the Developmental State: The Vicissitudes and Implications of East Asian Interventionism." In *Developmental States: Relevancy, Redundancy or Reconfiguration?*, edited by L. Low, 29–40. New York: Nova Science Publishers.

Bell, Daniel. 2000. *East Meets West: Human Rights and Democracy in East Asia*. Princeton NJ: Princeton University Press.

Bello, Walden. 2000. "The Asian Financial Crisis: Heroes, Villains and Accomplices." In *Principled World Politics: The Challenge of Normative International Relations*, edited by Paul Wapner and Lester Edwin J. Ruiz, 181–90. Lanham MD: Rowman & Littlefield.

Berg, Andrew. 1999. "The Asia Crisis: Causes, Policy Responses, and Outcomes." IMF Working Paper. https://www.imf.org/external/pubs/ft/wp/1999/wp99138.pdf.

Berthier, Serge. 2000. "Interview with Dr. Mahathir: The True Significance of the Financial Crisis of 1998." *Asian Affairs on Global Issues*. http://www.asian-affairs.com/Frameleft/crisis.html.

Birdsall, Nancy M., Jose Edgardo L. Campos, Chang-Shik Kim, W. Max Corden, Lawrence MacDonald, Howard Pack, John Page, Richard Sabor, and Joseph E. Stiglitz. 1993. *The East Asian Miracle: Economic Growth and Public Policy, Main Report*. New York: Oxford University Press. http://documents.worldbank.org/curated/en/1993/09/698870/east-asian-miracle-economic-growth-public-policy-vol-1-2-main-report.

Bollas, Christopher. 2011. *The Christopher Bollas Reader*. London: Routledge.

Brummer, Alex. 1997. "Malaysian Tiger Takes a Mauling." *Guardian Weekly*, September 7, 19.

Cox, Michael. 2012. "Power Shifts, Economic Change and the Decline of the West?" *International Relations* 26 (4): 369–88.

Coyle, Diane. 1997. "Why the Asian Model Has Gone off the Road." *Independent*, November 25. http://www.independent.co.uk/opinion/why-the-asian-model-has-gone-off -the-road-1296185.html.

Fox, Justin. 1998. "The Great Emerging Markets Rip-Off." *Fortune*, May 11, 100.

Freud, Sigmund. 1915. *Thoughts for the Times on War and Death*. Part 1, *The Disillusionment of War*. https://www.freud.org.uk/file-uploads/files/THOUGHTS%20FOR%20 THE%20TIMES%20ON%20WAR%20AND%20DEATH%20%201.pdf.

———. 1959. *Group Psychology and the Analysis of the Ego*. Translated by James Strachey. New York: Norton.

———. 1962. *Civilization and Its Discontents*. Translated by James Strachey. New York: Norton.

———. 2004. "Mass Psychology and the Analysis of the 'I.'" In *Mass Psychology and Other Writings*, edited by Adam Phillips, translated by J. Underwood, 15–106. London: Penguin Books.

Fukuyama, Francis. 1998. "Asian Values and the Asian Crisis." *Commentary*, February 27. https://www.commentarymagazine.com/articles/asian-values-and-the-asian-crisis/.

Gay, Peter. 1994. *The Bourgeois Experience: Victoria to Freud*. Vol. 3, *The Cultivation of Hatred*. New York: Norton.

Ghesquire, Henri. 2007. *Singapore's Success: Engineering Economic Growth*. Singapore: Thomson Learning.

Golub, Phillip. 2016. *East Asia's Re-emergence*. Cambridge: Polity.

Goodman, Roger, Huck-ju Kwon, and Gordon White, eds. 1998. *The East Asian Welfare Model: Welfare Orientalism and the State*. London: Routledge.

Halimi, Serge. 2015. "The Europe We Don't Want." *Le Monde Diplomatique*, August, 1–3.

Harvey, David. 1982. *The Limits to Capital*. Cambridge MA: Blackwell.

———. 1989. *The Condition of Postmodernity*. Cambridge MA: Blackwell.

Hiebert, Murray. 1999. "Under Control." *Far Eastern Economic Review*, January 28, 42–44.

Hoagland, Jim. 1997a. "From Boom to Bust." *Washington Post*, October 12.

———. 1997b. "Tinkering with an Economic Mess." *Washington Post*, November 30.

Hutton, Will. 2013. "Westerners Don't Rule, but Their Values Do." *Guardian Weekly*, March 22.

Inoue, Tatsuo. 1999. "Liberal Democracy and Asian Orientalism." In *The East Asian Challenge for Human Rights*, edited by Joanne Bauer and Daniel. Bell, 27–59. Cambridge: Cambridge University Press.

International Monetary Fund. 2012. "IMF Adopts Institutional View on Capital Flows." *IMF News*, December 3. http://www.imf.org/external/pubs/ft/survey/so/2012/pol120312a. htm.

Jacques, Martin. 2009. *When China Rules the World: The End of the Western World and the Birth of the New Global Order*. New York: Penguin Press.

Jayasankaran, S. 1997. "Hit the Brakes." *Far Eastern Economic Review*, December 18, 14–15.

Jayasankaran, S., and Murray Hiebert. 1997. "Malaysian Dilemmas." *Far Eastern Economic Review*, September 4, 18–21.

Jomo, Kwame Sundaram. 2001. "From Currency Crisis to Recession." In *Malaysian Eclipse: Economic Crisis and Recovery*, edited by Kwame Sundaram Jomo, 1–46. London: Zed Books.

Kaplan, Ethan, and Dani Rodrik. 2001. "Did the Malaysian Capital Controls Work?" NBER Working Paper no. 8142. Cambridge MA: National Bureau of Economic Research. http://www.nber.org/papers/w8142.

Kapoor, Ilan. 2008. *The Postcolonial Politics of Development*. London: Routledge.

Kasese-Hara, Mambwe. 2004. "Human Development in 'Underdeveloped' Contexts." In *Critical Psychology*, edited by Derek Hook, 540–58. Landsdowne, South Africa: University of Cape Town Press.

Khanna, Parag. 2008. *The Second World: Empires and Influence in the New Global Order*. New York: Random House.

Khor, Martin. 2008. "The Malaysian Experience in Financial-Economic Management: An Alternative to the IMF-Style Approach." In *Capital Market Liberalization and Development*, edited by José Antonio Ocampo and Joseph Stiglitz, 205–61. Oxford: Oxford University Press.

Kohut, Heinz. 1973. *The Search for the Self: Selected Writings of Heinz Kohut: 1950–1978*. Vol. 2. New York: International Universities Press.

Krugman, Paul. 2015. "The Asian Crisis versus the Euro Crisis." *The Conscience of a Liberal* (blog), *New York Times*, August 28. http://krugman.blogs.nytimes.com/2013/08/28/the-asian-crisis-versus-the-euro-crisis/?_r=0.

Lee, Eddy. 1998. "The Asian Financial Crisis: The Challenge for Social Policy." Geneva: International Labour Office.

Lim Kok Wing, Robert Ho, and Mee Fah Yee. 1998. *Hidden Agenda*. Kuala Lumpur: Limkokwing Integrated.

Mahathir, Mohamad, and Ishihara Shintaro. 1995. *The Voice of Asia: Two Leaders Discuss the Coming Century*. Translated by Frank Baldwin. Tokyo: Kodansha International.

Mahbubani, Kishore. 2002. *Can Asians Think? Understanding the Divide between East and West*. South Royalton VT: Steerforth Press.

Mallaby, Sebastian. 1998. "In Asia's Mirror." *National Interest* 52, 13–22.

Mallet, Victor. 1999. *The Trouble with Tigers: The Rise and Fall of South-East Asia*. London: HarperCollins.

Mamdani, Mahmood. 2008. "Lessons of Zimbabwe." *London Review of Books*, December 4, 17–21.

McClintock, Alex. 2015. "Greek Bailout 'a New Versailles Treaty', Says Former Finance Minister Yanis Varoufakis." ABC, July 13. http://www.abc.net.au/radionational/programs /latenightlive/greek-bailout-deal-'a-new-versailles-treaty':-yanis-varoufakis/6616532.

Mead, Walter Russell. 1998. "The Real Asian Miracle; Asia Devalued." *New York Times Magazine*, May 31. http://www.nytimes.com/1998/05/31/magazine/the-real-asian-miracle -asia-devalued.html?pagewanted=all.

Meesook, Kanitta, Il Houng Lee, Olin Liu, Yougesh Khatri, Natalia Tamirisa, Michael Moore, and Mark H. Krysl. 2001. *Malaysia: From Crisis to Recovery*, Occasional Paper 207. Washington DC: International Monetary Fund.

Milner, Anthony. 2000. "What Happened to 'Asian Values'?" In *Towards Recovery in Pacific Asia*, edited by Gerald Segal and David Goodman, 56–68. London: Routledge.

Mirsky, Jonathan. 1998. "Asian Values, a Fabulous Notion." *New Statesman*, April 3, 26–27.

Nougayréde, Natalie. 2015. "If Greece and Russia Feel Humiliated, That's Something Europe Cannot Ignore." *Guardian*, June 18. http://www.theguardian.com/commentisfree /2015/jun/18/greece-russia-humiliated-europe.

Panitch, Leo. 2014. "The US Still Decides the Future of Capitalism, Not the G20, and Not the Brics Nations." *Guardian*, August 27. https://www.theguardian.com/commentisfree /2014/aug/27/the-us-still-decides-the-future-of-capitalism-not-the-g20-and-not-the -brics-nations.

Rachjman, John, ed. 1995. *The Identity in Question*. New York: Routledge.

Radelet, Steven, and Jeffrey Sachs. 1998. "The Onset of the East Asian Currency Crisis." NBER Working Paper no. 6680. Cambridge MA: National Bureau of Economic Research.

Rose, Jacqueline. 2004. "In Our Present-Day White Christian Culture." *London Review of Books*, July 8, 14–17.

———. 2005. *The Question of Zion*. Princeton NJ: Princeton University Press.

———. 2007. *The Last Resistance*. London: Verso.

Sen, Amartya. 1999. "Human Rights and Economic Achievement." In *The East Asian Challenge for Human Rights*, edited by Joanne Bauer and Daniel Bell, 88–99. Cambridge: Cambridge University Press.

Sheridan, Greg. 1997. *Tigers: Leaders of the New Asia-Pacific*. St. Leonards, NSW: Allen & Unwin.

Shin, Hee Young. 2015. "The IMF and Troika's Greek Bailout Programs: An East Asian View." *Real-World Economics Review*, no. 73, 76–91.

Smith, Helena. 2015. "Was This Humiliation of Greeks Really Necessary?" *Guardian*, July 12. http://www.theguardian.com/world/commentisfree/2015/jul/12/was-this-humiliation-of-greeks-really-necessary.

Soros, George. 1997. "Mahathir vs. Soros." *Far Eastern Economic Review*, October 2, 32.

Stiglitz, Joseph E. 2001. "Monetary and Exchange Rate Policy in Small Open Economies: The Case of Iceland." Working Paper no. 15. Reykjavík: Central Bank of Iceland

——. 2006. *Making Globalization Work*. New York: Norton.

——. 2015. "A Greek Morality Tale." Project Syndicate, February 3. https://www.project-syndicate.org/commentary/greece-eurozone-austerity-reform-by-joseph-e--stiglitz-2015-02?barrier=true.

Trading Economics. 2017. "Foreign Exchange Reserves." https://tradingeconomics.com/country-list/foreign-exchange-reserves.

Wheeler, Colin. 1995. "Malaysia: Special Report." *Financial Post*, August 26, 29.

Zingales, Luigi. 2012. "Crony Capitalism and the Crisis of the West." *Wall Street Journal*, June 6. http://www.wsj.com/articles/SB10001424052702303665904577450071884712152.

Zuckerman, Mortimer. 1998. "Japan Inc. Unravels." *US News and World Report* 125 (7): 77.

3   Beyond the End of the World
Breaking Attachment to a Dying Planet

Robert Fletcher

> Ideology isn't simply imposed on ourselves. Ideology is
> our spontaneous relationship to our social world, how we
> perceive its meaning and so on. We enjoy our ideology. . . .
> To step out of ideology, it hurts; it's a painful experience. You
> must force yourself to do it. . . . This is a paradox we have to
> accept: the extreme violence of liberation, that you must be
> forced to be free. If you trust your spontaneous sense of well-
> being you will never get free. Freedom hurts.
>
> Žižek, *The Pervert's Guide to Ideology*

How to move our glObal society from its current ecocidal trajectory to a
more sustainable path is one of the most urgent questions in the world today.
Researchers have approached this question in a variety of ways, alternately
emphasizing political, economic, social, and psychological obstacles in the
face of sustainable living. Each of these perspectives has its place within
a comprehensive approach to addressing the question. In this chapter,
however, I suggest that psychoanalytic theory can illuminate aspects of
this issue that other approaches have failed to adequately appreciate thus
far. Specifically, psychoanalysis helps us to understand how unconscious
processes influence perception, belief, and action in ways that elude our
conscious deliberation. Over the past two decades, a small yet growing body
of work has begun to apply a psychoanalytic perspective to discussion of
environmental issues. Building on this literature, as well as other recent

research bringing a psychoanalytic perspective into the social sciences, this chapter highlights the ways that the process of attachment to the status quo tends to inhibit efforts to introduce change. Importantly, psychoanalysis tells us that this attachment can occur even in situations that subjects consider negative and claim to want to leave. This is because breaking attachment requires a process of mourning, of facing the pain of loss necessary to let go of present circumstances and embrace a novel future. To avoid this pain, we tend to deny our attachments. More than mere denial, in fact, we often engage in a process of "disavowal," simultaneously acknowledging and denying our ties and the pain this causes. This disavowal makes truly addressing attachment difficult, since it allows subjects to maintain that they are in fact addressing the attachment when in reality a deep-seated commitment to it remains.

In this chapter, I apply this psychoanalytic perspective to what is undoubtedly the most urgent environmental challenge facing the planet today: the increasingly problematic impacts of anthropogenic climate change. I begin by describing the extent of the problem and the wholly inadequate responses it has inspired to date. This is so, I then contend, because truly redressing the problem would require such dramatic transformation of our global socioeconomic system that it would be virtually unrecognizable in its present form. To avoid full acknowledgment of this necessity, the global community has increasingly engaged in what Klein (2014) calls "magical thinking": positing ostensive solutions to the problem that paradoxically present the forces in large part responsible for it—chief among which is a neoliberal capitalist economy demanding continual growth—as its remedy as well. I show how psychoanalysis can help illuminate this situation by demonstrating how desire for *jouissance* can compel attachment to a situation—even one that subjects find distasteful and claim to want to leave—such that they will engage in all manner of psychological gymnastics to maintain this attachment. Chief among the psychic mechanisms facilitating this dynamic is disavowal, whereby subjects claim to be acknowledging a situation while simultaneously denying it as well. Such disavowal is particularly difficult to counter as it enables subjects to believe that they are honestly facing a situation that they continue to unconsciously evade in order to escape the pain of loss of attachment that would otherwise ensue. Unable to face up to the reality of loss, this disavowal then forces desire to turn back on itself, becoming instead what Lacan called "drive," in which attachment moves from the object of desire to the very experience of this object's loss, a state of melancholia compelling continual repetition of failure to attain the object in question. In addition to illuminating these dynamics, psychoanalysis tells us that in order to overcome this impasse one must be compelled to come to terms with the loss, requiring a process of "traversing the fantasy" facilitating disavowal and entering into mourning for the end of attachment. To do this, it helps if subjects are presented with an alternative object of desire that is sufficiently compelling to inspire willingness to face the pain of loss. This has significant implications for climate change politics, as I discuss in closing, suggesting that a major obstacle in the face of effective policy is the lack of an alternative vision of a new, desirable society beyond the apocalyptic, dystopian images commonly presented in discussions concerning life in a warmer future world.

A final caveat before I continue. It is clear that while climate change is a global problem, there exists massive inequality in terms of both who causes it and how its impacts are and will be experienced (Agarwal and Narain 1991; Klein 2014). While in the following I often speak in the collective "we," I am certainly not implying that we are all in the same boat equally, but merely that the implications of, and hence actions needed to address, climate change are inherently global in scale.

Confronting a Dying Planet

The extent of the ecological devastation humans have wrought on our planet is daunting to fully acknowledge. This is true with respect to a wide variety of environmental issues (see, e.g., Millennium Ecosystem Assessment 2005), but nowhere is it more apparent than in the case of anthropogenic climate change. It is now widely accepted that raising global atmospheric temperatures more than two degrees Celsius above preindustrial levels creates the potential for impacts that may spiral out of control because of feedback processes such as the melting of polar ice caps and arctic tundra, spontaneous rainforest combustion, and so forth. Likely consequences of this change include massive human displacement due to sea level rise, increased intensity and unpredictability of weather events, and loss of agricultural capacity in many food-vulnerable areas (Intergovernmental Panel on Climate Change [IPCC] 2014).

There is disagreement concerning how much carbon dioxide the atmosphere can accommodate before exceeding this two-degree rise but common estimates range between 350–550 parts per million (PPM). In 2014 the planet exceeded 400 PPM for the first time in recorded history, and we continue to release CO_2 at ever-increasing rates. Hence, many commentators are beginning to acknowledge that remaining within the two-degree window is less and less likely. Accomplishing this would require immediate and drastic action to dramatically reduce greenhouse gas (GHG) emissions in industrialized societies around the world. Conservative estimates suggest that global emissions would need to peak by 2025, then drop to half of current levels by 2050 (IPCC 2014). Less restrained assessments assert that global emissions must in fact peak by 2017 and quickly reduce to 90 percent of current levels thereafter (Klein 2014). Critics warn that even this may allow for a global temperature increase of three to four degrees owing to climate effects already set in motion by past action (Jordan et al. 2013).

If the extent of the problem is difficult to fully accept, the degree of socioeconomic transformation necessary to achieve even more conservative reductions in GHG emissions is more difficult still. To put the issue into perspective, consider this assessment of Britain's 2008 Climate Change Act envisioning a relatively modest emissions reduction of at least 34 percent over 1990 levels by 2020: "Assuming a GDP [gross domestic product] growth of 2% p.a., a year-on-year annual rate of decarbonization of 5.3% is required to reach the Act's target; whereas there is no record of any economy having achieved greater than 2.0%, and then only for short spells. In sum, this Act requires the UK to achieve the impossible" (Prins et al. 2009, 9). Extrapolate this to other industrialized nations and for the more stringent targets that are really needed and one begins to appreciate the enormity of the challenge. Bluntly stated, truly reversing current climate trajectories would require dramatic transformation in political, economic, and social structures at every level and throughout the glObe. As Klein (2014) asserts, it would require changing virtually everything about our way of life within contemporary capitalist society.

The prospect of such change becomes more daunting still when one considers the overwhelming failure of past efforts to address the issue. For in fact world leaders, long acknowledging the potential dangers of climate change, have been organizing to reduce global emissions for more than twenty-five years now, via the United Nations Framework Convention on Climate Change (UNFCCC), enacted at the Rio Earth Summit in 1992. Yet to date this convention has failed entirely to achieve its intended aim to reduce GHG emissions a mere collective 5 percent over 1990 levels; on the contrary, global emissions have risen substantially throughout the period during which they were intended to diminish (Klein 2014).

The Paris Agreement enacted at UNFCCC's Twenty-First Conference of the Parties (COP-21) in December 2015 may correct for this to some degree, offering a new glObal compact in which nearly every nation in the world has promised (albeit in a nonbinding framework) to substantially reduce emissions according to nationally determined contributions (NDCs). Yet analysts of these commitments concur that if fully realized in their current form, they are likely to result at best in a 2.7- to 3-degree temperature increase (see, e.g., Goldenberg et al. 2015), thus potentially allowing for many of the fearsome feedback effects IPCC (2014) predicts. And as with the UK Climate Act noted earlier, achieving even the inadequate goals codified in the Paris Agreement would require dramatic socioeconomic change in most societies. Hence, in all likelihood the sobering truth is that we remain firmly on a path toward climate catastrophe in the not-so-distant future.

Neoliberalism's Lifeblood

There is an important reason why it remains so difficult to move toward the change that almost everyone now agrees is needed. In *Lifeblood*, Matthew Huber (2013) presents a sobering analysis of the extent to which global soci-

Robert Fletcher

ety is grounded fundamentally in the use of fossil fuels. Taking the United States as his main focus, Huber shows that not only is the vast majority of capital accumulation fundamentally founded in fossil fuel exploitation (see Malm 2016), but even our very identities as neoliberal subjects—our sense of freedom and agency conditioned on unfettered mobility (Sheller and Urry 2006)—are deeply reliant on oil production and consumption. Moving to a "post-carbon" society, therefore, would entail loss of attachment not merely to our neoliberal capitalist economy, and the abundant opportunities for material consumption it provides so many of us, but to our very sense of self as well. Huber (2013) shows how this situation was in large part deliberately created, particularly in the postwar period. Many advanced industrial societies were redesigned around the ownership and use of personal automobiles as well as electricity-dependent home appliances in order to increase demand for, and thus dependency on, an (at that time) overabundant oil supply. As oil becomes more difficult to procure in sufficient quantities to sustain this created demand—and as the effects of its consumption become more apparent in the form of climate change—the consequences of this trajectory become increasingly dire yet resistant to redress. In short, one could assert with Stephen Healy that "peak oil is the end of a bender and climate change is our collective hangover" (2014, 187).

Magical Thinking

Klein (2014) was not the first to observe that, in the face of a growing global acknowledgment of the seriousness of climate change, rather than implement the dramatic restructuring needed to adequately address the issue, as well as the litany of other environmental ills on the ascent, political leaders around the world have sought instead to retrofit, in a sense, the mainstream capitalist economy. Such retrofitting seeks to internalize environmental and social costs through so-called market mechanisms—advocating, for example, for carbon offsets to address GHG emissions, biodiversity offsets to address habitat destruction and species loss, and geoengineering to capture and store atmospheric carbon and reflect solar radiation. A rapidly swelling body of research labels this approach "neoliberal environmentalism," among other monikers, noting that this has, over the past several decades, become the dominant approach to addressing degradation within the mainstream global ecology movement (see especially Heynen et al. 2007; Büscher et al. 2012). It is likely to remain a central component, in the form of expanded carbon markets, of the post–Paris Agreement climate governance framework as well (Böhm 2015). The irony of this strategy is that, from a critical perspective, it is in fact a capitalist economy predicated on continual growth in pursuit of ever-greater profit that is largely responsible for the same environmental and social problems it is now called on to fix within this neoliberal discourse (see especially Büscher et al. 2012). As I suggest elsewhere (Fletcher 2013b), this paradoxical situation evinces Fredric Jameson's astute assertion that it is increasingly "easier to imagine the end of the world than it is to imagine the end of capitalism" (2003, 76). Klein (2014) calls this neoliberal environmentalism "magical thinking," and what it entails, essentially, is an effort to deny the full extent of the transformation we know will be truly needed to address the problems in question. Or as Erik Swyngedouw eloquently phrases it, the logic holds that "we have to change radically, but within the contours of the existing state of the situation . . . so that nothing really has to change" (2010, 219).

Ideology, Fantasy, and Desire

The essential contradictions embodied in neoliberal environmentalism are apparent in growing evidence of its widespread failure to achieve intended results (Büscher et al. 2012; Fletcher et al. 2016). Rather than compromising the approach, however, such evidence tends to be obfuscated by using optimistic win-win rhetoric or by blaming improper state intervention for ineffective action (Fletcher 2013b). This obfuscation can be explained in a variety of ways. From a Marxist perspective, for instance, it is often framed as an ideological smokescreen disguising the reality that market mechanisms were never really intended to save the environment but merely to create an additional mode of capital accumulation (Harvey 2005; Büscher et al. 2012). For post-structuralists, on the other hand, failure to acknowledge market failure follows from Michel Foucault's analysis of the internal

Robert Fletcher

logic of neoliberal economics: "Nothing proves that the market economy is intrinsically defective since everything attributed to it as a defect and as the effect of its defectiveness should really be attributed to the state" (2008, 116). Psychoanalysis offers an alternate, yet complementary, interpretation of this situation, as described later.

Neoliberal environmentalism is generally grounded in a particular conception of human nature, namely, a so-called rational actor perspective, in which subjects are seen, by and large, as self-interested individuals coolly weighing the costs and benefits of alternative courses of action and choosing that which promises to maximize one's material utility (see especially Fletcher 2010, 2013b). From this point of view, promoting sustainability requires altering the structures in terms of which actors engage in this decision-making process in order to make the desired action the more beneficial choice. This approach is epitomized by the so-called nudge strategy for promoting social change, increasingly popular among international development planners (see, e.g., Banerjee and Duflo 2011). Meanwhile, most research concerning climate change communication has employed a version of the so-called education model of social change, entailing a conviction that provision of more facts concerning the realities of a situation will lead to greater awareness of the problem and, in turn, more effective action (cf. Weintrobe 2013a). This approach also assumes that the targets of such messaging are rational individuals who are able to coolly compare the facts on offer to empirical reality and shape their behavior accordingly.

Yet a growing body of research in behavioral economics, social psychology, and related fields demonstrates what psychoanalysts have long asserted, namely, that human behavior deviates substantially from the rational actor model and hence that rather than developing greater awareness and commitment to action, subjects tend to react to new information by becoming more firmly entrenched in their present perspective (see, e.g., Lakoff 2009). For psychoanalysts, this is explained by the fact that "much of our mental activity is unconscious, and that unconscious emotional dynamics can and do have consequences for the way we think and act in our conscious lives" (Benton 2013, 190). From a Lacanian perspective, in particular, humans are seen as fundamentally motivated by pursuit of *jouissance*, a libidinal mixture of pleasure and pain that adheres to fantasies that subjects therefore desire to fulfill (Fink 1995; see also chapter 7 in this volume). Such fantasies thus sustain a commitment to particular ideologies and states of being by promising provision of pleasure. For Lacanians, therefore, as Slavoj Žižek (2012) states in the epigraph, "Ideology isn't simply imposed on ourselves. . . . We enjoy our ideology."

Yet *jouissance*, by definition, is unattainable, offering merely a pale taste of the real thing (the illusory *objet petit a* to which it refers) that lies forever beyond one's grasp. In this dynamic, fantasy serves not only to compel a quest for the *objet* and the *jouissance* it promises but to explain as well why neither is actually attained. Hence, fantasy paradoxically produces rather than satiates desire (see also chapters 4 and 8). Thus Žižek writes, "In the fantasy-scene desire is not fulfilled, 'satisfied,' but constituted" (1989, 132), while Yannis Stavrakakis adds that fantasy should be seen "not only as a screen which promises to fill the lack in the Other, but also as what 'produces' this lack" (2007, 241). In this way, fantasy serves to obscure the unbridgeable gap between what ideology promises and what it actually delivers (see chapter 1), functioning as "a means for an ideology to take its own failure into account in advance" (Žižek 1989, 142).

Psychoanalysis and the Environment

From Joseph Mishan's (1996) formative "First Thoughts" on the relationship between psychoanalysis and environmentalism, consideration of the connection has progressed slowly but steadily, producing a small yet insightful stream of academic literature. Stavrakakis draws on Lacan to describe a "Green ideology" aiming "to refound and recreate the political, social and economic foundations of western societies on the basis of a political project that is constructed around a certain conception of nature" (1997a, 260). He views this ideology as symptomatic of the "limits to growth and economic expansion, limits imposed by the Real of nature" (Stavrakakis 1997b, 124), evidenced by the environmental crises giving rise to Green ideology itself. Meanwhile, Swyngedouw (2011) references Žižek (1992) to

Robert Fletcher

describe environmentalism as the "new opium for the masses" in its tendency to obscure the fundamentally political nature of ecological damage in positing purely technocratic solutions for these problems. Paul Robbins and Sarah Moore (2013) diagnose a growing "ecological anxiety disorder" manifest, for instance, in scientific debate concerning the merits of novel ecological systems. Building on all of this, elsewhere I have described how neoliberal environmental discourse resorts to fantasy to conceal the gap between its lofty promise and meager results in practice (Fletcher 2013a, b, 2014) as well as the way overpopulation serves as a scapegoat for the failure of sustainable development policies (Fletcher, Breitling, and Puleo 2014).

Increasingly, this literature has come to focus on climate change in particular. Hence, Swyngedouw (e.g., 2010, 2015) describes mainstream responses to climate change, in the form of carbon markets and related mechanisms, as a kind of "post-politics" that offers the fantasy of a purely technical fix for what are in reality deeply political issues demanding dramatic socioeconomic transformation. Mark Davidson analyzes mounting discussion of "sustainable cities" as a similar fantasy offering the (im)possibility of "continued economic growth without necessary reductions in carbon emissions" (2012, 14). Building on this, Healy (2014) describes the fossil fuel dependency propelling global warming as a form of "addiction," contending that this is sustained by a capitalist "economy of enjoyment" that lures subjects into deep attachment to an unsustainable society of which global warming constitutes a key symptom.

More ambitiously, Sally Weintrobe (2013a) has assembled a collection of psychoanalysts and others to explore the psychic mechanisms inhibiting effective climate change response. The key concept in this collection is, as one might expect, "denial." While denial has been a frequent topic in critique of climate change politics, most centrally with respect to efforts on the part of oil producers and others to impede or discredit scientific evidence affirming the problem (see, e.g., Oreskes and Conway 2011; Healy 2014), psychoanalysts focus on the ways in which particular subjects may impede their own awareness of events. Weintrobe (2013b) thus distinguishes three forms of denial. *Denialism* comprises "campaigns of misinformation about climate change, funded by commercial and ideological interests" (Weintrobe 2013b, 7), such as the ultraconservative Heartland Institute (Healy 2014). *Negation* "involves saying that something that is, is not" (Weintrobe 2013b, 7), as in efforts to directly refute the overwhelming scientific evidence documenting global warming. A third form of denial, *disavowal*, is more insidious, in that "reality is more accepted, but its significance is minimized" (Weintrobe 2013b, 7). Phrased differently, disavowal is a simultaneous admission and denial, or a state of "half-knowing," that operates according to the formula "I know very well, but still . . ." (Žižek 1989, 12). As a result, Weintrobe asserts, disavowal "is a more serious and intractable form of denial," for "while negation says no to the truth, it does not distort the truth. Disavowal, by contrast, can be highly organized at an unconscious level and can become entrenched. It distorts the truth in a variety of artful ways. Disavowal can lead us further and further away from accepting the reality of climate change. This is because the more reality is systematically avoided through making it insignificant or through distortion, the more anxiety builds up unconsciously, and the greater is the need to defend with further disavowal" (2013b, 7).

Such disavowal commonly manifests as perversion, a dysfunctional state involving a "turning away from the truth" (Layton 2010, 209) as "a way of not coming to terms with loss" (Hoggett 2013, 59; see also chapter 12 in this volume). In the case of climate change, Paul Hoggett thus asserts, "The majority of us in the West 'know' the facts, but we turn away from what we know" (2013, 60). Or more precisely, "We 'know' and yet we seem ill-equipped to bear the pain of what we know. In the perverse state of mind reality is not rejected outright but is simultaneously acknowledged and disavowed" (Hoggett 2013, 61). To facilitate this "half-knowing," rather than outright denying the problem disavowal characteristically "involves an entrenched 'quick fix' approach to problems" rather than serious inquiry into their complex causes and solutions (Weintrobe 2013b, 8).

This is, as I have suggested earlier and elsewhere (Fletcher 2013b), precisely how neoliberal environmentalism tends to function. By disavowing the reality of neoliberal capitalism's contributions to ecological degrada-

Robert Fletcher

tion, this discourse sustains the fantasy that degradation can be redressed through the same mechanisms that perpetuate it if we are only able to "get the market right" by internalizing environmental (and social) costs of production, thereby sending the proper market signals to producers and consumers. Visions of carbon markets and green cities smoothly paving the path to a post-carbon society thus serve as "palliative fantasies that offer an 'easy fix'" for a problem demanding substantial socioeconomic transformation (Healy 2014, 182).

In this respect, neoliberal environmentalism functions in much the same manner as Žižek's oft-cited example of the chocolate laxative, an actual product that claims to be the antidote to the problem—constipation—that it itself precipitates (Fletcher 2014). When Klein (2014) calls this approach "magical thinking," from a psychoanalytic perspective this indeed can be seen as an extension of an infant's magical efforts to avoid the reality principle and preserve a sense of omnipotence in the face of increasing awareness of its limited power to control the larger glObe (Mishan 1996).

Mourning and Melancholia

Advocacy of neoliberal environmentalism in order to preserve the status quo of mainstream capitalist society is rendered more paradoxical still by evidence that for a significant segment of the population, including many societal elites, this way of life is far from a satisfying one. Signs of discontent within modern society have been growing for some time (Freud 1962), expressed in all manner of media and cemented by a growing body of research demonstrating a fundamental disconnect between subjective happiness and material wealth beyond a certain minimum threshold (see, e.g., Anielski 2007). In other words, both those denied the benefits of modern society and those receiving them are rendered unhappy by its excesses. Why, then, do many remain so attached to a way of life that not only degrades the planet but makes them miserable as well?

For psychoanalysts, attachment is cemented by the *jouissance* it delivers. While this *jouissance*, as noted earlier, is rarely unequivocally pleasurable, rather offering pleasure and pain in equal measure, the fleeting pleasure it does provide reinforces commitment via the fantasy that the pain can be overcome and pure pleasure attained. Breaking attachment therefore requires the loss of both this fantasy of total fulfillment and the limited *jouissance* actually experienced. Facing this loss entails a process of mourning for the pain of separation and deprivation of pleasure (see chapter 11). To avoid this pain, we tend to retain attachment at all costs, or when forced to endure loss, we turn away from and repress the pain, in which case mourning is replaced by melancholia, a state of low-level depression precipitated by the inability to mourn and therefore dissipate the negative emotion (Freud 1925). Melancholia is supported by a variety of defense mechanisms, but one of the most significant is disavowal, which allows subjects to half-acknowledge their pain while simultaneously denying its significance. Manifest as perversion, this entails, paradoxically, a (largely unconscious) "'choice' to feel pain rather than suffer the painful truth" (Layton 2010, 309). One of psychoanalysis's most important insights is that this dynamic of attachment occurs even with respect to circumstances that subjects consider negative and that they may explicitly claim to want to end. In short, as Žižek asserts in the epigraph, attaining "freedom hurts."

From Desire to Drive

While fantasy is sustained by desire for the *jouissance* it promises, in the case of melancholia this dynamic changes: desire turns inward and become instead "drive," propelled by the inability to mourn for loss, in which case attachment turns from the object of desire—the *objet petit a*—to the *experience of loss itself*. As a result, this very experience of loss becomes the object perpetually pursued. In this way, drive becomes a self-destructive cycle in which one endlessly repeats a futile behavior while disavowing its negative effects. As Žižek describes, drive thus constitutes a "blind insistence that follows its course with utter disregard for the requirements of our concrete life-world" (2001, 98).

This move from desire to drive, Žižek claims, describes the trajectory of contemporary capitalism as a whole, whereby desire for *jouissance* promised by increased consumption in an "economy of enjoyment" is increasingly

Robert Fletcher

replaced by the endless repetition of a failure to attain enjoyment, instead becoming attached to this failure itself. In this way, drive "turns crisis into triumph, generating enjoyment, not from success, but repeated failure" (Kapoor 2015, 66). As with desire, it is the "libidinal kick (*jouissance*) which accompanies drive that helps explain capitalism's continued obstinacy and endurance" (Kapoor 2015, 67).

Desire and drive have thus come to complement one another as twin "drivers" of capitalist development operating at different levels. While desire grips us as particular "consumers, as subjects of desire, soliciting in [us] ever new perverse and excessive desires (for which it offers products to satisfy them) . . . drive inheres to capitalism at a more fundamental, *systemic* level: drive is that which propels the whole capitalist machinery, it is the impersonal compulsion to engage in the endless circular movement of expanded self-reproduction" (Žižek 2009, 61, quoted in Kapoor 2015, 69). This dynamic, Ilan Kapoor contends, accounts for capitalism's characteristic "circular drive to accumulate for the sake of accumulation" (2015, 66) even in the face of growing recognition of the environmental catastrophe created by drive.

Mainstream climate change politics seems to function in just this manner. Negotiations of the UNFCCC continually repeat a failure to achieve effective action, and industrial civilization as a whole thus continues its half-conscious journey toward self-destruction. A prime example here is provided by ExxonMobil. One of the largest oil companies in the world and one of the most profitable multinational corporations generally, copious evidence now demonstrates that ExxonMobil, along with other fossil fuel producers such as the infamous Koch brothers, have in fact been aware of the implications of fossil fuel emissions for climate change for decades yet have spent many millions of dollars to suppress or distort public discussion of them (see, e.g., Greenpeace USA 2013)—a classic case of Weintrobe's denialism. More recently, however, as evidence for climate change becomes increasingly pervasive and incontrovertible, the company's position has become more complicated. In a 2014 report, for instance, ExxonMobil explicitly acknowledged the decisive findings of the latest IPCC report issued the very same day, yet stated that these finding would be unlikely to provoke a significant regulatory response by most governments and hence that the company's primary obligation to its shareholders required that it continue to extract and sell all available oil despite the admittedly apocalyptic implications of doing so (see ExxonMobil 2014). This seems to signal a clear move from denialism to disavowal, in that the report does represent, on one level, an acknowledgment of climate change while still not accepting the serious implications of the phenomenon in terms of the dramatic impacts that should force any reasonable person to end actions contributing to the problem if it were fully acknowledged.

Even more recently, moreover, in the midst of the COP-21 summit, when it became clear that most of the world's nations were now committed to achieving a new global agreement and ExxonMobil had come under increasing attack from climate activists, the company reiterated a long-standing though lukewarm call for a universal carbon tax to compel the global market to begin moving away from fossil fuel dependence. Yet the implications of such a tax for the future of a company depending on oil production itself have not been addressed. If such taxes were high enough to be effective, they would make oil so expensive that a viable capitalist market for its purchase, as well as all of the other products tied to the price of oil, would collapse entirely. (The company calculates that to keep the planet within a 1.6-degree temperature rise would eventually necessitate a price of $2,000 per ton of CO_2, translating into a cost of approximately US$20 per gallon of gasoline [Eaton and Carroll 2015], which would of course be impossible for capitalist markets to accommodate.)

In this way, acknowledgment at one level facilitates continued (or even intensified) disavowal at another, framing the situation, as Žižek likes to quip, as "catastrophic but not yet serious" (1992, 27). Building on his general formula for disavowal, Žižek describes this perspective as maintaining that "I know very well (that the situation is catastrophic), but . . . (I don't believe it and will go on acting as though it were not serious)" (1992, 27). Thus, actors like ExxonMobil "know very well what they are doing, but still, they are doing it" (Žižek 1989, 26).

Robert Fletcher

Conclusion: Enjoying Climate Change

What all of this suggests, from the psychoanalytic perspective explored here, is that climate politics increasingly represents a glObal effort to disavow both the Real of capitalism as an economic system riddled with internal contradictions that make it inherently unstable unless continually expanding (Wilson 2014; Kapoor 2015) and the Real of nature as both a finite source of inputs for this system and a sink for its outputs whose fundamental limits have been exceeded (Stavrakakis 1997a). In this sense, the various forms of "magical thinking" outlined earlier could be understood as different stages in the process of disavowal. As Healy asks, "Could it be that the 'post-politics' of carbon markets described by Swyngedouw, the promises of an easy cure in the form of the utopian city described by Davidson, and the denials issued by the Heartland Institute, are simply a vacillation between admission and denial" (2014, 192), which is precisely what disavowal is about? In short, the neoliberal environmentalism increasingly dominating climate politics might be seen, like neoliberalism in general, as "an increasingly desperate struggle to hold reality together, against the traumatic incursions of the Real of Capital" (Wilson 2014, 315).

In response to this, the quintessential Lacanian injunction is to encourage subjects to "traverse the fantasy." As Michael Brearley summarizes this process, "the task of the ego (is) to wean itself away from its early reliance on magical and wishful thinking and painfully attempt to represent to itself what really is the case" (2013, 160). In the instance considered here, this would entail fully acknowledging the Real of capitalism as a self-destructive system driving us toward the brink of ecological catastrophe. And this, of course, would require consciously confronting the pain resulting from both loss of attachment to the capitalist society of enjoyment and recognition of the environmental devastation this society has wrought to break the cycle of melancholia and perversion. As Mishan asserted some time ago, "The psychic cost of such a move into recognition is the cost of the move from the paranoid-schizoid toward the depressive position. The cost is the psychic pain of guilt at damage done, and the necessity of mourning of our grandiose fantasy of self-sufficiency and immortality. Without such a move we risk eco-catastrophe, because we cannot assess the true threat" (1996, 65). Or as Healy puts it, we need to experience "a kind of hitting bottom in our relation to oil addiction as a precondition for moving beyond it" (2014, 193).

More than a lack of practicable alternatives, in other words, it may be our unconscious attachment to the contemporary capitalist order despite our expressed desire to transcend (or at least substantially transform) it that helps to hold it in place, raising the sobering prospect that many of us may not be nearly as willing to make the dramatic changes we know are necessary to develop a just and sustainable world as we would like to believe (see chapter 4). From the psychoanalytic perspective advanced in this chapter, achieving effective change requires generating the desire for attachment to a new situation sufficient to motivate subjects to face the pain of and then undergo the process of mourning necessary to break attachment to present circumstances. As Margaret Rustin phrases this dilemma, "Moving out of the paranoid-schizoid into more depressive ways of thinking and feeling can be found too painful to endure, if there are no internalized good objects to sustain a belief in the existence of good objects outside the self" (2013, 175). Yet if this new desire is merely for further unfulfillable fantasies, then nothing will have been gained. Hence, the aim must be to mobilize novel forms of "post-fantasmatic enjoyment" capable of traversing fantasy and accepting the impossibility of either achieving or escaping *jouissance* (Byrne and Healy 2006). Žižek (2010) suggests that this requires moving through Kübler-Ross's (1969) classic stages of grief from denial through anger, bargaining, depression, and finally to full acceptance.

Herein lies the crux of our present predicament. Assessments of our environmental problems overwhelmingly tend to envision an apocalyptic future in which depletion of natural resources will lead to either fierce competition for, or strict rationing of, what is left—a perspective that Swyngedouw (2010) evocatively calls forecasting "apocalypse forever." Both situations are generally depicted as quite grim and pleasure-less. It is difficult for even those of us gravely concerned by ecological degradation and highly motivated to address it to be inspired by such prospects, particularly when this entails giving up a lifestyle that does in fact provide the promise (if not achievement) of *jouissance* in myriad forms. And so while we may in fact claim that we desire the dramatic change we know is needed, we may secretly fear this change as well, engaging in our own disavowal concerning the depth of our commitment to the cause. Thus, Renee Aron Lertzman highlights "the power of unconscious desires: that we may in fact want our cars and cheap flights and also want to avoid global climate-induced catastrophes" (2013, 120), generating a deep-seated ambivalence toward the change we (half-)know is needed.

One of our most urgent present challenges, therefore, is to develop a vision of a sustainable society sufficiently motivating to compel a large and increasing number of subjects to become willing to undergo the process of mourning requisite to breaking attachment to the modern industrial capitalist system currently suffocating the earth—to create "a subject who desires nonexploitation" (Byrne and Healy 2006, 256) while keeping our "desiring eyes set on the communist horizon" (Dean 2012, 22). In this respect, Healy (2014) identifies several potentially "post-fantasmatic" forms of climate politics that may point in this direction. The Transition Town movement inspired by permaculturist Rob Hopkins (2008) has rapidly spread across Europe and North America in its vision to build low-carbon, fossil fuel–independent communities. At the same time, forms of so-called solidarity economy have expanded as well, "based on principles of mutual aid rather than competition, democratic social inclusion, and non-capitalist economic development" (Healy 2014, 193). Yet Healy's discussion of these dynamics remains quite speculative, inviting much greater analytical engagement with the movements in question. The potential of such alternatives to function as the basis of post-fantasmatic enjoyment, as Healy suggests, or even merely as transitional objects facilitating detachment from the status quo en route to an entirely different social order, is thus a vital focus of future inquiry.

Works Cited

Agarwal, Anil, and Sunita Narain. 1991. *Global Warming in an Unequal World: A Case of Environmental Colonialism*. New Delhi: Centre for Science and Environment.

Anielski, Mark. 2007. *The Economics of Happiness: Building Genuine Wealth*. New York: New Society Publishers.

Banerjee, Abhijit, and Esther Duflo. 2011. *Poor Economics: A Radical Rethinking of the Way to Fight Global Poverty*. New York: PublicAffairs.

Benton, Ted. 2013. "Discussion: How Is Climate Change an Issue for Psychoanalysis?" In *Engaging with Climate Change: Psychoanalytic and Interdisciplinary Perspectives*, edited by Sally Weintrobe, 190–95. New York: Routledge.

Böhm, Stephen. 2015. "How Emissions Trading at Paris Climate Talks Has Set Us Up for Failure." *The Conversation*, December 14. https://theconversation.com/how-emissions-trading-at-paris-climate-talks-has-set-us-up-for-failure-52319.

Brearley, Michael. 2013. "Discussion: Unconscious Obstacles to Caring for the Planet: Facing Up to Human Nature." In *Engaging with Climate Change: Psychoanalytic and Interdisciplinary Perspectives*, edited by Sally Weintrobe, 160–64. New York: Routledge.

Büscher, Bram, Sian Sullivan, Katja Neves, Jim Igoe, and Dan Brockington. 2012. "Towards a Synthesized Critique of Neoliberal Biodiversity Conservation." *Capitalism, Nature, Socialism* 23 (2): 4–30.

Byrne, Ken, and Stephen Healy. 2006. "Cooperative Subjects: Toward a Post-fantasmatic Enjoyment of the Economy." *Rethinking Marxism* 18, 241–58.

Davidson, Mark. 2012. "Sustainable City as Fantasy." *Human Geography* 5 (2): 14–25.

Dean, Jodi. 2012. *The Communist Horizon*. London: Verso.

Eaton, Collin, and Susan Carroll. 2015. "Exxon Mobil Backs Carbon Tax." *Houston Chronicle*, December 7. http://www.houstonchronicle.com/business/energy/article/Exxon-espouses-carbon-tax-amid-Paris-climate-talks-6682461.php.

ExxonMobil. 2014. *Energy and Carbon: Managing the Risks*. http://cdn.exxonmobil.com/~/media/global/files/energy-and-environment/report---energy-and-carbon---managing-the-risks.pdf.

Fink, Bruce. 1995. *The Lacanian Subject: Between Language and Jouissance*. Princeton NJ: Princeton University Press.

Fletcher, Robert. 2010. "Neoliberal Environmentality: Towards a Poststructuralist Political Ecology of the Conservation Debate." *Conservation and Society* 8, 171–81.

———. 2013a. "Bodies Do Matter: The Peculiar Persistence of Neoliberalism in Environmental Governance." *Human Geography* 6, 29–45.

———. 2013b. "How I Learned to Stop Worrying and Love the Market: Virtualism, Dis-avowal and Public Secrecy in Neoliberal Environmental Conservation." *Environment and Planning D: Society and Space* 31, 796–812.

———. 2014. "Taking the Chocolate Laxative: Why Neoliberal Conservation 'Fails For-ward.'" In *Nature™ Inc.: Environmental Conservation in the Neoliberal Age*, edited by Bram Büscher, Wolfram Dressler, and Robert Fletcher, 87–107. Tucson: University of Arizona Press.

Fletcher, Robert, Jan Breitling, and Valerie Puleo. 2014. "Barbarian Hordes: The Overpop-ulation Scapegoat in International Development Discourse." *Third World Quarterly* 35, 1195–1215.

Fletcher, Robert, Wolfram Dressler, Bram Büscher, and Zachary R. Anderson. 2016. "Questioning REDD+ and the Future of Market-Based Conservation." *Conservation Biology* 30 (3): 673–75. DOI: 10.1111/cobi.12680.

Foucault, Michel. 2008. *The Birth of Biopolitics*. Translated by G. Burchell. New York: Palgrave Macmillan.

Freud, Sigmund. 1925. "Mourning and Melancholia." In *Collected Papers*, vol. 4, 152–70. London: Hogarth Press.

———. 1962. *Civilization and Its Discontents*. New York: Norton.

Goldenberg, Suzanne, John Vidal, Lenore Taylor, Adam Vaughan, and Fiona Harvey. 2015. "Paris Climate Deal: Nearly 200 Nations Sign in End of Fossil Fuel Era." *Guardian*, Decem-ber 12. http://www.theguardian.com/environment/2015/dec/12/paris-climate-deal -200-nations-sign-finish-fossil-fuel-era.

Greenpeace USA. 2013. *Dealing in Doubt: The Climate Denial Machine vs Climate Science*. https:// climateaccess.org/resource/dealing-doubt-%E2%80%93-climate-denial-machine -vs-climate-science.

Harvey, David. 2005. *A Brief History of Neoliberalism*. Oxford: Oxford University Press.

Healy, Stephen. 2014. "Psychoanalysis and the Geography of the Anthropocene: Fantasy, Oil Addiction and the Politics of Global Warming." In *Psychoanalytic Geographies*, edited by Paul Kingsbury and Steve Pile, 181–96. Farnham, UK: Ashgate.

Heynen, Nik, James McCarthy, Paul Robbins, and Scott Prudham, eds. 2007. *Neoliberal Environments: False Promises and Unnatural Consequences*. New York: Routledge.

Hoggett, Paul. 2013. "Reply: Climate Change in a Perverse Culture." In *Engaging with Climate Change: Psychoanalytic and Interdisciplinary Perspectives*, edited by Sally Weintrobe, 84–86. New York: Routledge.

Hopkins, Rob. 2008. *The Transition Handbook: From Oil Dependency to Local Resilience*. White River Junction VT: Chelsea Green Publishing.

Huber, Matthew T. 2013. *Lifeblood: Oil, Freedom, and the Forces of Capital*. Minneapolis: University of Minnesota Press.

Intergovernmental Panel on Climate Change. 2014. *Climate Change 2014: Impacts, Adaptation, and Vulnerability*. http://www.ipcc.ch/report/ar5/wg2/.

Jameson, Fredric. 2003. "Future City." *New Left Review* 21, 65–79.

Jordan, Andrew, Tim Rayner, Heiki Schroeder, Neil, Adger, Kevin Anderson, Alice Bows, Corrine Le Quéré, et al. 2013. "Going Beyond Two Degrees? The Risks and Opportunities of Alternative Options." *Climate Policy* 13, 751–69.

Kapoor, Ilan. 2015. "What "Drives" Capitalist Development?" *Human Geography* 8 (3), 66–78.

Klein, Naomi. 2014. *This Changes Everything: Capitalism vs. the Climate*. New York: Simon & Schuster.

Kübler-Ross, Elisabeth. 1969. *On Death and Dying*. New York: Simon & Schuster.

Lakoff, George. 2009. *The Political Mind*. New York: Penguin.

Layton, Lynne. 2010. "Irrational Exuberance: Neoliberal Subjectivity and the Perversion of Truth." *Subjectivity* 3, 303–22.

Lertzman, Renee Aron. 2013. "The Myth of Apathy: Psychoanalytic Explorations of Environmental Subjectivity." In *Engaging with Climate Change: Psychoanalytic and Interdisciplinary Perspectives*, edited by Sally Weintrobe, 117–33. New York: Routledge.

Malm, Andreas. 2016. *Fossil Capital*. London: Verso.

Millennium Ecosystem Assessment. 2005. *Millennium Ecosystem Assessment: Ecosystems and Human Wellbeing*. Washington DC: Island Press.

Mishan, Joseph. 1996. "Psychoanalysis and Environmentalism: First Thoughts." *Psychoanalytic Psychotherapy* 10, 59–70.

Oreskes, Naomi, and Erik M. Conway. 2011. *Merchants of Doubt*. New York: Bloomsbury.

Prins, Gwyn, Malcolm Cook, Christopher Green, Mike Hulme, Atte Korhola, Eija-Riitta Korhola, Roger Pielke Jr., et al. 2009. *How to Get Climate Policy Back on Course*. London: LSE Mackinder Programme. http://sciencepolicy.colorado.edu/admin/publication _files/resource-2731-2009.17.pdf.

Robbins, Paul, and Sarah A. Moore. 2013. "Ecological Anxiety Disorder: Diagnosing the Politics of the Anthropocene." *Cultural Geographies* 20, 3–19.

Rustin, Margaret. 2013. "Reply: How Is Climate Change an Issue for Psychoanalysis?" In *Engaging with Climate Change: Psychoanalytic and Interdisciplinary Perspectives*, edited by Sally Weintrobe, 196–98. New York: Routledge.

Sheller, Mimi, and John Urry. 2006. "The New Mobilities Paradigm." *Environment and Planning A* 38, 207–26.

Robert Fletcher

Stavrakakis, Yannis. 1997a. "Green Fantasy and the Real of Nature: Elements of a Lacanian Critique of Green Ideological Discourse." *Journal for the Psychoanalysis of Culture and Society* 2, 123–32.

———. 1997b. "Green Ideology: A Discursive Reading." *Journal of Political Ideologies* 2, 259–79.

———. 2007. *The Lacanian Left: Psychoanalysis, Theory, Politics.* Edinburgh: University of Edinburgh Press.

Swyngedouw, Erik. 2010. "Apocalypse Forever? Post-political Populism and the Spectre of Climate Change." *Theory, Culture and Society* 27, 213–32.

———. 2011. "The Trouble with Nature: Ecology as the New Opium for the Masses." In *The Ashgate Research Companion to Planning Theory*, edited by J. Hillier and P. Healey 299–318. Farnham, UK: Ashgate.

———. 2015. "Depoliticized Environments and the Promises of the Anthropocene." In *The International Handbook of Political Ecology*, edited by R. L. Bryant, 131–45. Chechenham, UK: Edward Elgar.

Weintrobe, Sally, ed. 2013a. *Engaging with Climate Change: Psychoanalytic and Interdisciplinary Perspectives.* New York: Routledge.

———. 2013b. "Introduction." In *Engaging with Climate Change: Psychoanalytic and Interdisciplinary Perspectives*, edited by Sally Weintrobe, 1–15. New York: Routledge.

Wilson, Japhy. 2014. "The Shock of the Real: The Neoliberal Neurosis in the Life and Times of Jeffrey Sachs." *Antipode* 46 (1), 301–21.

Žižek, Slavoj. 1989. *The Sublime Object of Ideology.* London: Verso.

———. 1992. *Looking Awry: An Introduction to Jacques Lacan through Popular Culture.* Cambridge MA: MIT Press.

———. 2001. "The Rhetorics of Power." *Diacritics* 31, 91–104.

———. 2009. *The Parallax View.* Cambridge MA: MIT Press.

———. 2010. *Living in the End Times.* London: Verso.

———. 2012. *The Pervert's Guide to Ideology.* DVD. Directed by Sophie Fiennes. New York: P Guide Productions/Zeitgeist Films.

4   Integrative and Responsive Desires
Resources for an Alternative Political Economy

Eleanor MacDonald

The wealth of societies in which the capitalist mode of production prevails appears as "an immense collection of commodities"; the individual commodity appears as its elementary form. Our investigation therefore begins with the analysis of a commodity.

MARX, *Capital*

There is no freedom as long as everything has its price.

ADORNO, "Messages in a Bottle"

We live in a world suffused with market relations. Whether we are discussing personal relationships, governmental social policies, environmental issues, or global concerns, our words and actions seem invariably to turn to the language of investment, trade-offs, costs and benefits, income and expenditure, the bottom line. The glObal expansion of capitalism has generated a concomitant expansion of consumerism, converting all things and relations into property. Alongside the spread of capitalist economic relations, we can witness the spread of its cultural values and attitudes. This process includes not just the conversion of things into commodities, as Karl Marx argues, nor merely the corresponding narrowing of our reasoning into instrumental thinking, in the assessment of the thinkers of the Frankfurt School; it has also shifted our relationship to objects and others at the level of our affective response to them—our desires. In response, we would benefit from an awareness of other resources to be found in alternative forms of desire, both integrative and responsive. We need to think beyond the terms of ideology and discourse, as the ideas and meanings that circulate to support the spread of global capitalism, and consider how even our affective responses to others and to objects are implicated.

Volume 1 of Karl Marx's treatise *Capital* begins with the trenchant observation that what characterizes capitalist societies is that wealth appears within them as a tremendous agglomeration of commodities—of units characterized by the common denominator of exchange value, or "price" (1977, 64). The careful analysis Marx provides of the commodity form of wealth reveals its essential role both in the processes of capitalist exploitation and in the dissemblance of that exploitation. Marx's commentary on commodities shows the intrinsic connection between our perception of the world and power relations operative within that world. The revolutionary possibilities of worker solidarity, Marx hopes, will supplant this economy with a more human and more responsive one.

For Theodor Adorno, this analysis of the world as commodified—that everything has its price—is indicative of the flawed reasoning of a failed Enlightenment. Our relationship to the world, along with our capacity to know the world, has been damaged by a desire to control that world. Thus Adorno, along with Max Horkheimer, in their coauthored text, *Dialectic of Enlightenment*, provide a critique of "instrumental reason" (1982). In his *Negative Dialectics*, Adorno (1973) seeks an epistemological alternative such that we might perceive and respond to the world non-instrumentally. His further observations on aesthetics suggest that freedom can never be located within capitalist relations but might reside in our capacity for critical reasoning, as well as in the realm of autonomous art and in art as mimesis (Adorno 1997).

My argument in what follows draws substantially from the insights of these critiques of capitalism. I augment Marx's and Adorno's work by arguing that the problem of the commodity as the principle way in which we encounter the world not only lies in the realm of material relations (Marx) or purely in the realm of rationality (Adorno) but must also be countered at the level of our desire. For this, Freudian theory might provide useful conceptual tools. While economic analysis and critical reasoning are absolutely vital to analyzing and responding to the world's problems—poverty, disease, environmental damage, violence—our political responses are ineluctably influenced by unconscious drives, desires, affects. Rationally, we might argue that we need to make different choices, that there are a thousand ways in which we might need to relate to our global environment, to other species, and to each other in ways that are more respectful, that recognize the limits of our control, that do not seek profit maximization and the agglomeration of wealth as the principal goal. But political decisions are rarely, if ever, fully rational. Psychoanalytic theory, with its insights into the mechanisms and functioning of desire, could prove helpful in analyzing the unconscious appeal of the commodity form, of our desire to possess and control—that it is through understanding the mechanisms of desire, and of alternative forms of desire, that we may have some chance of challenging it (see chapter 3).

At the conclusion of his essay "On Narcissism," Sigmund Freud (1914) provides a rudimentary typology of desire. It can take the form, he says, of either anaclisis or narcissism. He encapsulates these two forms of desire, roughly, as the desire "to have" and the desire "to be." Each can take either active or passive form. In the first section of this essay, I summarize this typology and suggest some of its flaws and limitations. Its chief limitation is that Freud did not sufficiently explore or problematize three of his four categories of desire. Aside from the essay on narcissism, Freud gives significant attention only to the "active anaclitic" form. I argue that his prejudicial emphasis corresponds to the way in which desire primarily functions in Western society. Although Freud acknowledges that other forms of desire exist, his work normalizes (and reflects the normalization of) only one variant of desire.

In the second section of this essay, I develop my argument through a reworking of Freud's typology in which I rename several of his concepts and speculate about how the subordinate terms (narcissism and the passive forms of desire) might correspond to their subordination in Western culture (rather than, as Freud might suggest, corresponding to a pathology in which their subordination is requisite to social functioning). I then contemplate the ways in which desire responds to a range of human experiences that may be broader than what Freud envisages. These experiences may give rise to different cultural patterns of—"to be," "to have," "to belong." They may correspond to different modes of identification and social/material relations.

The third and final section of this paper relates the discussion of desire more explicitly to our relationship to our material environment in the context of global capitalism. My argument in this section is that alternative forms of desire might provide resources for alternative relations and experiences that could be useful in envisioning environmentalist and anticapitalist social transformation. I am especially concerned in this discussion with rethinking our relationship to the material, natural environment, of which we are a part and on which we entirely depend, despite our illusions of and attempts at mastery of it. My intention throughout the paper, including in this final section, is not to supplant one form of desire with another. Truthfully, I believe this would be impossible. Nor do I want to argue that all the solutions to the problems of capitalist society can be found at the level of desire itself. Capitalism has proved itself adept at seizing on all forms of desire to turn a profit from them. Rather, I hope to suggest that Western and globalizing capitalist culture has stultified the range of our unconscious affective responses to objects such that these are only partially realized or made capable of realization. Additionally, I argue that the subordinated forms of desire are acknowledged only insofar or inasmuch as they are assigned to others and repudiated or romanticized. Thus, we might reflect on the ways in which the leading and acknowledged form of desire serves to maintain forms of domination in our culture.

Freud's Typology of Desire

Freud (1914) distinguishes two types of desire—"anaclitic" and "narcissistic"—and adds that each can function either actively or passively, thus suggesting four possible experiences of desire. Although apparently a straightforward typology, further investigation indicates more complexity and offers an opportunity to problematize and rethink the ways in which this model has been adopted within psychoanalysis.

ANACLITIC DESIRE

The primary form of desire is "anaclitic." This is typically presented as the desire "to have" or "to take" the other as one's object. The term "anaclitic" was a neologism of Freud's English translator, James Strachey, who, along with many other colleagues in the psychoanalytic community, intended to offer English readers a word that sounded sufficiently medical and authoritative to be given a corresponding importance. The original German term was a common verb, *anlehung*, meaning "to lean on" or "to attach to." This form of desire had as its origins the original attachment of the infant to the person who was the source of survival and nourishment; in most cases, he assumed, this would be the mother. Infantile libido (sexual/life energy or, in the broadest terms, sexual desire), according to Freud, must attach "to one of the vital somatic functions" (1907).[1] Self-preservation— feeding—becomes the basis for a desire that is felt for what is then associated with nourishment: the breast, and subsequently the mother. In this shift from one object to the next ("food," "breast," "mother") not only does desire's object shift, but so too does its aim as the need for survival is supplanted by the desire for pleasure. But it is not the object nor the aim that is key to this form of desire; rather it is its *capacity to shift or transpose object-choice*. According to Freud, the infant transfers its desire from breast to nurse or mother and, at the critical stage of the Oedipal phase, to other and future objects of desire. Remarkably, this fungibility of object-choices is socially and culturally relevant as it makes possible individual adaptability to particular cultural and social conditions and the resolution of social conflict. When desire for an object is forbidden, taboo, or otherwise unavailable, the psyche has the capacity to transfer desire onto an alternative object.

Freud clearly links active anaclitic desire with men and masculinity. In his conventional version of the Oedipal drama, the male child represses and relinquishes his desire for his mother as a consequence of perceived

Eleanor MacDonald

rivalry with his father. That he has the capacity to do so is in part due to the transpositional capacity of anaclitic desire. But his ability to do so is also a consequence of his capacity to align himself with his father, thereby establishing an identification with him. Concomitant with this identification is the internalization of a superego that corresponds to and reinforces both the father's preeminence and the larger social order.

Freud anticipates that femininity will complement masculinity, that it will take the form of passive anaclitic desire—the desire to be possessed. He remained uncertain of how this state of desire would come about and considered it unreliable; he saw as other potential outcomes for women the possibility of active anaclitic desire (which he associated with female homosexuality) or loss of sexual desire entirely. He additionally surmised that women lacked men's motivation for internalizing the male superego, and thus that women were probably to be found morally inferior to (as well as libidinally weaker than) men (Freud 1933).

A further aspect of Freud's theorization of active anaclitic desire is that he regards it, at least in its most significant expression—that of heterosexual masculinity—as inherently dissatisfied. In his essay "The Universal Tendency to Debasement in the Sphere of Love," Freud notes that this "masculine desire," typical of the object choices made by men, is profoundly ambivalent. It is common—indeed, universally true if we are to take his title seriously—that men must separate sexual desire from love. Desire is apparently doomed to dissatisfaction. As Freud proclaims, "Those whom they love, they cannot desire, and those whom they desire they cannot love" (1912, 183). The "affectionate and sensual currents" are divided, such that either the man must love one person and desire another, or alternatively, he is able to desire the one whom he loves if she is lowered in his sight. It is normal, in other words, for men to psychically disparage women as a means to maintain their desire for them: "The main protective measure against such a disturbance which men have recourse to in this split in their love consists in a psychical debasement of the sexual object, the overvaluation that normally attaches to the sexual object being reserved for the incestuous object and its representatives. As soon as the condition of debasement is fulfilled, sensuality can be freely expressed, and important sexual capacities and a high degree of pleasure can develop" (Freud 1912, 183).

Throughout his work, Freud assumes this normative condition of active anaclisis for heterosexual men. He nowhere provides a complementary analysis of ambivalence among women or in same-sex male relationships. We are left to speculate about how such desire and relationships based on the confluence of various desires might function. Ultimately, Freud's speculations about active anaclitic desire lead him to a view of it as perennially dissatisfied:

> [We] must reckon with the possibility that something in the nature of the sexual instinct itself is unfavorable to the realization of complete satisfaction. If we consider the long and difficult developmental history of the instinct, two factors immediately spring to mind which might be made responsible for this difficulty. Firstly, as a result of the diphasic onset of object-choice, and the interposition of the barrier against incest, the final object of the sexual instinct is never any longer the original object but only a surrogate for it. Psychoanalysis has shown us that when the original object of a wishful impulse has been lost as a result of repression, it is frequently represented by an endless series of substitutive objects none of which, however, brings full satisfaction. This may explain the inconstancy in object-choice, the "craving for stimulation"—which is so often a feature of the love of adults. . . . The instincts of love are hard to educate; education of them achieves now too much, now too little. What civilization aims at making out of them seems unattainable except at the price of a sensible loss of pleasure; the persistence of the impulses that could not be made use of can be detected in sexual activity in the form of non-satisfaction. (1912, 189)

The picture that develops of anaclitic desire is thus complex. On the one hand, it is the typical and normative form of desire in Freudian psychoanalytic theory. It corresponds to his foundational Oedipal narrative, which relies on the capacity of the subject to alter object-choice according to an associative model, in which successive object-choices correspond to earlier, abandoned or repressed ones. This story line also accounts for a subject who has internalized the moral edicts of the culture through an identification with the presumed Oedipal rival, the father. On the other hand, the active anaclitic subject appears fated to perpetual dissatisfaction, and the objects or counterpart to that desire to a debased status.

NARCISSISTIC DESIRE

Like anaclisis, narcissistic desire is more complex and more ambivalent in Freud's formulations than is generally understood (see chapter 2). Freud followed Paul Nacke and Havelock Ellis in initially using the term in reference to men's sexual desire for other men. Where he differed from Ellis and Nacke was in his description of the origins of this desire. In articles written in 1905 and 1909, Freud pursued the explanation that the desire for another man was a consequence of a strong identification of the child with his mother and was an attempt to replicate that relationship in desiring another man in the way that his mother had once desired him: "[Male homosexuals] in the earliest years of their childhood, pass through a phase of very intense but short-lived fixation to a woman (usually their mother), and . . . after leaving this behind, they identify themselves with a woman and take *themselves* as their sexual object. That is to say, they proceed from a narcissistic basis and look for a young man who resembles themselves and whom *they* may love as their mother loved *them*" (1907, 144n1; italics in original). In a similar vein, a few years later, Freud writes, "The boy represses his love for his mother: he puts himself in her place, identifies himself with her, and takes his own person as a model in whose likeness he chooses the new objects of his love. In this way he has become a homosexual. . . . He finds the objects of his love along the path of *narcissism*" (1910, 100).

The most substantial comments that Freud made on the subject, however, came several years later in his 1914 article "On Narcissism: An Introduction."[2] In "On Narcissism," Freud initially provides a distinction between primary narcissism (a stage in infantile development, common to all humans, in which the child is both subject and object of its own pleasure) and secondary narcissism—its manifestation beyond infancy. For example, Freud continues to associate narcissism with male homosexuality, and his comments evidently pathologize it: "We have discovered, especially clearly in people whose libidinal development has suffered some disturbance, such as perverts and homosexuals, that in their later choice of love-objects they have taken as a model not their mother but their own selves. They are plainly seeking themselves as a love-object, and are exhibiting a type of object-choice which must be termed narcissistic" (1914, 81).

Yet Freud no longer links narcissism exclusively to male homosexuality. He suggests that narcissistic desire may also be the normal state of desire for women. Of women, he says:

[At least of the] type of female most frequently met with, which is probably the purest and truest one . . . the onset of puberty . . . seems to bring about an intensification of the original narcissism, and this is unfavorable to the development of a true object-choice. . . . Strictly speaking, it is only themselves that such women love with an intensity comparable to that of the man's love for them. Nor does their need lie in the direction of loving, but of being loved; and the man who fulfils this condition is the one who finds favor with them.[3] (Freud 1914, 82)

Narcissism may be, for Freud, "normal" for the "purest and truest" women, for homosexual men, and for perverts, but he does not stop at this assignment of narcissism to specific identities. Importantly, he goes on in the article to suggest that it is far more frequent and common than even those examples suggest. In outlining his typology of desire, Freud states:

A person may love:—
(1) According to the narcissistic type:
    (a) what he himself is (i.e. himself),
    (b) what he himself was,
    (c) what he himself would like to be,

(d) someone who was once a part of himself.

(2) According to the anaclitic (attachment) type:

(a) the woman who feeds him,

(b) the man who protects him,

and the succession of substitutes who take their place. (1914, 94)

Even more explicitly, he offers, "We have, however, not concluded that human beings are divided into two sharply differentiated groups, according as their object-choice conforms to the anaclitic or to the narcissistic type; *we assume rather that both kinds of object-choice are open to each individual, though he may show a preference for one or the other*" (Freud 1914, 88; emphasis added).

Indeed, narcissistic desire would appear to be ubiquitous. At different points in the article, Freud finds all of the following as manifestations of narcissism: a woman's vanity and love of herself; a man's sexual desire for other men; parents' love for and overvaluation of their children; various perversions and psychic illnesses, including megalomania, paranoia, and hypochondria; the ego's relationship to the ego-ideal, as a desire for what one might be or become; homosocial bonding; and the expectation or hope of anaclitic desire that it be requited, that one might be loved in return (Moore and Fine 1990).[4] Burness Moore and Bernard Fine, discussing narcissism as a psychoanalytic concept, comment that "[in] psychoanalytic literature *narcissistic* . . . came to be applied to many things: a sexual perversion, a developmental stage, a type of libido or its object, a type or mode of object choice, a mode of relating to the environment, an attitude, self-esteem, and a personality type, which may be relatively normal, neurotic, psychotic, or borderline" (1990, 124).

Not only does Freud oscillate between pathologizing and normalizing narcissism, between assigning it to particular identities and generalizing it, but he also fluctuates between examples in which the object-choice truly is the self (and therefore would conform to the conventional, pejorative usage of the term) and ones in which the object of desire is outside the self. This latter use extends to examples in which extreme (and admirable) selflessness may be the desire's most obvious quality (as may be the case in the love of a parent for their child).

Ultimately what distinguishes narcissistic from anaclitic desire seems neither to be the object of desire nor the identity of the narcissistic subject, but rather the mechanism or process of desire established in its psychic origins. And what is key to the narcissistic process is that it involves the capacity to internalize another and to respond and to desire from a place that seeks to reproduce that identification. Moreover, it would seem that the identification with the other is based not, as is the case with anaclitic desire, in an alignment with the *role* of another—the internalized rule or role of the father in the Oedipal scenario being the paradigmatic example— but in an effort to reproduce the *relationship* that was once in place, albeit from a different position within that relationship.

In proposing this, I realize that I am sharply deviating from the received and conventional use of the term "narcissism" in most psychoanalytic theory and in popular usage. But doing so permits me to question the pathologization of the term, better to capture what Freud presents as a fairly typical, indeed widespread, form of desire. Why does anaclitic desire receive popular approbation, despite its apparent tendency toward debasement of its objects and its apparent pattern of repeated, even endless, dissatisfaction, while meanwhile narcissistic desire gets cast as inferior, antisocial, and perverse, even while Freud indicates it may be ubiquitous as well as consonant with such laudable sentiments as selfless love for one's children or the esteem in which one might hold an idealized other? And further, why, given its ubiquity, does he develop narcissism as consistent with femininity and with male homosexual desire? What are the consequences of this elision of identities with modes of desire? Why, in addition to this, are the passive variations of both anaclitic and narcissistic desire collapsed into narcissistic desire, where they remain entirely undertheorized, and what potential insights might arise from a more careful parsing of their distinctive characteristics?

My response to these questions is entirely speculative. I argue that it is possible that the differential treatment of these variations of desire, and

Eleanor MacDonald

the normative privileging of desire based in possessiveness, dissatisfaction, and the individual internalization of the social order—in other words, of the active anaclitic form of desire—corresponds to the requirements of capitalist consumer culture. It is also thus possible—and here, my speculation goes further—that, in the alternative and subordinated forms of narcissism and passivity, one might locate some affective resources to draw on in challenging the dominant economic structure and corresponding culture. In suggesting this, I do not intend to reverse the valuation of forms of desire, to denigrate anaclitic desire, or to propose any ethical preeminence for narcissistic or passive desires. Instead, I am offering the view that no version or variant of desire offers any guarantee of just relationships or a just social order but that we would do well to consider the ways in which contemporary discourses and social practice diminish the capacity and range of our affective response to the broader world, and to that contemporary glObal.

An Alternative Typology of Desires

Following the arguments of the previous section, I would propose to make two radical alterations to Freud's topography of desire. The first of these is in this section. I recommend the value of renaming and reconfiguring Freud's typology of desires in a way that focuses on their actual and most fundamental distinctions: the etiology of each form of desire; its concomitant role in forming a relation of desire; and its role in the formation of a desiring subject. Speculative and cursory though it is, my reworking of the typology of desire gives a rough indication of how we could conceive of desire in richer and more diverse ways. I propose a range of etiologies for desire, in which each emergent form of desire positions the subject somewhat differently in relation to the object of desire, and each also leads down a different avenue in the process of identification. This is an experimental and radical reconfiguration of the typology, one in which I would also argue that there are advantages and disadvantages to every form of desire. The second alteration I will propose is in the next and final section, the purpose of which is to shift the attention onto the object of desire itself, an approach that may be vitally important to repositioning human subjectivity in relation to our environment.

Active anaclitic desire, I advise, would be more accurately and appropriately referred to as "associative" desire. It is through chains of associations, linking one object of desire to the next, that we are able to shift our attachments to objects. The use of the term "associative" has not only the advantage of being a more recognizable, common word; it also evokes the psychoanalytic therapeutic practice that reflects the chains of association that link a range of objects, concepts, and thoughts. In Freud's descriptions of anaclitic desire, in his depiction of the child transferring desire from the breast to the mother and beyond, in his discussion of the Oedipal bargain that resolves the castration complex, the relationship to the object appears to be one of control, possession, or acquisition. This is a fair response to the earliest origin of the desire—that on which it originally "leans," the experience of frank need—of food, for survival. Associative desire leaves need behind yet carries an echo of that need in all ensuing transpositions. Its ambivalence might be, in part, related to the fantasy of satiation that can never be realized. No lover can ever fill the lack that initiates individual consciousness and desire. Finally, as suggested in the preceding section, associative desire seems to produce a form of identification with others similarly situated—an alignment with the father in the abandonment of a rivalry with him (in Freud's resolution of the Oedipal complex), a banding of the brothers in his allegory of the origins of civilization (1921, 1930).

Narcissism has come to be defined only in terms of its most negative aspects. A handful of thinkers—Leo Bersani and Adam Phillips with their concept of "impersonal narcissism" (2008) and Imogen Tyler (2005) in her feminist rereading of narcissism—have tried to reclaim a meaning that is more neutral or positive. On the basis of Freud's early insights into the relational basis for narcissistic desire, I propose instead the term "integrative desire." This captures the identification that is inherent in the process through which "narcissistic desire" or "integrative desire" comes about. The relation to the object is one in which subjects are capable of seeing themselves taking up the position of "the other"; the capacity to do this and to feel a sense of desire or connection to that other is based in an earlier relationship in which the subject now replaces another.

If associative desire has its origin in the infant's survival needs, and in the succession of associations that are spawned in relation to that need, then arguably there is a different etiology for integrative desire. Such a possibility, I suggest, might be found in Freud's essay "Mourning and Melancholia" (1917), in which Freud expounds the process through which loss of another leads to identification with that other. The experience of grief is what causes the subject to internalize and thus to identify with another. In grief, Freud speculates, the unconscious refuses to accept the loss of the beloved other. In this refusal, the id sets up the lost other inside the ego, or as Freud more poetically states, "the shadow of the object falls upon the ego" (1917, 249):

There, [withdrawn into the ego], however, it [the libido] was not unemployed in any unspecified way, but served to establish an *identification* of the ego with the abandoned object. The shadow of the object fell upon the ego, and the latter could henceforth be judged by a special agency, as though it were an object, the forsaken object. In this way an object-loss was transformed into an ego-loss and the conflict between the ego and the loved person into a cleavage between the critical activity of the ego and the ego as altered by identification. (1917, 249)

This denial of loss through the internalization of the other sets up a lengthy process of mourning in which the unconscious id and superego inflict their anger (at loss) on the ego. Only slowly and painfully over time is the loss realized and accepted in the process of mourning; in the process of melancholia, the loss may never be fully resolved.

This depiction of loss as the origin of integrative desire may have explanatory potential within Freud's description of primary narcissism as a necessary stage in infantile development. When the infant moves from experiencing the absence of the other (the caregiver) not as a lack in itself (as hunger or need) but as the loss of another (to be mourned), the building of the ego in the structure of the psyche begins, as the infant works to become that lost other. This is the advent of primary narcissism in which the infant relates to itself as both subject and object of desire. It is thus different from autoeroticism, in which the sense of self and other remains undifferentiated. This process of identification, however, sets up two additional processes. First, it brings about heightened ambivalence toward the other (for that other's inevitable absences). This ambivalence can be toward that other but toward the self when the self, through grief, has internalized that other. In this mechanism, we see the precursor to the superego in the emerging ability of the psyche to castigate its own ego. This is the "special function of the ego" to which Freud avers. Second, the distinction of subject and object (outside, but also within the psyche) initiates the infant's capacity to take new objects on the basis of their likeness to the self, to the past self, or to the desired self in ways that enhance the nascent ego's efforts to become its own lost object.

The identificatory aspect of associative desire, I have already suggested, might be captured by the term "alignment," in that the experience of a common object of desire aligns subjects with each other. In integrative desire, the force of identification appears to run far deeper and might be best captured by the words "incorporative" or "introjective." A person, losing a lover, might take to wearing that lost other's clothes, sleeping on the lost other's side of the bed, even (unconsciously) adopting speech patterns or changing taste preferences. Enduring grief and loss, one might imagine one sees the world through the lost other's eyes. And while this relation of grief and identification after a permanent loss would be profound, the experience of grieving and the concomitant incorporation of another can occur among infants and young children in a far more quotidian way. For a young child, loss need not be permanent; it might only be a fleeting few moments for an infant or toddler to feel that the world has come to an end without the beloved caregiver and to initiate or carry forward the necessary work of internalizing and incorporating aspects of that other.

This approach suggests that associative and integrative desires are distinct because each arises from a different experience. Put simply, *a lack is not the same as a loss*. Yet both lack and loss fuel desire. In the case of lack,

Eleanor MacDonald

the desire arises in response to the demand to fulfill a need; in the case of loss, the demand is to restore a relation. And each desire is in its own way doomed (and, arguably, thus sustained). Just as a constant hunger might trouble all efforts to fulfill a need, so might continued grief haunt efforts to reestablish what has been lost. As Freud puts it later in the same essay: "By taking flight into the ego, love escapes extinction" (1917, 257).

Finally, the question of "passive" desires—either anaclitic or narcissistic in nature—requires yet further conjecture. Freud remained perplexed about passivity, which he saw as equivalent to femininity. Is the heightened likelihood of femininity or passivity in women the consequence of too circuitous an Oedipal journey, in which young girls' egos suffer too many rejections, he wondered? Or are there constitutional factors at work to make women (albeit not only women) passive or feminine in their desires? At points, as suggested earlier, Freud collapses narcissism and passivity together, resulting in a binary framework for desire: active/passive, anaclitic/narcissistic, male/female, heterosexual male / homosexual male, normal/pathological, civilized/primitive, and so forth. Yet it seems like something—possibly many things—valuable may be lost in this dualistic reduction of the original model.

One might surmise that having the capacity to internalize the subjectivity of another, as proposed in the theorization of integrative desire, might open up the capacity to experience oneself through the eyes of the other and to desire to respond to that other. To the degree that the infant experiences itself as needing the caregiving and protective other, the desire to respond to that other might correspond to a felt need for that other, just as associative desire links desire with need. And to the degree that the infant must encounter and undergo the loss of the other, experiencing that loss as real (even if brief) or potential, the infant may desire to respond to the other's desire as a way to will the other into place. Survival might depend on being what the other desires to have or being who the other desires to be. Rather than characterizing these desires as passive, they might better be described as "responsive." Their corresponding identificatory mode might be characterized as "relational," in as much as their purpose and their desire is to sustain a relationship that is based in need and fear of loss.[5]

The Object as the Material and Natural World

The previous section provided a renaming and reframing of the possibilities for a desiring subject. The *source* of the desire—in lack, loss, or confusion—would direct desires to develop as associative/acquisitive, integrative/introjective, or responsive/relational. The identification of the subject would thus arise respectively in its quest to align itself with the other, incorporate the other within itself, or receive and respond to the other's desires. For the most part, in outlining this alternative typology, I have presumed the "other" to be caregivers, parents, and their subsequent replacements, those toward whom we experience and direct our desires. My reworking of Freud's typology of desire involved a radical revision and renaming of its major concepts. The second revision I propose in this final section is that we shift toward greater consideration of the "other" of our desires as encompassing the nonhuman world. I submit that we have a libidinal and affective relationship to the world around us. This relationship to object-others is culturally produced. In capitalism, our relationship to objects is frequently commodified; we perceive and respond to objects as exchange values. Our acquisitive relationship to objects is thus intensified, as is our capacity for associative desire. Alternative ways of desiring the world of others and objects—desiring in ways that are both incorporative and responsive—might prove more problematic, even impossible to align with the existing order as these modes of desire involve a loss or repudiation of mastery over the natural and material world, along with a requirement to be more open and receptive to its needs and desires.

The transposition of "object" of desire from human to nonhuman remains well within Freudian theory, in which objects of desire as such regularly figure. Objects populate our dreams and fantasies. Metaphorically and metonymically, objects feature in our imagination, our language, and our unconscious. Advertisers are well aware of our capacity to substitute things for humans. Reification is ever-present. Capitalism would appear to correspond seamlessly with the modality of associative desire; globalized capitalism extends its economic reaches and concomitantly the cultural normalization of the exclusivity of associative desire (see chapters 2, 3, and 8). Not only does this form of desire correspond to the mechanisms of association in which a desire for one object can be transferred onto or augmented by the desire for another, but also the insatiability of desires serves the world of capitalist accumulation. Further to this, associative desire, in its positioning of the subject in alignment with other subjects who share common desires, appears to reflect a number of features of the subject within capitalism: individual competitive striving to attain more and better objects; a desire for mastery over the object; rampant consumerism; an internalization of the role of consumer (as against citizen, for example) and solidarity with others similarly positioned; an abiding attachment to the existing order. We are the "possessive individualists" whom C. B. Macpherson (1962) describes in his critique of liberal contract theory and ideology.

The risks of the preeminence of this form of desire are everywhere in sight. We are exhausting the planet's productive capacities along with its capacity for the assimilation of waste. Simultaneously, we are at risk of losing the capacity for any sort of solidarity (including that of democratic citizenship) that might work to change the order of ownership, production, and distribution or that might curtail the level of planetary damage that we are causing in our drive to acquire.

The problem that may arise in shifting to the other subordinated forms of desire is that our rational apprehension of the world tends both to consider human society and the natural world as separate and to view the natural world as without agency, in the sense of intentionality and subjectivity. To propose that we develop alternative ways of interacting with that world that draw on the affective and libidinal energies of integrative and responsive desire may seem like recommending that we engage in some sort of magical thinking or resacralization of the natural world.

The Enlightenment's dominant form of rationality, despite its promise of freedom, is what Adorno and Horkheimer (1982) decry as "instrumental rationality"—a way of understanding the world with an intention to control it, a rational approach to objects that treats them in terms of their instrumental use, rather than as ends in themselves, a rationality that is incapable of responding to questions of moral values. There is a place for such rationality, but they argue, it should never have become the exclusive or dominant form of reason. Adorno develops, in *Negative Dialectics*, an alternative epistemology in which he argues that we must come to understand the object as "preponderant" (1973).[6] The concept that we have of the object and the object itself are distinct. Rather than deny our capacity to know the object outside our concept of it, as Kant's theory does, we should, according to Adorno, attempt to recognize the "nonidentical" relationship of our concepts to the objects themselves; we must be, in his words, "fearlessly passive."[7]

Alongside his advocacy of critical reason through negative dialectical approaches to the object, Adorno sought an alternative relationship to the object through the mimetic opportunities afforded in art. He condemned the "culture industry," as he termed the rise of bland and mass-produced entertainment, for its production of conformity, its denial of suffering, and its reduction of art to mere pleasure (Adorno 1982). He believed in the possibilities of autonomous art for its complexity, its expression of nonidentity, and the demands it actively makes on the subject who views or listens to it. This reversal of subject and object, such that we respond to the artistic demands of the artwork itself, corresponds to the experience of responsive desire.

Integrative desire might, similarly, be located in the aesthetic experience of mimesis, in which the subject psychically becomes object. Brian O'Connor, in his treatise on Adorno, offers that "[in] mimetic behavior the subject loses itself in an 'object of desire.' . . . The self driven by an affective interest in the world expands beyond itself" (2012, 157).[8]

These parallels between the project of the Frankfurt School thinkers and the discussion of alternative forms of desire could be instructive. There are resonances and parallels between integrative and responsive desires, and the realm of childhood play and magical thinking, the aesthetic experiences of autonomous art, and explorations of non-identitarian rationality.

Eleanor MacDonald

Equally or better, one might find correspondences to Marx's advocacy of non-alienated work relationships, ones in which worker solidarity might overcome the isolated and competitive pressures of capitalism to give way to genuine empathy and collective spirit.

According to the preceding critique, however, one would not need "magical thinking," autonomous art, or even solidarity in the workplace per se, for a broader range of desire to be experienced. Indeed, my argument suggests that both these modalities of desire are felt by all of us, even while they are rarely acknowledged in the dominant culture. When and where their existence is recognized is typically when they are assigned to subordinated groups: women, queer people, indigenous people, children, people deemed insane or ill.

In a culture that respected and honored experiences of vulnerability and grief, the forms and experiences of desire corresponding to these might be more accessible and widely recognized. There is growing anthropological and ethnographical work that explores alternative relationships to land and objects, whether on an individual or cultural level (Henare, Holbraad, and Wastell 2007; Turkle 2007; Povinelli 1997; Cruikshank 2005). That our culture minimizes recognition of our affective relationship to the land and to objects, that it diminishes our capacity for feeling a sense of connection and vulnerability, or of loss and belonging, is I believe, a significant component in our incapacity to ground alternative relationships to our larger environments and the material world in which we live (see chapter 3).

Effectively, Freudian theory, in the normative justification it offers for active anaclitic desire (which I call here, associative), its pathologization of narcissistic desire (here, defined as integrative), and its undertheorization of passive (or responsive) desire, presents a dehistoricized paradigm of desire that does not acknowledge the full range and complexity of desire while it simultaneously conforms to the cultural and consumerist orientation of capitalism. The globalization of capitalist economy and capitalist consumer culture diminishes our knowledge and recognition of alternative cultural and political forms in which other relationships of desire, acquisition, and identification prevail. Without any wish to romanticize indigenous or traditional cultures, I would propose that they present alternative negotiations of desire, manifested in different forms of identification and ownership. Indigenous representation of the meaning given to property ownership, for example, characteristically focuses on an intensification of identification in one's relationship to land or to significant or sacred objects—relationships in which the object is configured as agent, as owning the subject—one belongs to the land as much or more than the reverse (Hann 1998; Hookimaw-Witt 2010; Weiner 1992; Wilmsen 1989). These cultural representations thus conform more to integrative and responsive configurations of desire than to the acquisitive form that overrides all others in globalized capitalist culture. Only by exploring alternative economies and cultural forms, based in a different balance of desire, might we move beyond the "immense collection of commodities" that, for Marx, signals the most obvious indicator of capitalism and that, for Adorno, stands as evidence of our unfreedom.

Conclusion

At an especially rich moment in the formation of his thought, Freud offered a limited, yet surprisingly rich, typology of desire that acknowledged that desire takes several different forms. Yet he normalized only one of these forms, the one that best corresponds, it seems, to the definition of masculine citizenship in contemporary Western culture: independent, competitive, rule-oriented, and acquisitive. My task in this paper has been to trouble his received typology of desires in a number of ways: first, by making the different forms of desire equivalent in value; second, by showing how each form of desire has its own etiology, establishes its own relationship to its objects of desire, and results in its own process of identification; and finally, by considering the implications of different desires when we consider each as foundational to our cultural relationship to the material world. While entirely speculative in nature, the project has not been purely academic but is instead critically motivated to expand our capacity to revisit and rework our affective relationship to the world around us. Drawing from the psychoanalytic insight that our rational judgment is easily impaired by our unconscious drives, this paper attempts to proffer affective and libidinal resources that might enhance our relationship to the glObal through supporting a greater sense of connectedness and vulnerability to it.

Notes

1. Other examples of Strachey's "medicalization" or "scientization" of the original terminology are the terms "ego," "id," and "superego," which were translated from the far more straightforward terms "I," "it," and the neologism "above-I" to signify the sense of a monitoring agency internal to the self. The word "cathexis," typically used to describe the way that desire is not free-floating but attaches strongly to a particular person or object, was adapted from its original Greek (in which it meant "retention") and used to translate the common German word used by Freud, *Besetzung*, meaning "to invest" or "to occupy" or "to hold," in the sense that an army might occupy a territory or someone might "hold" a seat for a friend (Ornston 1985). While Freud chose, in nearly every case, common language to express his ideas, there are some instances in which he, too, borrowed from Latin to develop new psychoanalytic terminology. He adopted the term "libido," which in Latin means "wish" or "desire," rather than using German terms with the same meaning. His naming of "narcissism"—discussed at length in this chapter—was adapted for psychoanalytic use from the Greek myth of Narcissus.

2. This article was one of a series of about a dozen that Freud wrote between 1914 and 1917 in which he significantly revised his earlier understanding of the psyche. During this period he developed his concept of the superego and reconfigured his understanding of the ego as the aspect of the psyche that struggles to respond to internal and external forces.

3. In these remarks, Freud blurs his distinction between narcissism and passivity. Passivity is the principal aspect of femininity for Freud and remains, for him, frustratingly difficult to understand. His connection of femininity to narcissistic desire is one of several attempts to make sense of the former.

4. Moore and Fine (1990) continue, "In addition, the concept of a separate line of development for narcissistic libido and object libido became a fundamental theoretical basis for the self psychology school, which accounted for various personality features as narcissistic structures resulting from transformations of narcissism. Such broad usage led to confusion and it became apparent that a more restricted use of the term would be advantageous."

5. Responsive desire, in this formulation, bears resemblance to Jean Laplanche's "general theory of seduction" (1999) in which the unconscious itself is produced as a consequence of the infant's incapacity to respond to the enigmatic and unassimilable desires of the parents. I depart from him in viewing "seductive messages" as *entirely* causal of the unconscious but share his view that these incessant messages from the parent are inescapable. They are neither abusive nor incestuous, but an inevitable consequence of the introjective/incorporative/narcissistic and possessive/associative/anaclitic relationships that caregivers/parents will have with infants. My sense is that the child cannot be immune to these desires and will develop affective responses to them.

6. "The nonidentical cannot be directly accessed as something positive in itself. It is the conceptually negative result of the defined negation of the notion of identity" (Adorno, cited in Schweppenhäuser 2009, 47).

7. "Approaching knowledge of the object is the act in which the subject rends the veil it is weaving around the object. It can do this only where, fearlessly passive, it entrusts itself to its own experience. In places where subjective reason scents subjective contingency, the primacy of the object is shimmering through. The subject is the object's agent, not its constituent" (Adorno 1982, 505; see also Lee 2005). As one commentator, quoting from this passage remarks, puts it, "Adorno's use of language here is highly suggestive—an experience that verges on erotic surrender" (Lee 2005, 75).

8. This capacity to lose oneself in the object, or lose oneself in the other, is captured well in Walter Benjamin's description of "the hidden child" who becomes the environment in which he plays. "The child's heart pounds. It holds its breath. Here the material, tangible world enfolds it. That world becomes terribly clear to the child, wordlessly close. . . . The child standing behind the curtain itself becomes something swaying, something white, a ghost. Crouching under the dining-room table turns the child into the wooden temple idol, with the carved legs forming the four columns. And behind a door it is a door itself; wearing the door as a heavy mask it will cast, as a wizard, a spell on anyone entering unawares." (2009, 74).

Works Cited

Adorno, Theodor. 1973. *Negative Dialectics*. Translated by E. Ashton. New York: Continuum Press.

———. 1982. "Subject and Object." In *The Essential Frankfurt School Reader*, edited by A. Arato and E. Gerbhardt, 497–511. New York: Continuum.

———. 1993. "Messages in a Bottle." *New Left Review* (200): 5–14.

Eleanor MacDonald

————. 1997. *Aesthetic Theory.* Edited by G. Adorno, R. Tiedemann. Translated by R. Hullot-Kantor. Minneapolis: University of Minnesota Press.

Adorno, Theodor, and Max Horkheimer. 1982. *Dialectic of Enlightenment: Philosophical Fragments.* Translated by J. Cumming. New York: Continuum.

Benjamin, Walter. 2009. *One-Way Street and Other Writings.* Translated by J. A. Underwood. London: Penguin.

Bersani, Leo, and Adam Phillips. 2008. *Intimacies.* Chicago: University of Chicago Press.

Cruikshank, Julie. 2005. *Do Glaciers Listen?: Local Knowledge, Colonial Encounters, and Social Imagination.* Vancouver: University of British Columbia Press.

Freud, Sigmund. 1907. "Three Essays on the Theory of Sexuality." In *Standard Edition of the Complete Psychological Works of Sigmund Freud*, translated by James Strachey, 7:130–243. New York: Norton.

————. 1910. "Leonardo da Vinci and a Memory of His Childhood." In *Standard Edition of the Complete Psychological Works of Sigmund Freud*, translated by James Strachey, 11:63–137. New York: Norton.

————. 1912. "On the Universal Tendency to Debasement in the Sphere of Love." In *Standard Edition of the Complete Psychological Works of Freud*, translated by James Strachey, 11:170–90. New York: Norton.

————. 1914. "On Narcissism: An Introduction." In *Standard Edition of the Complete Psychological Works of Sigmund Freud*, translated by James Strachey, 14:67–102. New York: Norton.

————. 1917. "Mourning and Melancholia." In *Standard Edition of the Complete Psychological Works of Sigmund Freud*, translated by James Strachey, 14:243–60. New York: Norton.

————. 1921. "Group Psychology and the Analysis of the Ego." In *Standard Edition of the Complete Works of Sigmund Freud*, translated by James Strachey, 18:69–143. New York: Norton.

————. 1930. "Civilization and Its Discontents." In *Standard Edition of the Complete Works of Sigmund Freud*, translated by James Strachey, vol. 21. New York: Norton.

————. 1933. "Femininity." *Standard Edition of the Complete Psychological Works of Sigmund Freud*, translated by James Strachey, 22:112–35. New York: Norton.

Hann, Chris M., ed. 1998. *Property Relations: Renewing the Anthropological Tradition.* Cambridge: University of Cambridge.

Henare, Amiria, Martin Holbraad, and Sari Wastell, eds. 2007. *Thinking through Things: Theorising Artefacts Ethnographically.* London: Routledge.

Hookimaw-Witt, Jackie. 2010. *The World Is Ours: Aboriginal Feminism Interpreted from Women's Role of Sacred Responsibility to the Land.* Kanata, Canada: JCharlton.

Laplanche, Jean. 1999. *Essays on Otherness*. London: Routledge.

Lee, Lisa Yun. 2005. *Dialectics of the Body: Corporeality in the Philosophy of T. W. Adorno*. New York: Routledge.

Macpherson, Crawford Brough. 1962. *The Political Theory of Possessive Individualism*. Oxford: Clarendon Press.

Marx, Karl. 1977. *Capital: A Critique of Political Economy*. Vol. 1, *The Process of Capitalist Production*. Translated by Ben Fowkes. New York: Vintage Books.

Moore, Burness E., and Bernard D. Fine. 1990. *Psychoanalytic Terms and Concepts*. New Haven CT: Yale University Press.

O'Connor, Brian. 2012. *Adorno*. Abingdon: Routledge.

Ornston, Darius. 1985. "The Invention of 'Cathexis' and Strachey's Strategy." *International Review of Psychoanalysis* 12, 391–98.

Povinelli, Elizabeth. 1997. "Do Rocks Listen?: The Cultural Politics of Apprehending Australian Indigenous Labour." *American Anthropologist*, n.s., 97 (3): 505–18.

Schweppenhäuser, Gerhard. 2009. *Theodor W. Adorno: An Introduction*. Translated by James Rolleston. Durham NC: Duke University Press

Turkle, Sherry. 2007. *Evocative Objects: Things We Think With*. Cambridge MA: MIT Press.

Tyler, Imogen. 2005. "Who Put the 'Me' in Feminism? The Sexual Politics of Narcissism." *Feminist Theory* 6 (1): 25–44.

Weiner, Annette B. 1992. *Inalienable Possessions: The Paradox of Keeping-While-Giving*. Berkeley: University of California Press.

Wilmsen, Edwin N., ed. 1989. *We Are Here: Politics of Aboriginal Land Tenure*. Berkeley: University of California Press.

PART 2 Cultural Anxieties

5 "I Love Death"

War in Syria and the Anxiety of the Other

Anna J. Secor

The conflagration in Syria that began in 2011 with antigovernment protests is today a thoroughly internationalized armed conflict in which at least 300,000 people have lost their lives and 11 million people have been displaced. This chapter examines how the war in Syria props up glObal circuits of anxiety and enjoyment. I argue that the affective geopolitics of the conflict has called forth a masochistic register in which what is sought is the Other's anxiety (Lacan 2014, 152) on the glObal stage—for example, in the circulation of the photograph of the dead Syrian child, Alan Kurdi, washed up on the Turkish beach in September 2015. This photograph—the site of unbearable loss—became the support, the fantasmatic prop, for a glObal eruption of affect and politics. The image of Alan Kurdi thereby participates in what I am calling an eroto-politics in which anxiety is the affective experience of the lethal side of *jouissance*. Further, the eroto-politics of the Syrian war is masochistic, I argue, insofar as, in the debasement of the body-as-object, its blind aim is the anxiety of the Other—that is, of God. I further elaborate this point through an analysis of a music video, "I Love Death" (2014) by the Syrian performance artist (and refugee) Batool Mohamed. I argue that this video, posted on YouTube, makes explicit the position of Syrian bodies as the support for an obscene enjoyment, not only within the orbit of the immediate violence, but in the glObal field.

The affect of anxiety (as we all know) signals danger, but psychoanalytically it also poses a topological question.[1] For Sigmund Freud, anxiety was primarily to be understood as a signal occurring in the ego and warning of an *inter-*

nal danger. Jacques Lacan elaborates on Freud but much complicates Freud's mapping of external and internal. Lacan argues that even if the anxiety signal is occurring in the ego, it refers to a desire that originates *somewhere else* and puts the very being of the subject into question. Anxiety for Lacan originates with the Other who addresses the subject as lost; it solicits the loss at the core of the subject (Lacan 2014, 152–53). In the address to the subject as lost, what makes me anxious is that the Other does not acknowledge me or even misrecognize me but instead interrogates me right where I come up empty-handed—that is, at the very spot where my fantasy is hooked, at the rim of the empty vase where *objet a*, the object-cause of desire, appears to bloom. Thus, anxiety is a specific manifestation of the desire of the Other as it takes root in my disintegration. Anxiety is the pulsing signal of the Other that comes back to say: "Right there in the spot around which you spin your fantasy of coherence, there is nothing but the speck of dust I left behind."

By tracing the route (or routes) of anxiety through glObal circuits, and by showing how "politics" arises in response to the paradoxical intimacy of alterity, this paper performs a kind of psycho-topology. Virginia Blum and I use the term "psycho-topology" to capture the always already psychical dimension of material space (Blum and Secor 2011). Key to this conception is the relationship between the subject and the Other, whose very externality becomes the origin of the subject's interiority. A psycho-topology analyzes how space takes shape, acquires form and meaning, through an open process of unfolding in which (to borrow Karen Barad's words) "relations of exteriority, connectivity, and exclusion are reconfigured" (Barad 2007, 141). This dynamic topological reconfiguring, in which there is no geometrical relationship of absolute exteriority but rather a continual enfolding, materializes psychic coordinates as much as it does locational ones. In relation to the glObal circulation of events of the Syrian war, my discussion of *anxiety*—an affect closely bound to the Mobius twist of interior-exterior that both makes and troubles the subject—is an attempt to demonstrate psycho-topological becoming.

Anxiety, emitting from the point where a radical alterity inhabits the subject, can be elicited precisely by the folding of geopolitical spatiality. If

Anna J. Secor

geopolitics creates glObal maps of friends and enemies, spatially arraying enclosures of "us" and "them," an attention to anxiety opens these cartographies to a topological dynamism, to the entanglement of here and there, us and them (Carter and McCormack 2006; Dixon 2014; Muller 2013; Pain 2009; Puar 2009). It is for this reason that I follow the arc of anxiety across the field within which the violence and displacement of the Syrian war is "served up" to international (and especially Western) publics. In doing so, I am employing a vague "we"—we who encounter the shock of the image, we who respond, in Europe and North America primarily, but by no means exclusively. This vague "we" will sometimes paper over the ways in which "we" "might be affected differently by what gets passed around," as Sara Ahmed puts it in her discussion of affective contagion (Ahmed 2010, 39). My hope is that you will tolerate this imprecise "we" as an opening gambit—a cut, a differentiator, an event (Barad, Lacan, Deleuze)—in a field of potential, one intended not to shut down alternatives but to proliferate possibilities for thought and politics.

Alan Kurdi: The Image of Anxiety and the Passage to Action

According to the International Organization for Migration, more than 3,770 migrants were reported to have died trying to cross the Mediterranean in 2015. More than eight hundred of these lost their lives in the Aegean crossing from Turkey to Greece. When a small, inflatable boat carrying sixteen Iraqi and Syrian refugees attempting transit to the Greek island of Kos capsized off the Turkish coast in the early morning hours of September 2, 2015, a three-year-old Kurdish boy from Syria became one of this number.

Washed up on the shore, Alan Kurdi's corpse became the object of a series of photographs by Turkish journalist Nilüfer Demir. The image of the child's drowned body lying face down in the surf went viral. By the morning of September 3, it appeared on the front pages of newspapers across Europe (fig. 1; Parkinson and George-Cosh 2015). The photo and accompanying story of a father's bitter loss elicited editorial condemnation of Western powers for their inaction in the face of the mounting refugee crisis. President Recep Tayyip Erdogan of Turkey took the opportunity to

Fig. 1. A Turkish police officer stands next to Alan Kurdi's dead body off the shores in Bodrum, southern Turkey, on September 2, 2015, after a boat carrying refugees sank while on its way to the Greek island of Kos. Photo by Nilufer Demir, AFP Collection, Getty Images.

castigate European powers for their failure to address either the conflict in Syria or the resulting displacement of millions of people. European leaders, including David Cameron and François Hollande, expressed emotional responses to the photo and called it a reminder of the world's responsibility toward the refugees. In the UK an online petition urging Cameron to increase quotas for asylum seekers surged from 40,000 to 300,000 signatures in one day. In Canada, reports that the Kurdi family had been denied asylum in Canada effected a shift in the national election campaign toward questions of immigration policy. Internationally, migrant and refuge aid organizations reported a huge swell of charitable donations.

The photograph, with its glObal affective pull, has been compared to Nick Ut's Pulitzer Prize–winning 1972 photograph of a nine-year-old Vietnamese girl running from a napalm attack, naked and in burning agony (fig. 2).

Anna J. Secor

Fig. 2. 1972 Pulitzer Prize–winning photograph by Nick Ut of children (including nine-year-old Kim Phuc [*center*]) fleeing South Vietnamese forces on Route 1 near Trang Bang after an aerial napalm attack. Associated Press photo by Nick Ut.

It has also been compared to Kevin Carter's Pulitzer Prize–winning 1993 image that drew world attention to the famine in the Sudan. In this arresting photo, a starving Sudanese child, her skeletal frame curled into a ball, is stalked by a vulture as she tries to crawl to a feeding station a kilometer away (fig. 3; Logan 2015). Each of the photographs presents the viewer with a child's debased body, and each is famous not merely as art but for the ways in which its circulation spurred affective and political response. Thus, when Brendan O'Neill (2015), in a blog post for the *Spectator*, wrote that the Kurdi image was no better than "a snuff photo for progressives, dead-child porn," he could have equally been referring to these previous Pulitzer Prize–winning images. O'Neill (2015) suggests that the Kurdi image incites some kind of perverse pleasure and that its circulation is "designed not to start a serious debate about migration in the 21st century but to elicit a self-satisfied feeling of sadness among Western observers." Indeed, the

Fig. 3. 1994 Pulitzer Prize–winning photograph by Kevin Carter of a starving girl being stalked by a vulture in Sudan. Photo by Kevin Carter, Sygma Premium Collection, Getty Images.

complex that places this image (and others like it) as an occasion for the release of feeling calls for further interrogation.

The image as it circulated incited an eruption of affective politics—that is, politics framed not by ideology but as a *passage a l'acte* riding on a surge of feeling. This event manifests what Brian Massumi calls the role of "images as the conveyers of forces of emergence, as vehicles for existential potentialization and transfer" (2002, 43). Massumi places the mass circulation of images within the context of an affective theory of late capitalist power, wherein they perform as relays for the transmission of potential that is then inhibited in its emergence as part of the cultural-political functioning of the media and connected apparatuses. This idea of the image as the bearer of affective power owes a debt to Walter Benjamin's "dialectical image," or the image that emerges in a flash to threaten the preservation of the status quo with the instantaneous irruption of the now (2002, 473, N9,7). As an event, the image of the dead child can be seen as just such a blast of now-

Anna J. Secor

time—though whether the measures taken in the wake of the explosion dislodge the "continuity of history" is a question to which I will return (Benjamin 2002, 474, N9a,6).

But first, what affect is transmitted in the circulation of the Kurdi image? O'Neill, the journalist quoted earlier, refers to "a self-satisfied feeling of sadness." But rather than sadness, I will argue that *anxiety* is the primary affective register of the image within the political-economic context of its circulation. And I wager that my focus on anxiety makes sense, psychoanalytically speaking: for Lacan (2014), anxiety is really *the* affect, the only one that matters. It is that which does not deceive. Sorrow, anger, joy, shame—these may be red herrings, leading the conscious subject away from that which it cannot bear. But anxiety is always true.

Second, *how* does the Kurdi picture solicit anxiety? And what is the topological structure of that anxiety? According to Lacan, if we are anxious, it is because we have been confronted with the unbearable loss at the root of our desire. This loss is not the loss of a little boy's life. Although we see ourselves as being moved by his death, in our effusions we are not mourning Alan Kurdi so much as we are being stirred to anxiety. So how, then, does this photograph, in the sociopolitical context of its circulation, make us anxious? In other words, how does it confront us with the Real of human inconsistency, with the fear of the radioactive Otherness that inhabits us?

Manifestly, the image calls forth expressions of responsibility, of shared humanity, of an obligation to *act*. It speaks the language of what Didier Fassin calls "humanitarian reason": "the vocabulary of suffering, compassion, assistance, and responsibility to protect forms of our political life" (2012, 2). The child is the hook for this humanitarian discourse because, as Miriam Ticktin explains, "The quintessential humanitarian victims bear no responsibility for their suffering. Their innocence is what qualifies them for humanitarian compassion. As innocents, they are pure, without guile, and without intent—they are seemingly outside politics and certainly outside blame for their misfortune. Yet who are these perfect victims? Interestingly, children are usually the face of humanitarianism; they are represented as innocent victims of famine, war, or natural disaster" (2015, para. 4).

Kurdi serves as such an innocent victim of the war in Syria and the international regime that lets refugees die and wash up on the shore like so much "wreckage, dreck, and waste" (Rich 1991, 4). The innocence of the dead body is what gives the photograph its affective charge. The obscenity of *India Today*'s photograph of Chinese dissident artist Ai Wei Wei posing as Kurdi on the shore of Lesbos arises from the dissonance between the scripted innocence of the dead child and the staged manipulation attributed to the (live) man (fig. 4; Chung 2016).

What follows the "viral" circulation of the Kurdi image—the surge of statements, signatures, money—is a discharge of political action that rides the affective wave. Like the student that ejaculates when he hands in his final exam (Lacan 2014, 169), the political rush comes at the height of our anxiety. Why? Because, for Lacan, *jouissance* protects the imaginary body from encountering the impasse of the Real (see chapters 3 and 7). The surge of action—however short-lived or rhetorical—following the international dissemination of the photograph thus appears as a response to the intimate geopolitical anxieties incited by the circulating image. In this response, there is an attempt to annul the anxiety produced by the unbearable pain of lack with actions that serve to (re)constitute a consistency of meaning around the image of the dead child.

In the passage to action that follows the Alan Kurdi photo, there is a moment of bliss—a moment when the boundary between us seems to dissolve, when humanity appears as one—followed by the inevitable end of this ecstatic transport and the return to the stability of the known order. The affect of anxiety moves the subject along the trajectory between *jouissance* and its lethal end (detumescence, castration, or death). Thus, in eroto-politics, short bursts of political action give pleasure in the first moment and then offer us a return to known consistencies in the second moment. The trajectory between these moments assuages our anxiety and deflects our encounter with the traumatic real.

To this point I have been staging my analysis as though there is a dyadic relationship between the image and our desire. Yet I do not think this is an adequate topological structure for either a political-geographic under-

Anna J. Secor

Fig. 4. 2016 photograph of Ai Wei Wei by Rohit Chawla. Photo by Rohit Chawla, *India Today*. Used with permission of Living Media India Limited.

standing or a psychoanalytic understanding of the anxiety that the image calls forth. It is not just between the image and our lack (our desire) that the anxiety and the *jouissance* of action take place. The image does not exist in isolation; what we are talking about when we talk about the Kurdi photograph is the image and the socio-symbolic-political context of its circulation. The image of Kurdi is thus bound to its affective load—to the anxiety that signals an opening to the impasses of the Real—through a third party, through the Other. Because, although it is true that we become anxious, the image does not primarily aim at *our* unwinding; what puts us on the hook is the desire of the Other, and thus it is *the Other's anxiety* that is the primary target of the photo. In other words, the image does not provoke our anxiety directly; it does not itself interrogate us at the point of our desire. But instead it works on us through its call for *God's* anxiety—that is, the anxiety of the Other whose law it is that recognizes in the child's corpse a debasement of the human.

It is thereby that we can say that the eroto-politics of the event of this photograph is masochistic. In the *Anxiety* seminar, Lacan (2014) points out that the aim of the masochist is masked by the fantasy of being the object of the Other's *jouissance*. It is not, Lacan claims, the Other's pleasure that the masochist seeks, but rather the *anxiety* of the Other. What is sought out is the Other's response to the subject's "fall into his final misery," his appearance as a "poor bodily scrap" (Lacan 2014, 163), an object among other valueless objects. The Kurdi photo provokes anxiety in presenting precisely such an object; the child is dead, washed up, the body deposited on the beach like so much trash.

If this picture makes God anxious, it is because it reveals the fragility of the symbolic order that ascribes meaning to childhood (such as innocence), to children's sweet and lovable bodies, to some kind of glObal order of care and responsibility (Fassin 2012). And we, in turn, become anxious in the face of the anxious Other because we feel that the Other's anxiety fixates on our own lack. Our lack of action. Our lack of compassion. Our lack of politics. Our lack of coherence as subjects. The Other interrogates us precisely where we fail, where we paper over our lack with a fantasy of love, of humanitarianism, of glObal "order." And so our own position as the object cause of the Other's desire is called into question. In other words, on the hook of this image, we are confronted with a loss, not of the small boy, but of coherence and meaning. And so the masochistic call to the anxiety of the Other makes us anxious in the very place where the Other lodges its signal, at the very core of our being. This is the psycho-topology of anxiety politics: the crumpled fold of our subjectivity (entangled with the debased object and the Other who doesn't see us as we want to be seen) enacts an affective geopolitics within which the reality of war and displacement become subsumed in the drive to repair, slapdash, the imaginary humanitarian order. "Politics" appears to be nothing other than a fantasy through which, in the face of our disintegration, we temporarily reconstitute the stability of our identities and the coherence of the imaginary structures within which we become recognizable to ourselves (Edelman 2004).

Anna J. Secor

Fig. 5. Screen shot of Batool Mohamed in the 2014 Bidayyat video, "I Love Death." "I Love Death," YouTube video, 4:18, posted by Bidayyat, April 30, 2014, https://www.youtube.com/watch?v=mDen2jaze9m.

"I Love Death": Laying Bare the Fantasy

The video clip (Mohamed 2014) opens with a series of still images: A neck kerchief with the Youth Baath Pioneers (YBP) insignia. Television color bars with "Syria" written across the top in English. A big pink rose. A mural depicting a boy and a girl wearing YBP outfits, holding a torch high between them. The words "I love death" (in Arabic) appear in front of the mural.

A woman appears in front of the mural in close up. Her face is very made up and beautiful. The camera pulls back and we see that she is wearing fancy clothes and many necklaces. Her nails are polished bright pink. She speaks into a microphone.

FANCY WOMAN: My beloved children, birds of heaven and angels of earth. We will now listen to one of the most promising talents of our youth. She is one of the bright lights and flowers of our nation. Let's all listen to the song she chose to perform today. Let's meet her.

The fancy woman pulls a girl dressed in a YBP uniform up from out of frame by one of her two ponytails, tied with ribbons on the sides of her head.

FANCY WOMAN: What is your name?

Speaking very fast and saluting, the girl answers:

BATOOL MOHAMED: This is Comrade Batool Mohamed, the pioneer in elo-
quence, oratory, and singing throughout the region.
FANCY WOMAN: Of course our great young comrade dedicates her song to
our great and beloved commander, the guardian of childhood and youth.
Let's listen to her.

The woman steps aside, and Batool comes to the microphone. She childishly adjusts the ponytail with which she had been yanked up and stands up very straight, her arms rigidly at her sides. A man at a keyboard also in a YBP uniform gives her a sign and begins to play a jaunty rhythm. The camera cuts to a man wearing black robes and a black mask standing in front of a mural of children wearing YBP uniforms. The mural depicts a black flag waving over the children on which is written (in Arabic), "There is no God but God." The man in black is dancing. The camera cuts back to Batool at the microphone. She places her hands on her heart and begins to sing a choppy, barely melodic song.

BATOOL MOHAMED: I love to die
By the bullets
Of a Kalashnikov
Or a sniper.
My head and eyes explode.
I want to make my prayers before it is too late.
I love to die
While I'm lost in thoughts.
Accidentally I am hit by
A mortar.

Anna J. Secor

Fuck ideas, we are here to get lost.

We don't give a shit, there's no tomorrow.

I love to die

By a knife

Based on the religion written on my ID card.

They chop me up,

Then stitch me together,

Amuse themselves with my blood.

I love to die

In explosions.

My skin gets grilled, and my body parts fly all over.

I love to die

By chemical gasses.

It's the ultimate kick.

Like this my cold dazed body arrives at the doors of heaven.

God judges me while I'm lying in front of him.

Heaven is out of order

But hell is blazing fiercely

Thanks to your reforms, dear Bashar.

Peaceful, peaceful . . .

Death, death, death and humiliation are on sale.

Today only half the price.

Peaceful, peaceful, peaceful . . .

While Batool sings, the camera returns to the masked man in black who now has a second man in black with his legs wrapped around his waist. They play a kind of rhythmic patty cake with each other. A third joins them. The men's dances begin as goofy disco-like moves but become vaguely obscene as they put their hands on their heads and wiggle their hips. The keyboardist grooves to his own music and eventually starts playing the keyboard with his feet. The camera occasionally cuts to the fancy woman, seated in a chair. Early on she is nodding in approval of Batool's song, but in the later cuts she often appears bored, arranging her clothes and fanning herself, until she realizes that the camera is on her and she arranges her face and body into a look of pleased attentiveness.

Batool maintains the cheerful and eager-to-please demeanor of the young pioneer. She mimes many of the violent deaths she is singing about, pretending to wield a Kalashnikov, widening her eyes, pounding her fist into her hand to indicate a mortar, repeating stabbing gestures at her own body when she sings about the knife. She makes expansive gestures to emphasize the distribution of her blood and body.

She smiles while she sings, perky and rhythmic in her gestures.

Throughout the song one gesture recurs: that of making a heart with one's hands, holding it first in front of the chest and then pushing it outward. Batool makes this gesture and so do the men in black. The hand-hearts spawn colorful animated hearts filling the screen. The keyboardist makes a heart with his feet after he starts using them to play music, and it is oddly disconcerting.

At the end of the song, Batool, the young pioneer, salutes. Standing in formation with the fancy woman, the keyboardist, and the three dancing men in black, the video ends as they clap rapidly in unison.

The video I have described is performed by Batool Mohamed, a young Syrian performance artist and current refugee in Istanbul. It was published on YouTube on April 30, 2014, and has had over 32,000 views. The text accompanying it frames the video as in opposition to Bashar al-Assad's one-party rule and also as a critique of the turn to jihadist slogans by such groups as ISIS and al-Nusra. It is a critique that emphasizes the struggle of Syrian youth for creative expression at a moment when their bodies, whether dismembered or displaced, have become fuel tossed on the fire of the war.

My interests in the video are askew from the way it is framed by its makers. In my view, the video satirizes not only the way the Assad regime and the fascist Islamist order arrange youth subjects in gleeful collaboration with their own undoing, but also the way Syrian youth must produce themselves in the form of "dead-child porn" in order to elicit an affective and political response. Thus, the video satirically performs a masochistic eroto-politics that aims at the anxiety of the Other. Once again, we have the figure of the child, a youth who dedicates herself to the nation and to multiple violent deaths. Her innocence is telegraphed in her ponytails, her cheerful demeanor, the hearts offered out from the body to the viewer and the childish graphic that emits from them. The young pioneer assures us that she loves death and invites her own mutilation, dismemberment, and death. This masochistic eroto-politics thus manifests the death drive, the drive to abolish every drive (Laplanche 1970, 107; see also chapters 8 and 11 in this volume).

While "I Love Death" is satirical, it is also a surface across which plays a queer negativity, one that pushes us beyond "futurism's unquestioned good" as embodied in the child; in Lee Edelman's words, the value of queer negativity "resides in its radical challenge to the very value of the social itself" (2004, 6). This queering aims precisely at the image of the child, taken to be the very figure of politics in our era, an image that serves to regulate political discourse, to fix us within a future-oriented social order (Edelman 2004). It is thus in a twist of queer negativity—"Fuck ideas, we're here to get lost. We don't give a shit, there's no tomorrow"—that Mohamed's performance calls out the voyeuristic appropriation of violent (child) death for political consumption. Death—and especially child death—has become a prop for a fantasy in which this most traumatic debasement is what (finally) calls forth the anxiety of the Other. Mohamed's satiric message can be read: If the world wants dead-child porn, well then the youth of Syria would enjoy nothing more than to provide it.

Conclusion: The Catastrophe of the Status Quo

Folding the trope of childhood "innocence" back on itself, and reflecting the backlash against immigrants to Europe that took hold shortly after the Kurdi affair, Charlie Hebdo's January 2016 cartoon suggested that Alan Kurdi would have grown up to be an "ass groper" in Germany (Meade 2016). The Hebdo cartoon makes reference to the New Year's Eve coordinated attacks on women in Cologne that, at the time, were attributed to refugees—though more recently it has come to light that, of the fifty-eight suspects arrested in connection with these attacks, only three were from Iraq or Syria. Regardless of its false premises, the intense backlash against asylum seekers to Europe that erupted following the Cologne attacks merely months after the Kurdi outpouring demonstrates that the circulation of the Kurdi photograph did not mark a long-term reorientation of the affect and politics surrounding the Syrian war and its displaced millions. Rather it was merely one in the series of events that emerge on the glObal stage eliciting anxiety—if not the anxiety of a lost humanitarianism, then the anxiety of lost security—and spurring chaotic, short-lived bursts of "politics" that do not, ultimately, add up to a sustained course of action. In response to the anxiety of the unbearable real of loss, the death drive propels us to cling to known consistencies; as Ellie Ragland puts it in *Essays on the Pleasures of Death*: "We defend whatever gives us fixity—a sense of being grounded— over the dialectic of movement where freedom, truth, and change lie" (1995, 87). In the grips of anxiety politics, it seems that "we" would rather die than blast open the homogeneity of our times.

Brian Massumi has suggested that "affect holds the key to rethinking postmodern power after ideology" (2002, 42). That is, ideology "no longer defines the global mode of functioning of power" but is instead one modality within a broader field wherein ideological effects are produced by non-ideological means; that is, they are produced affectively (Massumi 2002, 42). Massumi sees the move from an ideological to an affective theory of power as a shift away from deriving position from back-formed possibilities and toward an openness to continuous heterogeneous realities, "a gesture for the conceptual enablement of resistance in connection with the real" (2002, 263n24). And indeed this is the affective work of Benjamin's dialectical image that emerges suddenly "in the now of its recognizability," a dialectical experience that "dissipate[s] the semblance of eternal sameness, and even of repetition, in history" (2002, 473, N9,5, N9,7).

Yet here I have traced out a particular psycho-topology in which the irruption of the image, the arc of the event, yields a return—not to sameness

Anna J. Secor

exactly but to a repose wherein we await the reemergence of the desire to act in one direction or another. There is *movement* all right in this emergent psycho-topology, but insofar as it is yoked to the death drive, the topological unfolding of masochistic eroto-politics does not "rescue" us from what Benjamin calls the "catastrophe": the status quo (2002, 473, N9a,1). In Benjamin's words, "The rescue that is carried out by these means [by the flash of the dialectical image]—and only by these—can operate solely for the sake of what in the next moment is already irretrievably lost" (2002, 473, N9,7). In the rush to inadequate action that follows the event of the Kurdi image, there is no lasting retrieval of humanitarianism, no resurrection of the value of a child's life; we are not rescued from the debasement and horror, the lack of coherence and meaning, that this image flashes before us. The anxiety that masochistic eroto-politics provokes is not the basis for a sustained critique of the glObal order, nor for a reorientation of glObal practices regarding war and displacement. If the death drive is the drive to abolish every drive, masochistic eroto-politics is a politics to abolish all politics.

Notes

1. Throughout this chapter, I follow Lacan to refer to anxiety as an affect (Lacan 2014). Psychoanalytically, affect is the (mobile, displaced, and often misrecognized) effect of unconscious desire and drives. While I acknowledge that there are many more ways to define affect (from Spinoza to Silvan Tompkins) and that most current deployments pay little tribute to Lacan (cf. Berlant 2011), I find it to be functional and productive to bring a psychoanalytic understanding of anxiety to the questions of politics, geopolitics, and ideology (e.g., Massumi 2002; Ahmed 2010) that are animating social theoretical work on affect today.

Works Cited

Ahmed, Sara. 2010. *The Promise of Happiness*. Durham NC: Duke University Press.
Barad, Karen. 2007. *Meeting the Universe Halfway: Quantum Physics and the Entanglement of Matter and Meaning*. Durham NC: Duke University Press.
Benjamin, Walter. 2002. *The Arcades Project*. Cambridge MA: Harvard University Press.
Berlant, Lauren. 2011. *Cruel Optimism*. Durham NC: Duke University Press.

Blum, Virginia, and Anna J. Secor. 2011. "Psychotopologies: Closing the Circuit between Psychic and Material Space." *Environment and Planning D: Society and Space* 29 (6): 1030–47.

Carter, Sean, and Derek P. McCormack. 2006. "Film, Geopolitics and the Affective Logics of Intervention." *Political Geography* 25 (2): 228–45.

Chung, Stephy. 2016. "Ai Weiwei Poses as Drowned Syrian Child Alan Kurdi in Photograph." CNN, February 1. http://www.cnn.com/2016/02/01/arts/ai-weiwei-alan-kurdi -syria/.

Dixon, Deborah. 2014. "The Way of the Flesh: Life, Geopolitics, and the Weight of the Future." *Gender, Place and Culture* 21 (2): 136–51.

Edelman, Lee. 2004. *No Future: Queer Theory and the Death Drive.* Durham NC: Duke University Press.

Fassin, Didier. 2012. *Humanitarian Reason: A Moral History of the Present.* Berkeley: University of California Press.

Lacan, Jacques. 2014. *The Seminar, Book X: Anxiety.* Edited by Jacques-Alain Miller. Cambridge: Polity.

Laplanche, Jean. 1970. *Life and Death in Psychoanalysis.* Washington DC: Johns Hopkins University Press.

Logan, Nick. 2015. "These Images Changed Public Opinion. Has Alan Kurdi's Photo Done the Same?" Globalnews.ca, September 4. http://globalnews.ca/news/2204006/these -images-changed-public-opinion-has-alan-kurdis-photo-done-the-same/.

Massumi, Brian. 2002. *Parables for the Virtual: Movement, Affect, Sensation.* Durham NC: Duke University Press.

Meade, Amanda. 2016. "*Charlie Hebdo* Cartoon Depicting Drowned Child Alan Kurdi Sparks Racism Debate." *Guardian*, January 14. https://www.theguardian.com/media /2016/jan/14/charlie-hebdo-cartoon-depicting-drowned-child-alan-kurdi-sparks -racism-debate.

Mohamed, Batool. 2014. "I Love Death." YouTube video, 4:18. April 30. Posted by "Bidayyat." https://www.youtube.com/watch?v=mDen2JazE9M.

Mortimer, Caroline. 2016. "Cologne: Three out of 58 Men Arrested over Mass Sex Attack on New Year's Eve Were Refugees from Syria or Iraq." *Independent*, February 15. http://www .independent.co.uk/news/world/europe/cologne-only-three-out-of-58-men-arrested -in-connection-with-mass-sex-attack-on-new-years-eve-are-a6874201.html.

Muller, Martin. 2013. "Text, Discourse, Affect, and Things." In *The Ashgate Research Companion to Critical Geopolitics*, edited by J. Sharp and K. Dodds, 49–68. Farnham, UK: Ashgate.

O'Neill, Brendan. 2015. "Sharing a Photo of a Dead Syrian Child Isn't Compassionate, It's Narcissistic." *Coffee House* (blog), *Spectator*, September 3. http://blogs.spectator.co.uk/2015/09/sharing-a-photo-of-the-dead-syrian-child-isnt-compassionate-its-narcissistic/.

Pain, Rachel. 2009. "Globalized Fear? Towards an Emotional Geopolitics." *Progress in Human Geography* 33 (4): 466–86.

Parkinson, Joe, and David George-Cosh. 2015. "Image of Drowned Syrian Boy Echoes around World." *Wall Street Journal*, September 3. http://www.wsj.com/articles/image-of-syrian-boy-washed-up-on-beach-hits-hard-1441282847.

Puar, Jasbir K. 2009. "Prognosis Time: Towards a Geopolitics of Affect, Debility and Capacity." *Women and Performance* 19 (2): 161–72.

Ragland, Ellie. 1995. *Essays on the Pleasures of Death: From Freud to Lacan*. New York: Routledge.

Rich, Adrienne. 1991. *An Atlas of The Difficult World*. New York: Norton.

Ticktin, Miriam. 2015. "The Problem with Humanitarian Borders." *Public Seminar*, September 18. http://www.publicseminar.org/2015/09/the-problem-with-humanitarian-borders/#.VyuetljolzJ.

6   Empowering Women
A Symptom of Development?

Chizu Sato

The empowerment of less privileged women in the global South has been a major development objective for more than two decades. A succession of technologies has been deployed to empower these women, including, but not limited to, adult literacy, participatory appraisal, microfinance, human rights, and public-private partnerships (PPPs). While the technologies of empowerment shift, the less privileged women targeted in the global South are consistently recognized as potentially rational entrepreneurs who can multiply investments in a manner that benefits their own, familial, communal, and national well-being. Today, investing in women is "smart economics" (World Bank 2006, 2012) in that the empowerment of women is good for both development and business. Paralleling the sequence of technologies used for women's empowerment, feminist academics who study this empowerment have elaborated a sequence of critical analytic tools, for example, gender efficiency and practical and strategic gender needs (Moser 1989), the essentialization of Third World women (Mohanty 1991), social relations (Kabeer 1994), governmentality (Rankin 2001), feminization of poverty (Chant 2006), neoliberalization of feminism (Prügl 2015), postfeminism (Calkin 2015b; Elias 2013), and transnational business feminism (Roberts 2012, 2015), among others. These and other feminist interventions have contributed to our understanding of women, empowerment, and development. However, the repetition of both practice and critique does raise the question: What can we learn from this dialectic?

Analysis informed by transnational feminist literacy practices (Sato 2014, 2016) suggests that some aspects remain undertheorized within feminist interventions. First, most studies are class blind (Wolff 2003) or at best capitalocentric (Gibson-Graham 1996). Class—understood as processes of surplus production, appropriation, and distribution (Resnick and Wolff 1987)—is absent. When class is discussed, either capitalism is assumed or class is read as power from above or domination. This "class" presents capitalism as dominating or governing women in the global South and the capitalist class as able to accumulate capital. If discussed at all, noncapitalist class processes are seen as slight variations of capitalism—marginal to the point of irrelevance, processes on the way to becoming capitalist—or as existing within and functional to capitalism (e.g., Calkin 2015b; Mohanty 2003; Roberts 2012). This conception of "class," in which capitalism is taken for granted or essentialized, sharply limits the range of viable transformative strategies. Second, many feminist studies of PPPs use as data material composed by "partners" who are committed to their success. When these materials include the voices of participating women, these voices are both solicited and represented by partners. The conclusions based on this secondary material are, thus, limited to those supportable given these partners' perspectives. Combining the decision to work with partners' material with a notion of power or class as domination from above, these analyses tend to highlight the mechanism by which power from above impinges on women and tend to be structurally insensitive to expressions of women's agency other than that reported to partners. Third, feminist studies of empowerment often implicitly identify the source of problems as external. Problems may originate from, for example, global capitalism, neoliberalism, or Western liberal feminism (e.g., Calkin 2015b; Prügl 2015; Roberts 2012; K. Wilson 2015). Transnational feminist literacy practices enable us to see how this externalization might conceal interdependencies between problems identified (e.g., capitalism) and our academic conceptions of them (e.g., capitalocentrism and class as power) in a manner that constrains the range of political futures that are conceivable.

According to Lacanian psychoanalysis, the addition of new theoretical insights, such as those just endorsed, will not be adequate because they exclude what Jacques Lacan (1981) calls the Real. The Real, "the impossible" (Lacan 1981, 167) within the social structure, is something that may be approached but "always comes back to the same place" (49; see also the introduction and chapters 3, 5, 8, and 11 in this volume). Analyses that revolve around power reduce "society to its indwelling network of relations of power and knowledge" (Copjec 1994, 6).[1] In such historicist analyses, gender, class, and other processes intersect within networks of power that can never be escaped. This theorization is blind to the notion of negativity, upholding a subject who remains "undivided" (Spivak 1988, 274) as articulated within discourse. Lacanian subjects are psychically divided the moment they enter the social/linguistic structure. In Lacanian psychoanalysis, the social structure *as well as* its subjects cannot escape the Real. Ernesto Laclau and Chantal Mouffe (1985), drawing on psychoanalytic insights, suggest that politics that are insensitive to the Real—that is, social antagonisms—are doomed to fail as they can neither anticipate nor accommodate the inevitable yet unpredictable eruptions of the Real within discursively prescribed articulatory political practices. Lacanian psychoanalysis makes visible the empowerment of women in its sequence of forms as a *symptom*, a repressed content in positive social relations that comes back again and again to disturb the social structure. It highlights the role of enjoyment (*jouissance*) in that process, the excessive pleasure found, for example, in perpetually inadequate attempts to empower women (see chapters 3 and 7). The politics suggested by critics of women's empowerment has been insensitive to the dynamics of negativity, and the political futures envisioned by these critics necessarily have been delimited by this blindness. So what political futures might be conceivable were we to develop literacy in the dynamics of negativity when examining the empowerment of women in development?

This chapter draws on Lacanian psychoanalytic insights to extend transnational feminist critiques of women's empowerment in development. It sees the constantly evolving invention of new technologies of women's empowerment, as well as concomitant critiques, as a symptom of development, that is, as an effect of an intersubjective dialectics of desire within which women are constituted as subjects/objects of empowerment. Through practicing transnational feminist literacy that attends to the dynamics of negativity, I attempt to denaturalize our relationship with these ever-changing technologies and their critiques by suggesting the possibility of a different articulation of women's empowerment in the hopes of disrupting the mutually constitutive practices of those who empower, those empowered, and those who critique.

The chapter is divided into five sections. First, I offer a brief discussion of the historical conditions within which the signifier "empowerment" established itself. In the following two sections, I analyze how empowering women becomes a symptom of development and point to the problematic role of feminist academics in their reproduction of empowering women. In the conclusion, I discuss one vision of a transnational feminist solidarity that takes the dynamics of negativity into account.

The Construction of Intersubjective Networks

Development (capital D) is productively recognized as a social fantasy (Žižek 1990), a post–World War II scenario that papers over the Real, or social antagonisms, produced by long-standing but continuously shifting imperialist class struggles (Sato 2006). At least since the Fourth World Conference on Women in Beijing in 1995, empowerment has become a master signifier (the Lacanian *point de capiton*) or "a nodal point" (Laclau and Mouffe 1985) within development.[2] The signifier "empowerment" temporarily quilts or buckles together meanings of other signifiers (Lacan 2007), like education, health, income generation, microfinance, and human rights. Together, they help stabilize the inconsistent development apparatus such that it remains a workable field. This notion of shaping is exemplified in Sedgwick's metaphoric "Christmas effect" (as cited by Gibson-Graham 1996, viii).[3] The signifier "Christmas" provides a reference around which many institutions (e.g., the church, gift shops, Christmas-tree growers) have historically arrayed themselves in ways that are found to be workable. Empowerment, like Christmas, is a nodal point that provides a vessel assembling other signifiers in a manner whose operation defers, distracts attention from, or papers over eruptions of the Real.

Much like "Christmas," empowerment did not become a nodal point over night. The original articulation of women, empowerment, and development occurred in the mid-1980s. The term "empowerment" entered development as a result of the work of feminist activists and groups from and in the global South, such as Development Alternatives with Women for a New Era (DAWN). One intent of these groups was to empower themselves and other less privileged women in the global South in order to recognize and challenge intersecting local (e.g., caste) and external (e.g., structural adjustment programs [SAPs] sponsored by donors like the World Bank) oppressions (Sen and Grown 1987). Caroline Moser's (1989) work links DAWN's contribution to what she calls an empowerment approach, in which she advocates for the recognition of women in development. This early articulation of empowerment was taken up in the concerted construction of microcredit as *the* antipoverty panacea, exemplified by the post–Beijing conference success of the Grameen Bank. In this context, women, particularly those most harmed by SAPs, were found to be the best economic bet. This recognition facilitated the double process of weakening links between empowerment and DAWN-inspired bottom-up activism and of strengthening the links between empowerment, gender efficiency, and the market-based economy. Today, given the "success" of microcredit and the impressive track record of women's economic contribution both as workers and consumers at the bottom of the pyramid,[4] gender equality and women's empowerment are seen as integral to smart economics—they are good for both development and business.

"Gender equality and women's empowerment as smart economics" is now the Law within development. This Law was instituted and repeatedly enforced by a Master,[5] for example, Robert B. Zoellick, the eleventh World Bank president (2007–12). In a brochure targeting leaders of private-sector companies, Zoellick declares, "Gender equality in business is smart economics. Enlightened private sector companies recognize that. Gender equality

Chizu Sato

and women's empowerment are at the core of what we need do in development. It is not just a women's issue. Improved economic opportunities for women lead to better outcomes for families, societies and countries" (Global Private Sector Leaders Forum n.d.). The position from which Zoellick speaks is laden with authority that shapes how he is heard. With his statement Zoellick declares his expectations of and to his addressees, private-sector leaders. He demands that they "understand women's contributions to business profitability and to the community they operate in" and increase "women's opportunities in the private sector" (Global Private Sector Leaders Forum n.d.). His demand that private-sector leaders enroll women in their business efforts is excessive. It is in the service of his development that private-sector companies will form partnerships with public and nonprofit development organizations. Zoellick and his ilk articulate what private-sector leaders and the women needing empowerment must do to realize development.

The new Law of "smart economics" is situated in long-standing imperialist efforts to include, as past World Bank president James Wolfensohn put it, "more and more people into the economic mainstream" (cited in Bergeron 2003, 157). The theories and technologies of empowerment, participatory appraisal, social capital, microcredit, and today, public-private partnerships include those women who are recognized to be excluded from the "economic mainstream" in ways that are consistent with the Law of the Master. In this development, words like "inclusion" and "empowerment" become nodal points through which those who act appropriately cover over social antagonisms (e.g., imperialist class struggles and the impossibility of including all into the "economic mainstream") and thereby stabilize the social structure.

The Master requires an audience to address. In this case there are two: private-sector leaders and less privileged women in the global South. Private-sector leaders are addressed in such spaces as the Global Private Sector Leaders Forum, the World Economic Forum in Davos, and magazines like *Business Week* and *The Economist*. All of these spaces are public-pedagogical forums through which these private-sector leaders are called to be and interpellated as proponents of the Master's new Law. In taking up their symbolically assigned mandates, they become "enlightened" leaders. Evidence of this "smart" leadership is found in statements of magnates like Muhtar Kent, Coca-Cola chairman and CEO, and Mike Duke, Walmart president and CEO:

> The 21st century is the "Women's Century." Women's economic empowerment and entrepreneurial growth will drive the world's economy. It's not a matter of "if"—but rather a matter of "to what heights." For all of us in business, government, education and civil society—the implications will be vast and profound. Everyone's success will be contingent upon women's success. (Kent 2010)

> For Walmart, empowering women is also smart business. As we build the Next Generation Walmart, we must win the global war for talent. That means having the best men and women working at our company around the world. (Duke 2011)

By inserting women and empowerment into business speak on terms specified by the Master, private-sector leaders like Kent and Duke form chains linking the sets of signifiers native to their historical business practice to those of development. Through this articulation, they create sources of new knowledge: Kent, for instance, links women's empowerment with "national GDP [gross domestic product] growth, business growth, environmental sustainability, and improved human health" (Kent 2010). They then use their own substantial resources to implement the Law by setting up, for example, Coca-Cola's 5by20 (launched in 2010) and Walmart's Global Women's Economic Empowerment Initiative (launched in 2011).[6] These initiatives enact their desire for the new object—the "empowerment of women"—as conjured up within contemporary development. From a Lacanian psychoanalytic perspective, the enjoyment business leaders derive from their actions makes these initiatives possible: the material as well as symbolic rewards that come with performing as "enlightened" leaders. While their decisions are recognized as "freely" made, they are forced on them, from

Chizu Sato

a Lacanian psychoanalytic perspective, by the symbolic networks through which the leaders are necessarily articulated. If they do not follow the Law, they lose the symbolic status in these networks required to derive their specific pleasures.

Private-sector leaders, in turn, require an audience, which they find in the historically less privileged women of the global South.[7] For these women empowerment training sessions become one context in which they are taken up in pedagogical mechanisms whose success results in their enthusiastic assumption of the symbolic mandate given by private-sector leaders. Successful women are then asked to report how such training changed their lives and those of their families and communities. The following testimony of a young Indian trainee named Amandeep from a short video shown at launch of the Walmart Global Women's Economic Empowerment Initiative is a telling example: "I learned a lot at the Bharti Walmart Training Center, especially around topics like retail and wholesale. Also, good communication skills. Product knowledge. Member service. Always smiling face. These are some of the traits I learned. The work culture here is extremely good. It's like a family atmosphere here. I feel very proud of working with the No 1 retail company in the world" (Walmart 2011). In saying what is required of her, Amandeep affirms the Law and her place in a Development that her success creates. She was previously positioned outside the symbolic order (of "development"), but now she has been "included." Paralleling the private-sector leaders, she has taken up her symbolic mandate and with that sheds her status as a member of a "'vulnerable population'" (Wolfensohn, as cited in Bergeron 2003, 157) in need of "empowerment."

The voice-over at the end of the video in which Amandeep was featured tells us how her training enables her "independently" to create her own identity. These "freely" chosen identities are merely subjects giving voice to what is demanded of them as newly "empowered" women, to what is required of them if they were to be empowered. I want to suggest, in fact, that they are interpellated as "phallic" women (Salecl 1998, 67). For Lacan, the subject desires due to the failure or impossibility of full subjectivation and sexual difference depend on one's position in relation to desire (Lacan

1998). By virtue of their being newly enchained within the discourse of development, empowered women experience an enjoyment derived from *masquerading* as the idealized subjectivity assigned them. When inserted into the lack in the Other, these exemplars of "smart" entrepreneurial women help cover over social antagonisms and stabilize Development. In masquerading, these new entrepreneurial women make the Other complete, and thus, the Master may defer recognition of the impossibility of, for example, "smart economics" and of the inclusion of all into the "economic mainstream." Persistent repetition of performative acts that fail to realize their declared objectives is a symptom indicating the existence of a repressed content, content that cannot be represented in the power-laden symbolization process. The performative acts of these women create intersubjective networks among, but not limited to, women subjects/objects of empowerment, the development leaders, and the private-sector leaders. These intersubjective networks, supported by the enjoyment experienced by its subjects, produce fantasmatic consistency in the social structure.

On the Side of the Master

While the interlinking and mutually constitutive performances of the Master and his subjects may (re)produce social hierarchy, the relationship in this case is psychically symmetrical. The Master's subjects "independently" act in a manner that the Master both demands and recognizes. For example, on viewing the video featuring Amandeep, Walmart's Duke has the following comments: "As you saw, she's a graduate of one of our training centers in Punjab India and a sales associate at the Best Price Wholesale store in Amritsar. Now she's pursuing an MBA. She's writing her own future. And it'll be a better future for her and her family. I've been to our training centers in India. And let me say this: Nothing makes me prouder in this job than to see the faces of opportunity we provide to men and women around the globe" (Walmart 2011). What is not to be missed here is the repetitive-performative coproduction of reality: the Law interpellates its subjects, who, in performing their roles, retroactively confirm the Law. These subjects derive pleasure from doing what the Master commands and,

Chizu Sato

thereby, meeting his expectations while the Master derives pleasure from an obedience that secures his identity as Master. The Master and his subjects, thus, both derive enjoyment from their co-constitutive performances.

Lacanian psychoanalysis recognizes this mutual relationship as a *semblance*. Within a semblance the Real is removed, and the subjects are necessarily supported by *fantasy* ($ ◊ a$). Those who perform the Law are split ($) from their own desire upon entering the symbolic order, so they are marked by a symbolic lack. Split subjects, however, are unable to fully repress their own desire. It unpredictably erupts, troubling their speech and their acts. As a split subject, the Master does not know entirely what he is saying or performing. His speech always conveys something extra, a surplus (*objet a*, a piece of the Real) that, unknown to him, escapes his symbolization. While he seems to identify with and be fully satisfied by mirroring the performances of his subjects, he necessarily externalizes his own limit: he worries that he will fail to adequately accomplish the mandate assigned him within the symbolic order and that he will be unable to empower women. The anxiety produced by this irrepressible questioning is mitigated, but never resolved, by the perpetual invention of new technologies, such as microcredit and public-private partnership ($ ◊ a$). On this reading, smart economics is but one in a necessarily endless sequence of inadequate attempts to cover over the impossible gap created by the alienation of the Master from his own desire. The quest to include all in the "economic mainstream" is supported, on one hand, by the externalization of the internal limit of the split subject and, on the other, by the necessary and equally necessarily futile repression of the Real.

The enjoyment the Master derives from his impossible pursuit keeps him engaged in development. As a split subject, his desire can never be fully satisfied. As his desire is never fully met, he may derive perpetual enjoyment from its impossible pursuit. He is perpetually able to find opportunities to derive symbolically mediated enjoyment through recognition as a successful leader or enabler of women's empowerment. But what is critical in this analysis is his covert unsymbolizable enjoyment, the pleasures that come from being unable to include all people into the "economic development," that is, the pleasures that come from not being able to fully stabilize the symbolic order.

As seen in the quotes from previous World Bank presidents, class blindness marks the position of this Master. He presents and represents a capitalism that provides equal opportunity and democracy. The perpetual efforts of the Master to include those who are excluded, those who are outside the "economic mainstream," point to what threatens him. This Master is threatened by the unknown space "outside" the economic mainstream. According to neoclassical doctrine, the economic mainstream is efficient only once constraints are removed and one of these constraints is subjects who are excluded (Charusheela 2001). The Master, in order to be the Master, will demand removal of constraints as that will stabilize his symbolic order. In the case discussed here, the Master must demand the modernization of nonmainstream "precapitalist," "informal" economies. Today the Master is using the technologies of microcredit and PPPs to precipitate a transformation of "precapitalist" and "peripheral" economies, a transformation that is promised to bring those who are "excluded" into the "economic mainstream," and for these technologies the activities of women are thought most promising.

As much as fantasy depends on perpetual pursuit of an impossible goal, in this case full inclusion and its integrity also requires selective blindness. Among others, the fantasy discussed here requires the presumption of capitalism (capitalocentrism) and blindness to class where that is understood as the process of production, appropriation, and distribution of surplus (class qua surplus; see chapters 3 and 8). Within a capitalocentric perspective, Amandeep is only seen as exploited by Walmart. From the perspective of class qua surplus, she, as a retail worker, does not produce surplus. Since exploitation (appropriation of surplus by the non-producer of the surplus) only occurs in production (Resnick and Wolff 1987), she is not exploited by Walmart (see also Erçel 2006; Mulder 2011; Ruccio 2003). Yet the absence of exploitation does not mean that there are no class or other struggles between a merchant capitalist (Walmart) and its non-surplus-producing employees. The struggle here is a nonclass one over unequal exchange, that

Chizu Sato

is, Walmart retains a disproportionate fraction of the surplus (received from its subcontractors) at the expense of its employees' wages, benefits, and working conditions (Mulder 2011, 256). This knowledge, found when class as surplus is permitted, must necessarily not be perceptible within the fantasy of the Master because the private-sector leaders he anoints must be recognized as providing equal opportunities to the excluded within development.

By externalizing limits and repressing the Real, the Master appears to derive absolute enjoyment. He appears to occupy a position that is different from that of the women he addressed. Contrary to development narratives that identify less privileged women as "lacking," not measuring up to the standards set by those who are "developed," the Master, from a Lacanian standpoint, is just as much a split subject marked by lack. This subject cannot recognize himself as merely a servant, a passive object for the Other's enjoyment. His enjoyment requires that he disavow his dependence on the Other. Repressed knowledge (e.g., his dependence on these women and the knowledge of class qua surplus) guarantees that he will not confront the Real. The Real will continue to be elided, it will remain excluded from the symbolic order, and it will continue to erupt in ways that guarantee the perpetual invention of new performative acts as is found in the case of women's empowerment in development over the last twenty years. His enjoyable yet futile pursuit sustains a dialectics of desire, constituting both his identity and that of his subjects: a dialectics in which his subjects, by definition, reliably desire what is valued in the symbolic order, thereby securing his position as Master. This interplay of desire defers indefinitely any recognition of the antagonisms inherent within the social structure.

On the Side of the "Empowered"

Now turning to the Master's addressee, those who are less powerful in the chain of signification within development must accept a subordinate symbolic position if they are to have any position at all. Since the 1980s a series of events and practices, from the Fourth World Conference on Women in Beijing to the Millennium Development Goals, the UN's Women's

Empowerment Principles, and now the Sustainable Development Goals, have consistently called for the empowerment of less privileged women in the global South, women who have been "excluded" from the economic mainstream, in order to advance development. When represented, these women are most often presented as in need of empowerment, and the steps to be taken are specified by the Master and repeated by his surrogates. When they are represented as "empowered," the success of those specified technologies, thus the Master's position, is retroactively confirmed. Again, from a Lacanian perspective, the speaking subject is split and cannot be fully articulated in language. Then, what we hear of these women is limited to that articulable in the language of the Master. The persistence of calls for women's empowerment indicates that some part keeps escaping. Something must be repressed in the symbolization process. To the extent that less privileged women subjects/objects of empowerment such as Amandeep enter the symbolic order of development, they become a passive object for the Other's enjoyment. The woman's knowledge and labor are only relevant on the terms through which her newfound identity as a subject in need of empowerment is constituted. She exists to the extent that she does what the Master / the Other demands of her. The resulting alienation from her own desires produces an inassimilable surplus (*objet a*), which is, predictably, not visible within the symbolic order. Alienation from her own desires, the by-product of the repression of her own desires, is the price a woman like Amandeep pays to be included in the "economic mainstream." It is this repression that facilitates a compulsive return and creates fundamental antagonisms in the symbolic order.[8]

Why does a woman like Amandeep pay this price? It is, again, because she is a split subject embedded within an intersubjective network in a manner analogous to the Master. In the beginning of the promotional video, avoiding early marriage, a social norm prevalent for young girls in her community, was presented as *the* reason why Amandeep joined the training program. As an educated young woman, she said "no!" to early marriage and "yes!" to the empowerment training and the possibility of an MBA. Through acts that demonstrated an increased "human capital," such as learning particular business manners and going through an MBA program, she enjoys material (e.g., income, an MBA) and symbolic (e.g., the identity of "empowered" woman) rewards. Symbolic rewards are confirmed retroactively by the Other's (e.g., the Walmart CEO and the World Bank president) symbolic recognitions of her. However, attempts to cover over social antagonisms with her acts always in part fail. Thus, these women must repeat their acts again and again. Her repeated performative acts provoke the desire of the Other for her, since her acts fill in the gap in the Other, thus providing enjoyment for the Other. When women like Amandeep masquerade, they simultaneously sacrifice their own desire and gain the desire of the Other. This is why empowering women is a symptom. It is a continually repeated response to the eruption of repressed content in positive social relations enacted in order to stabilize Development. As with the Master, women also derive covert enjoyment from repressing their own desire (e.g., chatting with her friends in the field and resting). The enjoyment of these masquerading women keeps them trapped in vicious intersubjective dialectics of desire whose operation in turn impairs availability of the knowledge of the injustices (e.g., unequal exchange) involved in their everyday lives.

The aforementioned cycle of desire also signifies the impossibility of fully including the subaltern in the "economic mainstream." While large private-sector companies have sizable resources to spread their so-called success stories, the evidence tells us something different. For example, one participant in the Mexican Walmart empowerment project mentions that she constantly fears being seen as "successful" in her community because that success would make her a target for drug cartels (Tornhill 2015). Another young woman who participates in the Girl Effect campaign in Brazil is reported to have gotten pregnant while going through her training (Moeller 2013).[9] There are additional reported occurrences of absences and dropouts from the empowerment projects (Gupta and Rajshekhar 2005; Moeller 2013; Tornhill 2015). All of this tells us, at a minimum, that some women resist, bypass, or even reject the symbolic mandate of development. These failures are evidence that the Law is not fully effective. What the symbolic mandate declares to be the desires of these women does not entirely equal what they desire. In comparison with the articulable desire of the self-identified Master and of women subjects/objects of empowerment in the Master's representations, some part of the desire of these women is located elsewhere, outside the symbolic order that the Master recognizes.

However, not only the Master but also feminist academics who focus on the positive, articulable desire of development's success stories, seem unable to read negativity or surplus represented by women's desires. Upholding such negativity may make it possible to recognize the radical instability at the center of the subject and, by extension, at the center of the social structure.

On the Side of Feminist Academics

I have discussed how intersubjective dialectics of desire between the Master and his subjects sustains Development. Turning to feminist academics, we find ourselves on the opposite side of the Master and his ilk: we academics elaborate analytic tools we use to critique the evolving technologies of women's empowerment. This positioning may make it possible to imagine us as outside the intersubjective dialectics of desire that constitute Development. However, the persistence of calls for empowerment despite over twenty years of significant efforts suggests our critical analyses remain unthreatening. Academics' tendency to work with partners' data and to assume the dominance of capitalism constrains feminist analyses to the illumination partners' perspectives on capitalist terms (Sato 2016). These feminist critics' reading practice encourages them to recognize subjects—be they the Master or his flocks—as self-identified and as capable of extending capitalism within the closed circuits of power/knowledge. This form of critique, as discussed by Gibson-Graham (1996, 2006), has the perverse effect of reinforcing the hegemony of its object. In the case discussed here, these forms of critique consolidate the position and identity of the Master and his flocks. When feminists represent the subject as undivided, it is not possible to recognize the unspoken psychic struggles such as those I delineated earlier—the subaltern's multiple if not contradictory desires. We readily criticize the perversities of development practice that subordinate women in the name of their empowerment. In doing so we become unable to read the dynamics of negativity that I have just described. We risk, then, doing precisely what we criticize: keeping the subaltern's desires at bay. We end up joining hands with the very Master we disparage by turning less privileged women into a fetishistic object (Žižek 2008).

Transnational feminists have criticized fellow feminists for blindly exercising their power in an effort to "rescue" their less privileged sisters. They have called instead for building transnational feminist solidarity between less and more privileged women by making "glObal capitalism" a common object of struggle (Mohanty 2003). By examining the representational practices of partners, recent feminist critiques of empowerment projects argue that these practices (re)produce a "rescue" relationship between "Third World" women and "First World" women that makes feminist solidarity difficult if not impossible (Calkin 2015a; Koffman and Gill 2013; MacDonald 2016). Bringing forward insights from the psychoanalytic perspective just introduced, however, the relationship between less privileged women and more privileged feminist academics is recognizable as that constituting a Master and his subjects. That is, this relationship may be understood psychically as solidarity: feminist academics require less privileged women to sustain their identity, and we are able to maintain this pleasurable status by remaining illiterate in the dynamics of negativity—the dynamics of the subaltern's and our own desires. In this sense, our solidarity may be an ever so slightly different power-laden intersubjective recognition a Master cultivates with his subjects.

Instead of pointing the finger at fellow feminists, let me explain by using myself as an example. I recognize that I am a subject of development. Through my socialization process and academic acculturation, I have acquired a particular "cultural archive" (Said 1993). In this Western consumer culture, "development" tends to be represented as desirable and "sexy" (Cameron and Haanstra 2008), obscuring imperialist injustices past and present. On the one hand, we are exhorted to "help" others. Moral obligation toward the distant, if not exotic, less privileged other is encouraged via instruments like cause marketing (Hawkins 2011; Richey and Ponte 2011; Wilson 2015), celebrity humanitarianism (Kapoor 2012), or celebrity-endorsed products. We are told what to do to help others: engage in compassionate consumption (Wilson 2015) and, in so doing, imagine global sisterhood (Hawkins 2011).[10] On the other hand, there are enormous pressures to perform within our increasingly corporatized universities. We are told what we must do to succeed: good teaching evaluations, publications in journals with high impact factors, big research grants. Publicly and professionally, we may challenge capitalism, neoliberalism, or modernist development, but privately, we obey what we challenge, including the dictates of corporatized universities or tenure regulations.

In my case, the conditions conducive to the cultivation of an imperialist morality are well established. When I hear someone like Zoellick say, "Progress in the area of women's economic empowerment is still far, far too slow. Whether it is the question of employment, opportunity, pay, or access to finance, there is a tremendous amount of work to do to level the playing field for women" (World Bank 2008), the intersubjective networks through which we are articulated encourage me to agree with the statement. If I, or my peers, come to agree with such an assertion, even slightly, we become vulnerable to the superego's command to "Enjoy!" Our internalized compulsive moral law pushes us to take pleasure in following the Law. In my case, I am typically invited to derive narcissistic enjoyment by performing the role of the critic: one who condemns "neoliberal capitalism" while simultaneously arguing for gender equality and women's empowerment and building a tenure file. However, do we not covertly desire women's perpetual failure to empower themselves so that we may continue performing our role as critic or savior? Were women successfully able to empower themselves, it would put an end to our source of enjoyment. In short, do we not want to continue to derive narcissistic pleasure from taking on the white man's burden, now repackaged as the "cosmopolitan white" burden (cf. Abu-Lughod 2002; Saraswati 2010)?[11]

Our inability to read the dynamics of negativity comes at a cost. Our cosmopolitan imperialist morality—composed in part of proclamations in favor of and acts that are recognized as helping others—combined with our own covert narcissistic pleasures make it hard to turn our critical gaze to our own practice. We cover over our internal lack with our fetishistic object, in this case empowering less privileged women. We are, thus, able to continue living our daily lives relatively smoothly (Žižek 2008). As critics of development, we become part and parcel of the intersubjective dialectics of desire that make up Development. We might be able to recognize smart economics as an update to a centuries-old imperialist civilizing mission, but we remain unable to read the dynamics of negativity in which we are constituted. We adopt those analytics that are functional to our pleasure, such as capitalocentrism and historicism, while repressing others, such as class qua surplus and literacy in the dynamic of negativity, whose proper use would threaten our enjoyment. With our conduct we provide conditions that support the continued existence of social antagonisms such as class and other injustice.

Faced with the truth of our complicity with that which we criticize or loathe, we may so easily retreat into denial, we may be overcome and paralyzed with guilt, or we may withdraw from development altogether. These reactions blind us to our necessary co-constitution with the Other. My point here has been to encourage reflection on our own desire, to recognize and better come to terms with that which we often unconsciously avert—the Real, or social antagonisms. When we recognize ourselves as necessarily constituted in and deriving pleasure through pernicious intersubjective dialectics of desire, we are better equipped to access the relevance of existing analytic tools and politics, such as class qua surplus and postcapitalist politics. In taking advantage of these tools, we may find futures that we, today, are not able to see. For example, even though women's performances conform to the Master's expectations, through the lens provided by class qua surplus it is possible to ask if the class processes in which these women are engaged are all "capitalist." Shakti Ammas, female micro-distributors of Hindustan Unilever products in rural areas, while financially supported by Hindustan Unilever, are independent merchants; many of them collaborate with their male family members to forge possibly cooperative merchanting businesses (Hindustan Unilever 2012). Coca-Cola 5by20 supports women-run cooperatives (e.g., three hundred waste collection cooperatives in Brazil) in which the members appropriate the fruits of their own labor. Seen through a capitalocentric perspective, these private-sector-induced economic activities precipitate transitions from the precapitalist to the capitalist practice. From a postcapitalist perspective (Gibson-Graham, Cameron, and Healy 2016), acknowledging James Ferguson's argument that neoliberal strategies need not result in neoliberal outcomes, the same economic activities may be seen as an array of idiosyncratic co-optations of productive and merchant capital that support the emergence of postcapitalist politics. There is no reason to romanticize these "noncapitalist" economic practices: there may be nonclass struggles, for example, between the capitalist partners and noncapitalist "beneficiaries" and among "beneficiaries." The value of these analytics may be that they enable us to cultivate our desire for a postcapitalist politics (Gibson-Graham 2006; see also Healy 2010; Madra and Özselçuk 2015) within intersubjective networks through which unforeseen yet potentially more democratic futures can be imagined.

Conclusion: A Transnational Feminist Literacy in the Dynamics of Negativity

This chapter presented the constant reinvention of technologies for women's empowerment together with their critiques as a symptom of development: as an effect of an intersubjective dialectics of desire constituting those who empower, those who are empowered, and their critics within Development. The point of this analysis has not been to repudiate the dialectics of desire constitutive of Development but to consider the productivity of an understanding of these dialectics. I propose to expand transnational feminist literacy by becoming more literate in the dynamics of negativity. Lacanian psychoanalysis enables us to recognize the practice and effects of contingent and unspoken psychic struggles, which then illuminate both women's and our own struggles and agency quite differently. This lens helps us see subjects of development as differently enchained within a common symbolic order, and as a result, we are all divided and often possessed of contradictory desires. It highlights psychic interdependencies we silently cultivate and the way our enjoyment so often depends on the Other. Recognizing these psychic interdependencies may allow us to identify novel and contextually appropriate strategies to transform the intersubjective networks in which we are formed from our respective locations.

Psychoanalysis is not a metalanguage. It alone does not provide political direction. Here I suggest literacy in economic difference informed by antiessentialist Marxian insights (e.g., class qua surplus and postcapitalist politics). Literacy in economic difference reveals an abundance of heterogeneous economic activities in which the women participating in empowerment projects engage. When it is possible to see a diversity of class and nonclass struggles between surplus-producing workers and non-surplus-producing workers, we become sensitive to textured class and nonclass injustices (see, for example, Mulder 2011). With this insight we are able to generate a greater diversity of and hopefully more effective strategies for transformation.

Literacy in the dynamics of negativity enriches our understanding of our own and others' agency, while literacy in economic difference both affords a more heterogeneous representation of the economic landscape, differentiating noncapitalist class processes from capitalist ones, and makes perceptible new political directions, such as linking empowerment with nonexploitation and other forms of class and nonclass justice. In new transnational feminist political imaginaries, solidarity is not understood as an imperialist "glObal sisterhood" or as formed in opposition to an essentialized conceptualization of "glObal capitalism," but as fidelity to the Real. At the heart of any political struggles there are always social antagonisms (Laclau and Mouffe 1985): the subaltern may escape symbolization, and empowerment may fail. These psychoanalytic insights nonetheless support our democratic struggles insofar as these insights force us to recognize and, with that, release us from the desperate futility of attempts such as the inclusion of all in the "economic mainstream" while motivating us to continue to imagine an engagement with the subaltern from our respective locations. Through practicing a transnational feminist literacy that is attentive to the dynamics of negativity, we might be able to imagine heterogeneous, more democratic and perhaps noncapitalist developments in which the subaltern and the non-subaltern derive uncompromising enjoyment based on mutual recognitions of desires.

Notes

My special thanks goes to Ilan Kapoor for reinvigorating my interest in Lacanian psychoanalysis and providing constructive criticisms and careful editing. The earlier version of the paper was presented as part of the three panels organized by Ilan at the Association of American Geographers' Annual Conference in 2016. I benefitted from the comments of and conversations among my fellow panelists and our audience. Peter Tamas provided support for various aspects of this study. However, all faults remain mine.

1. Copjec limits her critique to Foucault's *Discipline and Punish, The History of Sexuality*, "and essays and interviews of the mid to late 1970s, when Foucault reversed his position with respect to linguistic and psychoanalytic theory" (1994, 4).

2. In non-psychoanalytic discussions, a "buzzword" is used to discuss this phenomenon. See Cornwall and Brock (2005).

3. Gibson-Graham (1996) made the analogy between Christmas and capitalism.

4. The bottom of the pyramid indicates the four billion people who live on less than US$2.50 a day (Prahalad 2005).

5. This Master occupies the position of agent in Lacan's Master's discourse (Lacan 2007).

6. Collaborating with public and civil society organizations, Coca-Cola is set to involve five million women in their supply chain by 2020. Walmart's five-year commitment is to provide job training and education to women in its supply chain in the United States and beyond and to donate $100 million in grants to support women's economic empowerment.

7. The position of the Other can be also occupied by other actors in the networks, such as state officials in the global South and nongovernmental organization officers who receive funding.

8. To be sure, it is the return that confirms the existence of repression. In other words, there is no repression before the return. See Žižek (2008).

9. The Girl Effect is a corporate social responsibility campaign with the aim of empowering adolescent girls for poverty eradication, supported by the Nike Foundation,

the philanthropic arm of Nike Inc., in collaboration with the NoVo Foundation, the
United Nations Foundation, and other partners.

10. Today's imperialist consumption is not new. For example, British imperialism was
supported by consumption practices in the UK (Kothari 2014; McClintock 1995;
Ramamurthy 2012).

11. Saraswati (2010) argues that cosmopolitan whiteness indicates a globe-trotting
lifestyle regardless of actual race. Here I mean that the phenomenon once known
as the white man's burden is no longer restricted to literal white men. This same
burden is now available to those who exhibit cosmopolitan whiteness.

Works Cited

Abu-Lughod, Lila. 2002. "Do Muslim Women Really Need Saving?: Anthropological
Reflections on Cultural Relativism and Its Others." *American Anthropologist* 104 (3):
783–90.

Bergeron, Suzanne. 2003. "Challenging the World Bank's Narrative of Inclusion." In
World Bank Literature, edited by Amitava Kumar, 157–71. Minneapolis: University
of Minnesota Press.

Calkin, Sydney. 2015a. "Post-feminist Spectatorship and the Girl Effect: 'Go Ahead, Really
Imagine Her.'" *Third World Quarterly* 36 (4): 654–69.

———. 2015b. "'Tapping' Women for Post-crisis Capitalism: Evidence from the 2012
World Development Report." *International Feminist Journal of Politics* 17 (4): 611–29.

Cameron, John, and Anna Haanstra. 2008. "Development Made Sexy: How It Happened
and What It Means." *Third World Quarterly* 29 (8): 1475–89.

Chant, Slyvia. 2006. "Re-thinking the 'Feminization of Poverty' in Relation to Aggregate
Gender Indices." *Journal of Human Development* 7 (2): 201–20.

Charusheela, S. 2001. "Women's Choices and the Ethnocentrism/Relativism Dilemma."
In *Postmodernism, Economics and Knowledge*, edited by Stephen Cullenberg, Jack
Amariglio, and David F. Ruccio, 197–220. London: Routledge.

Copjec, Joan. 1994. *Read My Desire: Lacan against the Historicists*. Cambridge MA: MIT
Press.

Cornwall, Andrea, and Karen Brock. 2005. "What Do Buzzwords Do for Development
Policy?: A Critical Look at 'Participation,' 'Empowerment' and 'Poverty Reduction.'"
Third World Quarterly 26 (7): 1043–60.

Duke, Mike. 2011. "Women's Empowerment: Driving Inclusion and Opportunity." http://news.
walmart.com/executive-viewpoints/mike-duke-womens-economic-empowerment
-initiative.

Elias, Juanita. 2013. "Davos Woman to the Rescue of Global Capitalism: Postfeminist Politics and Competitiveness Promotion at the World Economic Forum." *International Political Sociology* 7 (2): 152–69.

Erçel, Kenan. 2006. "Orientalization of Exploitation: A Class-Analytical Critique of the Sweatshop Discourse." *Rethinking Marxism* 18 (2): 289–306.

Gibson-Graham, J. K. 1996. *The End of Capitalism (As We Knew It): A Feminist Critique of Political Economy*. Cambridge MA: Blackwell.

———. 2006. *A Postcapitalist Politics*. Minneapolis: University of Minnesota Press.

Gibson-Graham, J. K., Jenny Cameron, and Stephen Healy. 2016. "Commoning as a Post-capitalist Politics." In *Releasing the Commons: Rethinking the Futures of the Commons*, edited by Ash Amin and Philip Howell, 192–212. London: Routledge.

Global Private Sector Leaders Forum. n.d. "Promoting Women's Economic Empowerment." http://siteresources.worldbank.org/INTGENDER/Resources/336003-1232650627030 /WB_GPSLBrochure.pdf.

Gupta, Indrajit, and M. Rajshekhar. 2005. "ITC vs HLL." ITC, April 25. http://www .itcportal.com/media-centre/press-reports-content.aspx?id=460&type=C&news=itc-vs %20-hll.

Hawkins, Roberta. 2011. "'One Pack = One Vaccine' = One Global Motherhood?: A Feminist Analysis of Ethical Consumption." *Gender, Place and Culture* 18 (2): 235–53.

Healy, Stephen. 2010. "Traversing Fantasies, Activating Desires: Economic Geography, Activist Research, and Psychoanalytic Methodology." *Professional Geographer* 62 (4): 496–506.

Hindustan Unilever. 2012. "Project Shakti: It Is All about Empowerment." *Indian Management*, February, 87–89.

Kabeer, Naila. 1994. *Reversed Realities: Gender Hierarchies in Development Thought*. New York: Verso.

Kapoor, Ilan. 2012. *Celebrity Humanitarianism: The Ideology of Global Charity*. New York: Routledge.

Kent, Muhtar. 2010. "This Century Goes to the Women." *Huffington Post*. http://www .huffingtonpost.com/muhtar-kent/post_1057_b_762044.html.

Koffman, Ofra, and Rosalind Gill. 2013. "'The Revolution Will Be Led by a 12-Year-Old Girl': Girl Power and Global Biopolitics." *Feminist Review* 105 (1): 83–102.

Kothari, Uma. 2014. "Trade, Consumption and Development Alliances: The Historical Legacy of the Empire Marketing Board Poster Campaign." *Third World Quarterly* 35 (1): 43–64.

Lacan, Jacques. 1981. *The Four Fundamental Concepts of Psycho-analysis*. Edited by Jacques-Alain Miller. Translated by Alan Sheridan. New York: Norton.

———. 1998. *On Feminine Sexuality: The Limits of Love and Knowledge.* Edited by Jacques-Alain Miller. Translated by Bruce Fink. New York: Norton.

———. 2007. *The Seminar, Book XVII: The Other Side of Psychoanalysis.* Edited by Jacques-Alain Miller. Translated by Russell Grigg. New York: Norton.

Laclau, Ernesto, and Chantal Mouffe. 1985. *Hegemony and Socialist Strategy: Towards a Radical Democratic Politics.* London: Verso.

MacDonald, Katie. 2016. "Calls for Educating Girls in the Third World: Futurity, Girls and the 'Third World Woman.'" *Gender, Place and Culture* 23 (1): 1–17.

Madra, Yahya M., and Ceren Özselçuk. 2015. "Creating Spaces for Communism: Post-capitalist Desire in Hong Kong, the Philippines and Western Massachusetts." In *Making Other Worlds Possible: Performing Diverse Economies,* edited by Gerda Roelvink, Kevin St. Martin, and J. K. Gibson-Graham, 127–52. Minneapolis: University of Minnesota Press.

McClintock, Anne. 1995. *Imperial Leather: Race, Gender, and Sexuality in the Colonial Conquest.* New York: Routledge.

Moeller, Kathryn. 2013. "Proving 'the Girl Effect': Corporate Knowledge Production and Educational Intervention." *International Journal of Educational Development* 33 (6): 612–21.

Mohanty, Chandra Talpade. 1991. "Under Western Eyes: Feminist Scholarship and Colonial Discourses." In *Third World Women and the Politics of Feminism,* edited by Chandra Talpade Mohanty, Ann Russo, and Lourdes Torres, 51–80. Bloomington: Indiana University Press.

———. 2003. *Feminism without Borders: Decolonizing Theory, Practicing Solidarity.* Durham NC: Duke University Press.

Moser, Caroline O. 1989. "Gender Planning in the Third World: Meeting Practical and Strategic Gender Needs." *World Development* 17 (11): 1799–1825.

Mulder, Catherine P. 2011. "Wal-Mart's Role in Capitalism." *Rethinking Marxism* 23 (2): 246–63.

Prahalad, C. K. 2005. *The Fortune at the Bottom of the Pyramid: Eradicating Poverty through Profits.* Upper Saddle River NJ: Pearson Education.

Prügl, Elisabeth. 2015. "Neoliberalising Feminism." *New Political Economy* 20 (4): 614–31.

Ramamurthy, Anandi. 2012. "Absences and Silences: The Representation of the Tea Picker in Colonial and Fair Trade Advertising." *Visual Culture in Britain* 1 (3): 367–81.

Rankin, Katharine N. 2001. "Governing Development: Neoliberalism, Microcredit, and Rational Economic Woman." *Economy and Society* 30 (1): 18–37.

Resnick, Stephen A., and Richard D. Wolff. 1987. *Knowledge and Class: A Marxian Critique of Political Economy.* Chicago: University of Chicago Press.

Richey, Lisa Ann, and Stefano Ponte. 2011. *Brand Aid: Shopping Well to Save the World.* Minneapolis: University of Minnesota Press.

Roberts, Adrienne. 2012. "Financial Crisis, Financial Firms . . . and Financial Feminism?: The Rise of 'Transnational Business Feminism' and the Necessity of Marxist-Feminist IPE." *Socialist Studies/Études socialistes* 8 (2): 85–105.

———. 2015. "The Political Economy of 'Transnational Business Feminism': Problematizing the Corporate-Led Gender Equality Agenda." *International Feminist Journal of Politics* 17 (2): 209–31.

Ruccio, David F. 2003. "Globalization and Imperialism." *Rethinking Marxism* 15 (1): 75–94.

Said, Edward W. 1993. *Culture and Imperialism.* New York: Vintage Books.

Salecl, Renata. 1998. *(Per)versions of Love and Hate.* London: Verso.

Saraswati, L. Ayu. 2010. "Cosmopolitan Whiteness: The Effects and Affects of Skin-Whitening Advertisements in a Transnational Women's Magazine in Indonesia." *Meridians: Feminism, Race, Transnationalism* 10 (2): 15–41.

Sato, Chizu. 2006. "Subjectivity, Enjoyment, and Development: Preliminary Thoughts on a New Approach to Postdevelopment." *Rethinking Marxism* 18 (2): 273–88.

———. 2014. "Toward Transnational Feminist Literacy Practices." *Rethinking Marxism* 26 (1): 44–60.

———. 2016. "Two Frontiers of Development?: A Transnational Feminist Analysis of Public-Private Partnerships for Women's Empowerment." *International Political Sociology* 10 (2): 150–67.

Sen, Gita, and Caren Grown. 1987. *Development, Crises, and Alternative Visions: Third World Women's Perspectives.* New York: Monthly Review Press.

Spivak, Gayatri Charkravorty. 1988. "Can the Subaltern Speak?" In *Marxism and the Interpretation of Culture,* edited by Cary Nelson and Lawrence Grossberg, 271–313. Urbana: University of Illinois Press.

Tornhill, Sofie. 2015. "Gender Equality Incorporated? Coca-Cola and Wal-Mart's Initiatives for Female Empowerment in Mexico." In *Institutionalizing Gender Equality: Historical and Global Perspectives,* edited by Yuliya Gradskova and Sara Sanders, 127–46. London: Lexington Books.

Walmart. 2011. "How the Bharti Walmart Training Center Helped Amandeep Kaur Grow in the Retail Industry." September 13. http://news.walmart.com/media-library/youtube/how-the-bharti-walmart-training-center-helped-amandeep-kaur-grow-in-the-retail-industry-qy8t8pfswwm.

Wilson, Japhy. 2015. "The Joy of Inequality: The Libidinal Economy of Compassionate Consumerism." *International Journal of Žižek Studies* 9 (2). https://zizekstudies.org/index.php/IJZS/article/viewFile/815/820.

Wilson, Kalpana. 2015. "Towards a Radical Re-appropriation: Gender, Development and Neoliberal Feminism." *Development and Change* 46 (4): 803–32.

Wolff, Richard. 2003. "World Bank/Class Blindness." In *World Bank Literature*, edited by Amitava Kumar, 172–83. Minneapolis: University of Minnesota Press.

World Bank. 2006. "Gender Equality as Smart Economics: A World Bank Group Gender Action Plan (Fiscal Years 2007–10)." Washington DC: World Bank.

———. 2008. "World Bank Group to Increase Support to Women." http://web.worldbank .org/WBSITE/EXTERNAL/NEWS/0,,contentMDK:21727367~pagePK:64257043 ~piPK:437376~theSitePK:4607,00.html.

———. 2012. "World Development Report: Gender Equality and Development." Washington DC: World Bank.

Žižek, Slovaj. 1990. "Beyond Discourse Analysis." In *In New Reflections on the Revolution of Our Time*, edited by Ernesto Laclau, 249–60. London: Verso.

———. 2008. *Enjoy Your Symptom!: Jacques Lacan in Hollywood and Out*. London: Routledge.

7   Architectural Enjoyment
Lefebvre and Lacan

Lucas Pohl

Prologue

> Evil is in matter.
>
> <small>LACAN</small>, *The Ethics of Psychoanalysis*

In the early morning hours of February 2, 2014, the subways in Frankfurt, Germany, are more crowded than usual. Loaded with folding chairs, thermos flasks, and picnic baskets, thousands of people are not on their way to the next recreation area but are traveling to a place in the middle of the city. It is cold and foggy, but still, by 10 a.m. around thirty thousand people gather on the square, which is blocked for traffic on this day. The reason: the impending demise of a thirty-two-story tower building. It is why radio stations scramble for expensive hotel rooms with convenient views of the spot of interest and why newspapers have been reporting on this morning for weeks; why postcards, t-shirts, and books are sold and hundreds of champagne glasses are filled while camera tripods are set up; and why thousands of people stand on the square with a strange mix of enthusiasm, silent tears, and angry voices. Built in the 1970s as the highest university building of the country, the AfE-Turm for decades hosted thousands of university members and became a national symbol for student protests, the Frankfurt School, and brutalist architecture. After the university moved to another location in the city, the building was abandoned, and on February 2 it was blown up in the largest controlled building detonation in Europe.

Fig. 6. AfE-Turm shortly before its detonation. Photo by Lucas Pohl, February 2, 2014.

Before questioning how this "monster," as the media referred to this building (cf. Pohl 2015), serves as an example for architectural enjoyment, the next section promotes a critical dialogue between Henri Lefebvre and Jacques Lacan.[1] First, I discuss the basics of their notions of enjoyment by giving special attention to its political implications. Second, I exemplify how enjoyment takes place for Lefebvre and Lacan in terms of social practice. Then, by rereading J. G. Ballard's novel *High-Rise*, the focus switches to architecture, wherein its relation to space is of particular importance. Finally, I conclude by sketching a way to grasp architectural enjoyment in order to picture the utopian fantasies as well as the constitutive lacking structure that haunts a building.

Another Reading of Lefebvre and Lacan

Much has been said about the relationship between Lefebvre and Lacan, with most of these efforts involving a vehement critique of the latter. While Lefebvre is seen as one of the most important representatives of the critical treatment of space (Gregory 1997, 205), Lacan concentrates on ocular- and logocentrism and is therefore viewed as overestimating the visual (Imaginary) and linguistic (Symbolic) dimensions of social reality (Gregory 1997, 215). Lacan's position is questioned as being "apolitical, aspatial, and decorporealizing," while Lefebvre is sometimes presented as the more "ground-breaking" thinker (Blum and Nast 1996, 577). Lacan's subject seems fundamentally two-dimensional, renouncing the dimension of the body (Blum and Nast 2000, 184), whereas Lefebvre promotes his materialist project as an understanding of subjectivity and space that includes physicality and materiality: "Lefebvre does not deny the importance of (Lacan's) Imaginary and Symbolic spaces for the constitution of the self, but he wants to establish their material inscription in social space. He wants to include the underlying material, spatial and political forces that have the possibility to transcend the visual domain" (Simonsen 2005, 5).

Even though this chapter does not deny such notions, it nevertheless argues, mirroring Proudfoot and Kingsbury (2014, 244), that this critique

Lucas Pohl

of Lacan "only tells half of the story"; instead, I offer another reading of Lefebvre and Lacan by shifting the focus of comparison. Whereas most of the work on Lefebvre centers on his masterpiece *La production de l'espace*, this chapter draws on a text that has not yet received the same level of attention: *Vers une architecture de la jouissance*. This forgotten manuscript, written in 1973 and published in 2014, is not just a forceful text about bodies, space, and architecture, which from now on "needs to be read as part and parcel of Lefebvre's formulation of the theory of the production of space" (Stanek 2014, xvi); it should also be read as another puzzle piece in terms of Lefebvre's relation to psychoanalysis. There is hardly any other work in which Lefebvre writes so constructively (and less polemically) about psychoanalysis and its key concepts (e.g., the death drive). Therefore, in what follows I will argue that *Vers une architecture de la jouissance* serves as an important source for extending the existing state of research on enjoyment and architecture. This change of focus unavoidably involves a discussion of the Real, a Lacanian concept that Lefebvre tends to ignore, even if it is often seen as Lacan's "most elusive concept" (Blum and Nast 1996, 561; Gregory 1997, 210; Pile 1996, 137).

Enjoyment Is Somewhere

Jouissance is evil.

LACAN, *The Ethics of Psychoanalysis*

While Lacan spent much effort developing his notion of enjoyment (*jouissance*), he seems to have been just one of the few who employed the term during his lifetime.[2] As Robert Bononno, the translator of *Vers une architecture de la jouissance*, puts it, "jouissance, of course, has escaped the cage of Lacanian psychoanalysis," and "while Lefebvre was familiar with Lacan's work, nothing in *Toward an Architecture of Enjoyment* indicates his employment of the word in the sense(s) used by Lacan" (Bononno 2014, ix). In my attempt to discuss a perspective on architectural enjoyment, I will not just sketch the differences between Lacan and Lefebvre but also question this non-relation of their use of the term "enjoyment."

For both Lefebvre and Lacan, an approach to enjoyment is essentially related to a critical discussion of philosophy. While Lefebvre starts *Vers une architecture de la jouissance* by stating that philosophy "overlooks sensuality and sensoriality, sexuality and pleasure" and in this sense has "no place for enjoyment" (2014, 9), for Lacan it is philosophy that does not know anything about enjoyment (cf. Badiou 2013, 166). But what is enjoyment? Lacan states that "Jouissance is what serves no purpose" (1999, 3), and Lefebvre writes in direct reference to psychoanalysis that "pleasure supports mediation," whereas enjoyment "is merely a flash, a form of energy that is expended, wasted, destroying itself in the process" (2014, 115).[3] In this sense, enjoyment is primarily related to negativity (see chapter 6), but even if it appears for both "beyond the pleasure principle" (Lacan 1998, 184), here we are able to observe a first difference between Lefebvre and Lacan.

Lefebvre justifies a use of the term based on his unease with the word "happiness"; for that reason, one can "replace it with the word 'enjoyment' in the broad sense" (2014, 26), a sense that comprises happiness as well as serenity, voluptuousness, life, joy, and sensuality. To contrast this notion with Lacan, let us further question what it means to claim that enjoyment takes place *beyond pleasure*. For Lacan, the difference between pleasure and enjoyment cannot be compared to the difference between productive and nonproductive ways of life, and it is necessary to overcome such dualistic perspectives. Therefore, he raises the question of the death drive (Lacan 2006, 53; see also chapters 3 and 5 in this volume). Lefebvre on the contrary problematizes the death drive as a "negative life force," a drive to "return to the inorganic" that predominates in every living being, thus critiquing psychoanalysis as it changes "the symptom into an explanatory diagram" (2014, 104–6). Death in this sense seems the only solution to counter political power, but only if one ignores the subversive potential for enjoyment to become the meaning of life. Here, Lefebvre concludes that the way in which psychoanalysis destroys pleasure by casting it "into the clutter of the unconscious" and its hope to provide a "'surplus value' of enjoyment" are pursuits that do not teach us anything about space (2014, 106–7).

Lucas Pohl

From a Lacanian standpoint, such a reading of the death drive is problematic, insofar as the death drive is not an "instinct to return to the state of equilibrium of the inanimate sphere" (Lacan 1992, 212); it is not the will to destroy itself, but it enables a third way between life and death. Therefore, Slavoj Žižek states that the death drive reveals the "ultimate lesson of psychoanalysis": that "humans are not simply alive, they are possessed by the strange drive to enjoy life in excess, passionately attached to a surplus which sticks out and derails the ordinary run of things" (2006, 61; see also chapter 8 in this volume). Why does Lefebvre not mention this third way? One possibility is that Lefebvre followed a simplified reading of Freud and was not familiar with Lacan's reading of the death drive. Another possibility is that it is not simply a case of ignorance, but an ontological difference we can extract from the death drive. By following the latter option, I argue that it is the political project that differentiates Lefebvre from Lacan at this point.

Lefebvre's whole work is rooted in a critique of his present—to search for alternatives during the rise of global capitalism and the "worldwide tendency to uniformity" (1987, 8). By exploring the "possible-impossible," the "u-topia" of the everyday (Lefebvre 2003a, 186), he seeks to overcome philosophical and cosmological considerations, which he calls "abstract utopias," and opposes a "utopia of enjoyment" that is spatialized and "tends toward the concrete" (Lefebvre 2014, 100). In contrast to an abstract utopia, which generates a positive ideal, the "concrete utopia" is based on negativity—"It rejects" (Lefebvre 2014, 148)—and enjoyment serves as a starting point to realize this u-topia by rejecting the capitalist order through a nonproductive principle. Lacan would agree with Lefebvre that enjoyment is crucial for constituting a society, as "it is Jouissance whose absence would render the universe vain" (Lacan 2006, 694), and while enjoyment for Lacan also enables a critical encounter with capitalist society (cf. Lacan 2007), he nevertheless develops his notion of enjoyment in relation to the death drive, which cannot serve in a u-topian sense similar to Lefebvre's. While Lefebvre grasps enjoyment as an ontic rejection of its present, for Lacan enjoyment is ontic as well (2001, 327) but related to the death drive as its ontological background (1992, 127).[4] As enjoyment is linked to something ontologically inaccessible—the Lacanian name therefore is *objet a*—it becomes utopian in itself: an *a*-topia, as it constitutes a place based on an object that we never acquire.[5] In this sense, Lefebvre indeed presents a political way out of the death drive, as the drive is "the enemy of the good society" (McGowan 2013, 283), but to eliminate it, he also removes a central aspect of Lacanian political theory: the Real.

For Lacan, there is a fundamental lack in any subject and symbolic order because "as soon as we have to deal with anything in the world appearing in the form of the signifying chain, there is somewhere . . . which is the beyond of that chain" (1992, 212). *There is somewhere . . .* This seems to be the essential truth for Lacan to grasp something socially. However, it is crucial to understand such "things" not as localized and comparable to the social reality from where we speak. On the contrary: following Lacan's materialism, *somewhere* becomes "a-thing" (Lacan 2007, 159). This "thing"-like object is neither in nor out of social reality but stands as a marker of its limits, a positivized negativity that embodies the incompleteness of any identity. In this sense, *a*-topia is by no means less concrete than u-topia because, even if Lacan views enjoyment as structured around a real void, it is spatialized through the social reality. The Real is comparable to Lefebvre's notion of the possible-impossible as a "non-place . . . that gives meaning to the possible" (2003b, 179). As for Lefebvre, "the impossible arises . . . in the heart of the possible" while conversely there is no possibility that does not include "the project of the impossible" (2003a, 186). Consequently, the Real does not mean that there is another reality besides the one we live in.

Then what is the difference between u-topia and *a*-topia? The answer to this question lies in the possibility of entering the space of the possible-impossible. For Lefebvre, "every time you obtain enjoyment (and not merely satisfaction), every time you find a place genuinely pleasing and enchanting, every time you rediscover, with its native generosity, not exempt from cruelty, some part of the natural world, you enter this utopia" (2014, 132). As the lacking structure of reality is constitutive for Lacan, such a realization of the possible-impossible remains a fantasy. He therefore radicalizes

Lucas Pohl

Lefebvre's statement that "there is no place without an other place and the other place, without the elsewhere and the nowhere" (Lefebvre 2003a, 186) by inserting the real *objet a*, which disables any u-topia as it marks the impossibility to become a new symbolic order of society. That is the "evil" lesson through which psychoanalysis enters the field of politics: there is no place in society to create a u-topia of enjoyment based on a "possible object from information related to reality" (Lefebvre 2000, 151) because politics is grounded in the enjoyment of an impossible object related to the Real. But is there any possibility for change, then? Following Žižek (2006, 382), the revolutionary moment comprehends not a rejection of "something" but "the move from something to nothing, from the gap between two 'somethings' to the gap that separates a something from nothing, from the void of its own place," and as we will see in a later part of this chapter, it is this void that opens the space for an architectural enjoyment.

High-Rise—A Place to Enjoy

You think that we're secretly enjoying all this?

BALLARD, *High-Rise*

To formulate a geographic account of enjoyment, let us first question how enjoyment takes place for Lefebvre and Lacan through social practice.[6] To this end, I will provide an example by rereading *High-Rise*, a novel written by J. G. Ballard. The book was first published in 1975 and tells the futuristic story of a forty-story tower building in the suburbs of London by following different characters throughout their everyday lives.

If we focus on particular passages in the novel, we could come away with an impression of the high-rise as a prototype of a place built for enjoyment. It is more than just a residential building: it is a "vertical city" (Ballard 2014, 65) with its own socioeconomic order, as well as a supermarket, liquor stores, schools, swimming pools, a sauna, hairdressing salons, a bank, and restaurants. Consequently, people usually do not leave the high-rise, apart from going to work, an exception that is not considered by the protagonists. Except for a few pages, the story does not take place outside the building, and the longer residents live in the high-rise, the less they enter into the world outside the building. Going to work appears to be strange. One of the occupants, Robert Laing, visits his workplace for the first time in days and is "struck immediately by the cooler light and air, like the harsh atmosphere of an alien planet" (Ballard 2014, 142). Furthermore, parties and sex make up two crucial cornerstones of life for the inhabitants. As Anthony Royal, the architect of the high-rise explains, "Beginning with the lower floors, the parties spread upwards through the apartment block, investing it in an armour of light and festivity. Standing on his balcony, Royal listened to the ascending music and laughter. . . . Far below him, a car drove along the access road to the nearby high-rise, its three occupants looking up at the hundreds of crowded balconies. Anyone seeing this ship of lights would take for granted that the two thousand people on board lived together in a state of corporate euphoria" (Ballard 2014, 127). Throughout this cross-reading of *High-Rise*, the building certainly appears as a place of enjoyment in the Lefebvrian sense. It is portrayed as a place of leisure, serenity, voluptuousness, and sensuality—a place of nonwork, of wasting time without any sense of productivity. In this sense, the high-rise is a concrete utopia, as it embodies a spatial reality of rejection, a space from which the capitalist world outside appears "dreamlike in its unreality" (Ballard 2014, 79).

For anyone who is familiar with the novel, the misimpression of this reading is evident. Most of the narrative of *High-Rise* captures the destruction of this vertical city, so that the previous reading tells only part of the story. As the plot unravels, the ordinary life of the inhabitants changes rapidly. Death, rape, vandalism, violation, and conflict darken the setting, and the high-rise becomes a "Pandora's box" (Ballard 2014, 43) with the "ultimate goal" of creating a realm where the "most deviant impulses were free at last to exercise themselves in anyway they wished" (212). By considering Lefebvre, we could claim that this transformation of *High-Rise* is crucially determined by an "absence of enjoyment" because "to survive" people need a "bath of enjoyment from time to time," otherwise they "lose sight of needs themselves" and become "marked by the sign of death" (Lefebvre 2014, 132).

Lucas Pohl

But if we understand the first part of the book as a story about a place to enjoy, this consequently means that there would have been a change in terms of productivity to justify its breakdown. Otherwise, there is no recognizable reason that could explain why enjoyment becomes absent and everything spins out of control. At this point, we refer to Lacan by claiming that this other side beyond normality in *High-Rise* is not marked by an absence, but rather by an increasing or excess of enjoyment. If we reframe enjoyment through a drive that derails the ordinary run of things, the building becomes a place of enjoyment, not before, but after the uncontrollable. Do the inhabitants really suffer because they do not enjoy?

Richard Wilder, another resident, decides right at the beginning of the transformation to climb up the building. His motives are not revealed clearly, but he mentions that he developed a "powerful phobia about the high-rise": "He was constantly aware of the immense weight of concrete stacked above him, . . . conscious of each of the 999 other apartments pressing on him through the walls and ceiling, forcing the air from his chest" (Ballard 2014, 62–63). Here, it seems that some of the inhabitants recognize that the breakdown of the high-rise does not necessarily lead to an end but enables the start of a new life. Therefore, even if *High-Rise* is a story about fading vital functions, missing electricity, deserted staircases, shattered elevators, dead pets, abandoned supermarkets, and ruined swimming pools, it is not just a story about death. Probably, the most crucial lesson to take away from a Lacanian reading of the novel is this: *High-Rise* is not just a story about decline, ruination, and the "material failure" of the "deepening trend" toward verticality (Hewitt and Graham 2015, 929); instead, it envisions a third outcome, as it is also a story about the inherent possibility of change. Does *High-Rise* question how the social life of the inhabitants starts out as seemingly perfect and "degenerates into a violent dystopia" (Hewitt and Graham 2015, 931)? Or does it commence with a dystopian vision of social life in which nothing counts other than daily parties and thus to the contrary tells a story about the possibility of something impossible? The architect Anthony Royal speaks of a "new order" that has emerged as an internal rebellion fights against its present. The building in this sense does not just fall apart but transforms into something that was an inherent part of it from the beginning. It becomes an *a*-topia, as it realizes neither a good nor a new place but instead portrays the struggle with its own negation. On one of the last pages, Robert Laing "looked up at the face of the high-rise. All the floors were in darkness, and he felt happy at this" (Ballard 2014, 247).

This reading of *High-Rise* aims to illustrate how enjoyment is embodied through social practice following the notions of Lefebvre and Lacan. From both perspectives, the high-rise appears to be a place to enjoy. The Lefebvrian notion of enjoyment seems at best applicable in the beginning of the novel and in this sense becomes a product of the architect. While for Lacan enjoyment is also a product of architecture, it manifests itself in a different way as I will exemplify throughout the following pages. To demonstrate this difference, let us first apply the possible-impossible to the general relation between architecture and space in order to question the Real as it is rooted in the building itself.

The Dialectic of Architectural Space

Regarding the relation of space and architecture, Lefebvre is often interpreted as saying that architecture is not adequate to serve as a foundation of space. In *La production de l'espace*, for instance, he claims that "any definition of architecture itself requires a prior analysis and exposition of the concept of space" (Lefebvre 1991, 15). In this context, Nathaniel Coleman states that for Lefebvre architecture "is not so much space as space contains architecture" (2015, 62). When considering *Vers une architecture de la jouissance*, we are able to extend this definition because here Lefebvre grasps architecture as a "production of space" itself (2014, 3). Hence, architecture is no longer just a product of the "world of commodities" (Lefebvre 2003b, 90), but also a project that is "endowed with relative autonomy" (Lefebvre 2014, 27), where space "cannot consist of a building" (152). From that perspective, architecture is able to question the space it produces (Lefebvre 2014, 133), even if Lefebvre critically asserts that architecture operates with a "blank drawing paper," wherein the architect "confuses projection and project in a confused reality which he believes to be 'real'" (Lefebvre 2000, 190–91).

This "double perspective" (Stanek 2011, 250) or dialectical approach toward architecture as being both a product of its social conditions and its own production of space is crucial not just for *Vers une architecture de la jouissance*, but also for the way Lacan applies architecture.[7] His contribution to architecture can be surmised in one statement: "architecture can be defined as something organized around emptiness" (Lacan 1992, 135). What is this void that structures architecture? Is it the same blank space Lefebvre criticizes architecture for—an emptiness that is not able to grasp reality? To capture Lacan's observation according to the relation of architecture and the void, let us consider a passage out of the lecture *Je parle aux murs*:

> Architects exist for . . . building walls. And walls . . . are made to envelop a void. How are we to imagine what used to go on within the walls of the Parthenon, and a few other knick-knacks of which some of the crumbled walls still remain? . . . What used to go on in those festivals? It's quite unbelievable that we don't have the faintest idea. On the other hand, when it comes to the void, we have a very firm idea about this because everything that remains of what has come down to us from a tradition that is termed *philosophical* accords a major place to the void. There is even a certain Plato who made his entire idea of the world revolve around that . . . because he's the one who invented the cave. He transformed it into a darkroom. There was something going on outside, and, passing through a small aperture, shadows were formed by all that. . . . This is clearly a theory that lets us put a finger on what is involved with the object *a*. Suppose if you will that Plato's cave is equivalent to these walls within which my voice is making itself heard. It's quite clear that I derive jouissance from these walls. And it is in this respect that you all obtain jouissance. (Lacan 2017, 81–83)

In Lacanian terms, the void through which architecture is organized is not some illusionary space that fails to capture the "real"; on the contrary, it is Real, as it is both a condition for architecture as well as a space that is produced by architecture itself. The void *is* the space of architecture, just as for Lacan space "is part of the real" (2014, 283); it is the immaterial counterpart of architecture's materiality, its impossibility.[8] The connection between architecture and space is best described by appropriating the Lacanian formula of fantasy, where the subject is related to the *objet a* via the *poinçon* ($<>a$). Architecture assumes the role of the subject, whereby space becomes its lost cause *a*, with both paradoxically connected through an act of "envelopment-development-conjunction-disjunction" (Lacan 2006, 542). Therefore, Lacan supports Lefebvre by arguing that space does not consist of a building because, as soon as architecture is organized, space is produced as a leftover *a* that is related but impossible to complete by the architectural gaze.

Even if Lefebvre does not grasp the Real in the sense Lacan does, here both thinkers share a basic premise: they help to introduce the possible-impossible into a dialectic of architectural space. For Lefebvre—especially following *Vers une architecture de la jouissance*—architecture is simultaneously a product of society and a relatively autonomous production of space. For Lacan, architecture is organized around a void space that is both a product of architecture as well as its retroactive condition. At this point the assumption *there is somewhere* works for both Lefebvre and Lacan, with one difference: while Lefebvre condemns architecture for failing to capture the society as "real," Lacan recognizes this inconsistency as an ontological or hauntological condition of architecture. For him, architecture cannot include its (social) space in the same way that Plato's cave cannot include its outside. Even if the outside irrupts what is inside, society as the *extimate* space of architecture remains a-thing that appears as empty because the inside co-founded but "does not explain the outside" (Lacan 2007, 54).[9]

To exemplify this dialectic of architectural space, let us refer back to *High-Rise* because the novel contains an impressive sensibility for any over-simplified opposition between the building and its social space. Following the plot, it seems impossible to differentiate whether the building represents the social structure of its context or if the context and the inhabitants

Lucas Pohl

represent the building itself. In any case, the focal point of the book is not the building as such, but the people who are related to it. The overarching lesson here is that it is not architecture but society that decides whether the high-rise exists or disappears (see chapter 9). This notion is reflected in the role of the architect Anthony Royal, who planned the high-rise based on a "rigid hierarchy" that for him was "the key to the elusive success of these huge buildings" (Ballard 2014, 96). Thus, the building represents a specific social structure:

The 10th-floor shopping mall formed a clear boundary between the lower nine floors, with their "proletariat" of film technicians, air-hostesses and the like, and the middle section of the high-rise, which extended from the 10th floor to the swimming-pool and restaurant deck on the 35th. This central two-thirds of the apartment building formed its middle class, made up of self-centred but basically docile members of the pro-fessions. . . . Above them, on the top five floors of the high-rise, was its upper class, the discreet oligarchy of minor tycoons and entrepreneurs, television actresses and careerist academics, with their high-speed ele-vators and superior services, their carpeted staircases. It was they who set the pace of the building. (Ballard 2014, 69–70)

As the high-rise is divided into a lower, middle, and upper class, it appears as an architectural reincarnation of a stereotypical liberal society, and through this social structure, it becomes a symbol for the unnaturalness of built environments and the entanglement of architecture and society.

As fundamental as this message seems, it is crucial to highlight that such a reading of *High-Rise* reveals just half of the story. While the building on the one hand appears to be the central focus around which the plot develops, it simultaneously appears as a distinct reality separate from the outside, with an "internal time" and "psychological climate" (Ballard 2014, 9). Such an interpretation, in which the building becomes more than just the setting of the scene, is represented in the characters' thoughts themselves. In one conversation between Richard Wilder and his wife, for instance, she is staring through the window while contemplating, "In fact, it's not really the other residents. It's the building." (Ballard 2014, 59). In another scene, Wilder himself feels "rejected . . . by the high-rise" and recognizes that "he felt suddenly exhausted, as much by the building's weight and mass as by his own failure" (Ballard 2014, 92). The imposing dialectic *High-Rise* is working with becomes apparent here, since the building is both a materialized reincarnation of its social present *and* a built space that incarnates a relative autonomy with "a life of its own" (Lefebvre 2014, 27). While this duality tells us something about the social context of the structure, it does not capture or represent the society at all. Even though the high-rise remains a product of its architect and part of its social context, it nevertheless maintains a relatively distinct existence that lies beyond the control of the architect and inhabitants.[10]

Toward an Architectural Enjoyment

Finally, I seek to connect the first part of this chapter on enjoyment to the preceding sketch on architecture and space in order to follow the argument that enjoyment is the real substance of architecture. As previously stated, I argue that Lacan and Lefebvre reveal the potential of a dialectical reading of architectural space. Architecture is both a relatively autonomous production of space and a contextualized product of its present; it produces a space that enables architecture, while the space itself becomes the void of it. Therefore, architecture is lacking in the sense that it never completely pictures its *objet a*: the space in which it is localized.

At this point the coincidence that structures this chapter becomes apparent: "enjoyment" and "architecture" are not just two random terms that appear in the works of Lefebvre and Lacan. They share a crucial characteristic: they both produce and are produced by the possible-impossible. To grasp this curious relation, I claim that there is something in architecture that fosters enjoyment, just as there is something in enjoyment that promotes architecture. For this reason, Lefebvre asserts that any concrete utopia "begins with enjoyment and . . . can only be based on an architectural project" (2014, 148). Likewise, Lacan declares that "walls" can cause enjoyment (2017, 83). To prove this claim, wider comprehensive research is necessary, but at this point we can already demonstrate that both Lefebvre and Lacan provide helpful directions toward an approach on architectural enjoyment.

As a conclusion to this chapter, I would like to demonstrate how psychoanalysis can pave the way for future discussions within this discourse. Let us briefly consider the relation of Marxism to psychoanalysis, as Marx is one of the most important references shared by both Lefebvre and Lacan. In an interview, Lefebvre discusses the meaning of being a Marxist by stating that it is "a way of being" that involves the struggle and "mutual ambivalence of life and death" (2003a, 257). He argues that this means to "hold out a hand to psychoanalysts," but only by excluding the death drive, because "life wins" (Lefebvre 2003a, 257). While Lefebvre precisely recounts one of the most basic principles of Marxist thought, he nevertheless fails to acknowledge a crucial premise of psychoanalysis. Since the psychoanalytic subject is structured around a lack, psychoanalysis does not privilege death but transverses this opposition through a third way. While the Marxian utopia follows a flow of "pure productivity," the political project of psychoanalysis is rather to highlight the ruptures in the glObal and to recognize the "death in life," which contains "at once more suffering and more enjoyment" (McGowan 2013, 242). Consequently, it is reasonable to argue that Lefebvre grasps u-topias as places we can enter through architecture to overcome the present society, while for Lacan, there is no such thing as a place to enjoy, except for the void that structures reality. Since Lacan grasps enjoyment through the death drive, the utopia of enjoyment becomes inherently related to the founding lack of the signified subject and becomes, in this sense, *a*-topian, as it is not realized *somewhere* other than in the unfulfilled reality. Therefore, enjoyment takes place in architecture when architecture is confronted by space, as space is architecture's loss and negation. From a Lacanian point of view, we can then finally sketch a basic principle toward an architectural enjoyment; namely, as soon as there is architecture, there is space, and as soon as this space is *somewhere*, architectural enjoyment is possible.

Epilogue

Let us end with an example of how architectural enjoyment takes place in the city, thereby turning back to the prologue where this journey began. The case of the high-rise that was blown up on February 2, 2014, in Frankfurt is more than just the story of a building's detonation. While thousands of people were shocked, sad, happy, angry, and excited to see the old university building disappear, a flurry of commerce appeared as well: traders sold postcards with nostalgic motifs of the high-rise, a hotel sold DVDs with slow-motion recordings of the detonation, and a Twitter account materialized in the building's name, tweeting only minutes after the explosion: "In your hearts I live forever."

Is this not a great example of how a building is as much the product of its social practice as of its own existence, which lies beyond its control? And is this not the case of yet another building that does not simply fall apart but transforms into something inherently different? With regards to Giorgio Agamben, who states that "the fundamental architectural problem becomes visible only in the house ravaged by fire" (1999, 6), we could claim that it is this transformative moment when buildings become monstrous, whereby the dialectic of architectural space becomes apparent. In this sense, the novel *High-Rise* and the AfE-Turm in Frankfurt are prime examples to illustrate the irrational and devastating potential of architecture (see chapter 9). In times when cities worldwide grow constantly in terms of size, density, and verticality, on the one hand, and glObal crises of over-accumulation disturb the ordinary run of things, on the other, this monstrous capability of cities becomes increasingly apparent (see chapter 10). Therefore, it is necessary to question the *a*-topias, which arise from today's deathly driven realities to traverse all the "imaginary politics" (Pohl 2017) of coherency and stability that "local identities" are founded on.

To acknowledge that architectural space is powerful—a condition that local politicians, urban planners, and architects have to deal with—helps to transfer Žižek's claim that a "properly aesthetic attitude" today has to accept "the inertia of rotten material which serves no purpose" into the

Lucas Pohl

Fig. 7. AfE-Turm during its detonation. Photo by Lucas Pohl, February 2, 2014.

urban (2010, 35). Enjoyment in this sense becomes a key notion for politicians, planners, architects, and geographers across the glObe to recognize the Real of cities,[11] and as we have observed that there is no architecture without enjoyment, our view of architecture changes. Architectural space, as the manifestation of the Real, moves into our center of attention and therefore clears a path for further research on urban vacancy, decay, and destruction. To localize the void, we have to grasp architecture's ruination in the same way as its creation to finally introduce the death drive as a third way between life and death to architecture.

Notes

1. As part of a book project on the AfE-Turm, I worked on the medial discourse of the building months before the detonation to relate entrepreneurial local image politics with negotiations of dysfunctionally built environments as "urban monstrosities."
2. I will use both the terms "*jouissance*" and "enjoyment" interchangeably.
3. At this point, a discussion about the relationship between enjoyment and desire is appropriate. For Lacan, desire is, comparable to Lefebvre's claim, "involved in the larger scheme of things," whereby enjoyment is "always veiled and unfathomable" (Lacan 2013, 76–77). However, to stay within the scope of this chapter, I am unable to go into further detail on this issue, except to say that both terms are crucially connected, especially for Lacan. Desire concerns enjoyment, as "it is normative for desire . . . not to manage" it (Lacan 2014, 182). To relate desire and enjoyment as such enables the claim that there is no enjoyment without desire and vice versa because desire is constituted *not* to manage enjoyment as enjoyment is constituted *not* to be captured through desire. This is how I understand enjoyment, as a constitutive part of the lacking subject—an "'inherent' jouissance" that for at least the late Lacan "is, in a radical sense, the only possible jouissance" (Chiesa 2007, 183).
4. Thanks to Moritz Herrmann for giving me an impetus to think this through.
5. As Lefebvre's notion of u-topia is based on a separation of the Greek *topos* (place) and *u*, which derives from *eu* (good) and *ou* (no), where it suggests to define a "good non place" (Coleman 2015, 48), *a*-topia replaces the "good" by inserting a constitutive void represented by *a*.
6. Even if no one pictures enjoyment as a question raised by Lefebvre and Lacan, this is by far the first geographic contribution to Lacanian enjoyment. Paul Kingsbury (2005) pictures the "politics of enjoyment" regarding Jamaican tourism, Jesse Proud-

Lucas Pohl

foot (2010) gives an example of enjoyment as "extradiscursive" by reflecting on interviews during an international soccer competition in Vancouver, and Proudfoot and Kingsbury (2014) have published a work on "phallic jouissance" by focusing on masculine sexuation in submarine films, to mention just a few essential works.

7. During recent years authors have started to question the possibilities for a Lacanian perspective on architecture (cf. Binotto 2013; Hays 2010), and in this sense, one can recognize a slight change regarding the absence of Lacan in the discourse of architecture that Lorens Holm (2000, 29) has problematized.

8. Here a broader discussion on the difference between Seminar 7 and Seminar 10 could follow because a co-reading of Lacan's arguments on architecture, along with his statements on space, requires a debate about the difference between *the Thing* as the primordial void in Seminar 7 and Lacan's later notion of the dialectical *objet a*, the Real of the Symbolic. My reading here pursues a retroactive replacement of the *objet a* as the void through which architecture is organized.

9. "Extimacy" is a neologism Lacan developed "to designate in a problematic manner the real in the symbolic" (Miller 1994, 75) or, to put it in another way, to grasp something from the *inside* that lies *somewhere else*.

10. Therefore, it is reasonable that Ned Beauman in his introduction to *High-Rise* mentions two contradictory readings of the book: "the book is all about architecture" and "the book is not about architecture at all" (Ballard 2014, viii).

11. As mentioned, it is enjoyment that "serves no purpose" (Lacan 1999, 3).

Works Cited

Agamben, Giorgio. 1999. *The Man without Content*. Stanford CA: Stanford University.

Badiou, Alain. 2013. *Lacan: L'antiphilosophie 3*. Paris: Fayard.

Ballard, James Graham. 2014. *High-Rise*. London: Fourth Estate.

Binotto, Johannes. 2013. *TAT/ORT. Das Unheimliche und sein Raum in der Kultur*. Zürich: Diaphanes.

Blum, Virginia, and Heidi Nast. 1996. "Where's the Difference? The Heterosexualization of Alterity in Henri Lefebvre and Jacques Lacan." *Environment and Planning D* 14, 559–80.

———. 2000. "Jacques Lacan's Two-Dimensional Subjectivity." In *Thinking Space*, edited by Mike Crang and Nigel Thrift, 183–204. London: Routledge.

Bononno, Robert. 2014. Translator's note in *Toward an Architecture of Enjoyment*, by Henri Lefebvre. Minneapolis: University of Minnesota.

Chiesa, Lorenzo. 2007. *Subjectivity and Otherness: A Philosophical Reading of Lacan*. Cambridge MA: MIT Press.

Coleman, Nathaniel. 2015. *Lefebvre for Architects*. London: Routledge.

Gregory, Derek. 1997. "Lacan and Geography: The Production of Space Revisited." In *Space and Social Theory: Interpreting Modernity and Postmodernity*, edited by George Benko and Ulf Strohmayer, 203–31. New York: Blackwell.

Hays, K. Michael. 2010. *Architecture's Desire: Reading the Late Avant-Garde*. Cambridge MA: MIT Press.

Hewitt, Lucy, and Stephen Graham. 2015. "Vertical Cities: Representations of Urban Verticality in 20th-Century Science Fiction Literature." *Urban Studies* 52 (5): 923–37.

Holm, Lorens. 2000. "What Lacan Said Re: Architecture." *Critical Quarterly* 42 (2): 29–64.

Kingsbury, Paul. 2005. "Jamaican Tourism and the Politics of Enjoyment." *Geoforum* 36, 113–32.

Lacan, Jacques. 1992. *The Ethics of Psychoanalysis*. New York: Norton.

——. 1998. *The Four Fundamental Concepts of Psychoanalysis*. New York: Norton.

——. 1999. *On Feminine Sexuality: The Limits of Love and Knowledge*. New York: Norton.

——. 2001. *Autre Ecrits*. Paris: Editions du Seuil.

——. 2006. *Ecrits*. New York: Norton.

——. 2007. *The Other Side of Psychoanalysis*. New York: Norton.

——. 2013. *On the Names-of-the-Father*. Cambridge: Polity.

——. 2014. *Anxiety*. Cambridge: Polity.

——. 2017. *Talking to Brick Walls: A Series of Presentations in the Chapel at Sainte-Anne Hospital*. Cambridge: Polity.

Lefebvre, Henri. 1987. "The Everyday and Everydayness." *Yale French Studies* 73, 7–11.

——. 1991. *The Production of Space*. Oxford: Blackwell.

——. 2000. *Writings on Cities*. Malden: Blackwell.

——. 2003a. *Key Writings*. New York: Continuum.

——. 2003b. *The Urban Revolution*. Minneapolis: University of Minnesota.

——. 2014. *Toward an Architecture of Enjoyment*. Minneapolis: University of Minnesota.

McGowan, Todd. 2013. *Enjoying What We Don't Have: The Political Project of Psychoanalysis*. Lincoln: University of Nebraska Press.

Miller, Jacques-Alain. 1994. "Extimite." In *Lacanian Theory of Discourse: Subject, Structure, and Society*, edited by Mark Bracher, Marshall Alcorn Jr., Ronald Corthell, and Françoise Massardier-Kenney, 74–87. New York: New York University Press.

Pile, Steve. 1996. *The Body and the City: Psychoanalysis, Space and Subjectivity*. London: Routledge.

Pohl, Lucas. 2015. "Wie ein toter Wal - Zur Sprengung des AfE-Turms und der Unmöglichkeit urbaner Monstrosität." In *Turmgeschichten: Raumerfahrung und-aneignung im*

AfE-Turm, edited by Minna-Kristiina Ruokonen-Engler, Lucas Pohl, Anna Dichtl, Jessica Lütgens, and David Schommer, 144–59, Münster: Westfälisches Dampfboot.

———. 2017. "Imaginary Politics of the Branded City: Right-Wing Terrorism as a Mediated Object of Stigmatization." In *Negative Neighbourhood Reputation and Place Attachment: The Production and Contestation of Territorial Stigma*, edited by Paul Kirkness and Andreas Tijé-Dra, 27–41. London: Routledge.

Proudfoot, Jesse. 2010. "Interviewing Enjoyment, or the Limits of Discourse." *Professional Geographer* 62 (4): 1–12.

Proudfoot, Jesse, and Paul Kingsbury. 2014. "Periscope Down! Charting Masculine Sexuation in Submarine Films." In *Psychoanalytic Geographies*, edited by Paul Kingsbury and Steve Pile, 241–56. Farnham, UK: Ashgate.

Simonsen, Kirsten. 2005. "Bodies, Sensations, Space and Time: The Contribution from Henri Lefebvre." *Geografiska Annaler* 87B (1): 1–14.

Stanek, Łukasz. 2011. *Henri Lefebvre on Space: Architecture, Urban Research, and the Production of Theory*. Minneapolis: University of Minnesota.

———. 2014. Introduction to *Toward an Architecture of Enjoyment*, by Henri Lefebvre. Minneapolis: University of Minnesota.

Žižek, Slavoj. 2006. *The Parallax View*. Cambridge MA: MIT Press.

———. 2010. *Living in the End Times*. London: Verso.

8 Anamorphosis of Capital

Black Holes, Gothic Monsters, and the Will of God

Japhy Wilson

In *Representing Capital*, Fredric Jameson notes the impossibility of directly representing the totality of global capitalism, "in which the informing power is everywhere and nowhere all at once, and at the same time in relentless expansion, by way of appropriation and subsumption alike" (2011, 7). Despite the unrepresentability of capital, however, Jameson insists that its representation must nonetheless be attempted if we are to have any hope of grasping and addressing the seemingly inexorable dynamics of creative destruction that are producing and transforming our collective reality. To do so, he argues, we can draw on the methodology of psychoanalysis. Jameson notes that in *The Interpretation of Dreams*, Sigmund Freud "presupposes that any full or satisfactory representation of the drive is impossible," but points out that Freud nonetheless asserts "the possibility in the drive of some minimal expression" (2011, 7). Lacanian psychoanalysis similarly identifies the Real as a traumatic presence-absence that is excluded from the symbolic reality that it structures (Žižek 1989, 132–33), while simultaneously claiming that analysis has the capacity to bring elements of the Real into the Symbolic (Fink 1995, 25–26). Drawing on the work of Jacques Lacan, Slavoj Žižek has identified Capital as Real, arguing that the symbolic universe of capital embodies "the Lacanian difference between reality and the Real: 'reality' is the social reality of the actual people involved in the production process, while the Real is the inexorable 'abstract' spectral logic of Capital which determines what goes on in social reality" (1999, 331).

How, then, can the conceptual tools of psychoanalysis be deployed in the symbolization of the Real of Capital? In his lectures on *The Four Fundamental Concepts of Psychoanalysis*, Lacan discusses the methodology of anamorphosis as a means of interpreting the symptoms of the Real that return in distorted form within symbolically structured reality (Dolar 2015). Lacan appeals to Hans Holbein's sixteenth-century painting *The Ambassadors*, in which a formal scene of two ambassadors posing before a display of cultural artefacts is disturbed by a seemingly amorphous stain in the foreground of the picture. When viewed from an oblique angle, this "stain" is revealed as a human skull. Žižek argues that an analogously anamorphic shift in perspective is required to decipher the social symptom, understood as "an inert stain resisting communication and interpretation, a stain which cannot be included in the . . . social bond network, but is at the same time a positive condition of it" (1989, 75). This suggests that the Real of Capital may be more effectively communicated through the analysis of its distorted symptomatic appearances than through its direct representation. As Žižek argues, under such circumstances it is "precisely by 'looking awry' [that we can see] the thing in its clear and distinct form, in opposition to the 'straightforward' view that sees only an indistinct confusion" (1992, 11).

This chapter seeks to symbolize the Real of Capital, not through its direct representation, but by looking at capital awry, in the analysis of its social symptoms. I do so through the exploration of three specific objects: black holes, gothic monsters, and the divine providence through which the will of God is expressed in a fallen world. Each of these objects exerts an uncanny power of fascination within contemporary Western culture—a power that seems to have increased in recent years in the context of the permanent crisis of neoliberal capitalism. This power, I argue, can be explained in part by the metaphorical relation that these objects hold to the Real of Capital. This Real is repressed within the symbolic universe of capitalist society, and yet it "shines through" uncanny objects such as these, elevating each of them to the status of a "sublime object," which Žižek has defined as "the paradox of an object which, in the field of representation, provides a view, in a negative way, of the dimension of what is unrepresentable" (1989, 203). The chapter thus approaches the anamorphosis of capital on the basis of the premise that "we gain admittance to the domain of Truth only by stepping back, by resisting the temptation to penetrate it directly" (Žižek 2008, 145).

Black Hole Capitalism

The black hole has been described as "a signifier that pervades contemporary experience, conveying the 'gaps' and 'voids' in Western culture and psyche" (Hinton 2007, 433). Following the global financial breakdown of 2008, the black hole metaphor has been repeatedly deployed to capture the destructive fury of capital in crisis. The mainstream press has warned of "a huge black hole at the heart of capitalism" (Kane 2012); leftist websites have decried "the great black hole of casino capitalism" (Ford 2009) and "the black hole of the capitalist consciousness" (Santos 2010); and Yanis Varoufakis has described the crisis in Greece with the warning that "everything is going into a black hole" (quoted in Y. Smith 2012). The black hole has also been appealed to in recent attempts to capture the implosive-explosive dialectic of planetary urbanization and the more generalized ecological crisis of capitalism, with critical scholars describing how "space-time seems to collapse towards the event horizon of black hole cities" (Featherstone 2010, 128) and defining urban agglomerations as "entropic black holes sweeping up the productivity of a vastly larger and increasingly global resource hinterland" (Rees 2012, 261).

These invocations of the black hole do not develop the metaphor beyond the deployment of its immediate visceral power. Yet the proliferation of this metaphor in popular, political, and academic discourses, and the unconscious impact that it exerts upon us, together suggest the presence of something that our established understandings of capitalism are failing to capture. The black hole appears in these discourses as precisely the kind of anamorphic distortion that defines the psychoanalytic symptom: an incongruous object in the midst of symbolically constituted reality, through which the Real shines with a compellingly cryptic opacity. To bring this distortion into focus, we must twist our perspective in such a

Japhy Wilson

way that we are able to "see" the structural relationship between the black hole, the Real, and value, in relation to our cosmological, symbolic, and social universes. This is not as outlandish a proposition as it may at first appear. Like value theory and psychoanalysis, modern physics, "when carried out in a truly scientific spirit, is ordained and commanded by the Real, by that which does not work, by that which does not fit" (Fink 1995, 135; see also Tomšič 2015, 71–72). Let us begin, then, with the cosmological Real of the black hole.

Black holes are the eternal endgame of huge exhausted stars, whose explosive powers have lost their battle against their own gravitational forces. Smaller stars become red giants before shrinking into white dwarfs or neutron stars, in which the last structures of matter are able to retain their integrity. But the enormous mass of black holes causes them to enter a state of infinite collapse. According to Einstein's theory of relativity, gravity is generated by the distortion of space-time caused by the mass of the objects within it. The space-time around a black hole becomes so contorted that light cannot escape, and black holes are therefore invisible. The gravitational power of the black hole draws in vast amounts of matter from the galaxies that surround it. Having crossed the event horizon that marks the frontier of visibility, this matter continues to collapse toward the singularity, an impossible point of infinite density buried deep within the void of the black hole. Yet as matter approaches this point of no return, it sheds vast quantities of energy that pour back into space. Through this combination of gravity and energy, black holes structure the entire universe, and at the heart of almost every galaxy is a supermassive black hole (Bartusiak 2015; Scharf 2012).

Black holes are therefore "real holes in space-time" (Bartusiak 2015, 15), which are unobservable and unrepresentable and whose existence is only betrayed by their effects on the galaxies that surround them (Scharf 2012, 95–121). As such, they are the cosmological equivalent of the Lacanian Real. As already discussed, our symbolic universe is structured by a combination of symbolic and imaginary elements that defend us against a traumatic and unsymbolized Real. Just as black holes are invisible voids that structure the material universe, so the Real is "a hole, a gap, an opening in the middle of the symbolic order—it is the lack around which the symbolic order is structured" (Žižek 1989, 170). Like black holes, the Real is unobservable, and its existence "can be constructed only backwards, from its structural effects. All its effectivity lies in the distortion it produces in the symbolic universe of the subject" (Žižek 1989, 169; see also the introduction and chapters 3, 6, and 7 in this volume). Indeed, black hole imagery is frequently appealed to in the discourse of the analysand in psychoanalytic sessions, in which it tends to be deployed precisely at the point at which the Real is confronted as "an overwhelming opening in experience that exceeds one's capacity to signify" (Hinton 2007, 442). Žižek accordingly appeals to the black hole metaphor on repeated occasions, in defining the Real as "the central 'black hole' around which the signifying network is interlaced" (1992, 40), the "destructive vortex . . . which we cannot approach too closely" (2008, civ), and "the unfathomable X which . . . curves and distorts any space of symbolic representation and condemns it to ultimate failure" (1997, 124).

This understanding of the Real also resonates with Marx's theory of value. According to Marx (1976), the value of a commodity is entirely abstracted from its material use value, existing as a pure measure of the socially necessary labor time expended in its production, which is determined by innumerable acts of exchange conducted by private producers throughout the world market. Just as gravity structures the material coordinates of the universe, despite having no concrete materiality of its own, so the law of value determines the space-time of glObal capitalism, despite the fact that value is a social relation and not a quality inherent in discrete material "things." As Marx himself once argued, value, like gravity, is therefore "immaterial but objective" (quoted in Harvey 2013, 70). Building on this understanding of value, Chris Arthur has argued, "Capitalism is marked by the subjection of the material process of production and circulation to the ghostly objectivity of value" (2004, 154). Like the Lacanian Real, value is therefore an unobservable presence-absence that structures our entire social universe—"a void at the heart of capitalism" (Arthur 2004, 154), the existence of which can only be identified through observation of its material effects. This description again recalls the image of the black hole, which has been defined as "mass without matter . . . the mass disappears from our view; only its gravitational attraction remains behind to affect us" (Bartusiak 2015, 107). Furthermore, like a black hole, value not only structures the universe of glObal capitalism but also drags an ever-increasing mass of use values into its sphere of expanded reproduction, as "a shape opposed to all materiality, a form without content, which yet takes possession of the world the only way it can, through draining it of reality" (Arthur 2004, 167). This is the Real that shines through the sublime object of "black hole capitalism," contributing to the fascination that the black hole exerts in popular culture, and helping to explain the intuitive appeal of the black hole metaphor in the depiction of capitalist crises.

Neoliberal Gothic

The global financial crisis that provoked the metaphor of black hole capitalism was thought to have heralded the demise of neoliberal hegemony. Yet in the aftermath of this unprecedented annihilation of its material and ideological foundations, neoliberalism has risen from the grave and now staggers forward once again, as the only symbolic framework through which Western capitalism appears capable of articulating its increasingly spasmodic and dysfunctional reproduction. In the absence of a rational explanation for this uncanny persistence, critics have resorted to gothic representations of the undead. Colin Crouch (2011) has noted "the strange non-death of neo-liberalism"; Mitchell Dean (2014) has observed that "neoliberal regimes persist in an 'undead' form"; and Neil Smith (2012) has described neoliberalism as "dead but dominant." Among these morbid metaphors, the figure of the zombie has acquired peculiar prominence. Ben Fine (2008) claims that "the current phase of neoliberalism is zombie-like," in the sense that it is "both dead and alive at the same time"; Mark Fisher (2013) observes that "neoliberalism now shambles on as a zombie," noting that "it is sometimes harder to kill a zombie than a living person"; and Jamie Peck suggests that neoliberalism has "entered its zombie phase. . . . The living dead of the free-market revolution continue to walk the earth, though with each resurrection their decidedly uncoordinated gait becomes even more erratic" (2010, 109).

The newfound appeal of the gothic metaphor in critical political economy has been matched in popular culture, which in recent years has been filled with zombies, vampires, and other monstrous incarnations of the living dead. As Evan Calder Williams (2011, 72) has noted, "In these dark, anxious years, the undead are having their day in the sun: none more so than zombies; the contemporary vision of the walking dead horde has, without doubt, become the nightmare vision of our day." This is the case, not only in Hollywood productions like *World War Z* and American series such as *The Walking Dead*, but also throughout the cultural peripheries of global capitalism, including sub-Saharan Africa, where local culture industries are currently thriving on "unsettling tales of vampires and zombies and of extraordinary intercourse between the living and the dead" (McNally 2012, 175).

Like the black hole, the zombie thus appears within the symbolic order of contemporary capitalist society as a distorted symptom of *something else*, which remains to be deciphered. As such, it is only the latest of a series of gothic monsters who have haunted the history of capitalist modernity. In *Monsters of the Market: Zombies, Vampires and Global Capitalism*, David McNally analyses the relationship between gothic literature and capitalist social relations. Drawing on Marx's extensive use of gothic imagery in his critique of political economy, McNally interprets the key narratives of nineteenth-century gothic fiction as mythical renderings of the class relations of industrial capitalism that were being constituted at that time. Mary Shelley's *Frankenstein*, for example, is read as a metaphor for the role of the capitalist class (Dr. Frankenstein) in the creation of the proletariat (the Monster) from the disembodied fragments of a dispossessed peasantry (McNally 2012, 17–111). Vampire stories are also cast in class terms, with the vampires as capitalists feeding parasitically on the blood of the working class (McNally 2012, 113–73). And zombies, which only emerge in popular culture in the twentieth century, are identified as representations of the reduction of the global working class to meaningless labor and mindless consumerism (McNally 2012, 175–251).

From this perspective, gothic literature is just another ideological representation of the class relationship between capitalists and workers. "If vampires are the dreaded beings which might possess us and turn us into their docile servants," McNally concludes, "zombies represent our haunted self-image" (McNally 2012, 253). While this interpretation undoubtedly captures an important dimension of the monsters of gothic literature, it nevertheless remains faithful to what Evan Calder Williams calls "the parodic version" of Marxist ideology critique, according to which "everything is unidirectionally 'about' the economy in a banal and dogmatic way" (Calder Williams 2011, 79). Instead of automatically identifying "class struggle" as the material reality behind the ideological appearance of gothic monsters, these monsters can be understood as anamorphic distortions of the Real of Capital as an abstract form of domination.

Capital first emerges with the consolidation of what Marx conceptualized as the formal subsumption of labor to capital: the subordination of preexisting forms of production under the reign of wage labor. Formal subsumption, however, is limited to the production of absolute surplus value. This can only be increased through the expansion of the workforce and the extension of the working day and thus has concrete limits. The logic of inter-capitalist competition therefore drives toward the real subsumption of labor, which enables the production of relative surplus value, through the deployment of technologies that increase labor productivity and the rate of surplus value extraction (Marx 1976, 1019–38). Through the transition to real subsumption, as Postone (1993, 29–33) argues, the law of value increasingly compels all capitalists to obey the monolithic logic of "accumulation for accumulation's sake," and capital emerges as "an abstract form of domination."

From this perspective, the Real of Capital is an abstract, intangible presence-absence that dominates our reality without being symbolically included within it. Yet as Žižek argues, "In the opposition between reality and spectral illusion, the Real appears precisely as 'irreal,' as a spectral illusion for which there is no room in our (symbolically constructed) reality. . . . The inert remainder foreclosed from (what we experience as) reality returns precisely in the Real of spectral apparitions" (2008, xvi). It is therefore no coincidence that in England, the birthplace of industrial capitalism, the empowerment of capital as abstract domination through the shift from formal to real subsumption coincided precisely with the development of gothic literature, through which the Real of Capital began to appear in "spectral" and "illusory" forms. Indeed, Marx himself deploys gothic metaphors, not to depict class relations as McNally suggests, but precisely as a means of looking awry at the Real of Capital. In *Capital*, Marx describes value as "an animated monster which begins to 'work'" (1976, 302), depicting the automatic drive toward self-valorization as "a werewolf-like hunger for surplus labour" (353) and arguing that "the vampire will not let go while there remains a single . . . drop of blood to be exploited" (342).

This suggests that the relationship between Frankenstein and the Monster is not between the capitalist and the worker, but between our own alienated productive activity and the Real of Capital, which has "been endowed by living labour with a soul of its own, and establishes itself opposite living labour as an *alien power*" (Marx 1973, 454; emphasis in original). Equally, vampires should not be understood as mere metaphors for exploitative capitalists but are instead embodiments of the "ghostly objectivity" of capital itself (Marx, quoted in Arthur 2004, 153). Real subsumption is conceptualized by Marx as the subordination of living labor to dead labor. Dead labor is the value extracted from past labor and accumulated in the increasingly vast machineries through which relative surplus value is extracted in ever-greater quantities, looming above living labor as a spectral subject that continually "draws new vital spirits into itself, and realizes itself anew" (Marx 1973, 453). Capital is therefore "dead labour which, vampire-like, lives only by sucking living labour, and lives the more, the more labour it sucks" (Marx 1976, 342). In this context zombies appear, not as the working class exploited by capitalist vampires, as orthodox Marxist analysis would automatically suggest, but as a further embodiment of dead labor, which rises from the grave and is reanimated by the flesh of the living. If in the nineteenth century the solitary vampire was sufficient to convey the emergent power of capital as an abstract form of domination, by the late twentieth century the ever-greater

Japhy Wilson

masses of dead labor in relation to the living could only be adequately represented by infinite hordes of zombies swarming across the planet in blind pursuit of all remaining human meat and brains. It is for this reason, I would argue, that the zombie movie has become "the dominant vision of apocalypse in late capitalism" (Calder Williams 2011, 73).

Dead labor and the living dead are both embodiments of drive, which is defined by both Freud and Lacan in contrast to desire (see chapters 5 and 11). Whereas desire slides metonymically from one object to another, drive directly embodies *jouissance* in its repeated circling around a single object and is characterized by endlessly increasing tension and expansion in contrast to desire's pursuit of satisfaction and finality (Tomšič 2015, 121). This structure corresponds precisely to what Marx described as the "boundless drive" and "unceasing movement" of capital as an abstract form of domination (1976, 254), which compulsively repeats the circuit of capital in the endless expansion of surplus value production. As Žižek has argued, drive therefore "inheres to capitalism at a . . . fundamental, systemic level [as] that which propels the whole capitalist machinery" (quoted in Kapoor 2015, 69). Despite having its origins in the bodily drives, drive is fundamentally what Freud called "death drive," which is not a desire for death but a drive that exceeds death and all other limitations of material existence (Žižek 1997, 40–43), operating as "a blind persistence which follows its path with utter disregard for the requirements of our concrete life-world" (Žižek 2008, xvi). This definition of death drive embodies the irrational, excessive nature of *jouissance*, while simultaneously recalling Postone's description of capital as "blind, processual, and quasi-organic" and as "characterized by a constant directional movement with no external goal" (1993, 270, 278).

The relationship between capital and the death drive returns us to the metaphor of zombie neoliberalism. The neoliberal project was premised on the liberation of the death drive of global capital from all external constraints, but this very process unleashed the forces that drove the project to destruction in the form of the glObal financial crisis. The predicament of the neoliberal ideologue thus recalls that of the sorcerer's apprentice of Goethe's gothic poem, "who is no longer able to control the powers of the nether world that he has called up by his spells" (Marx and Engels 2002, 225). "The strange non-death of neo-liberalism" can accordingly be compared to the disintegration of the symbolic universe characteristic of psychosis, in which the fantasy frame has collapsed and all that remains is the automatic operation of the drive. In the aftermath of the disintegration of their symbolic universe, the Real of Capital continues to animate "the living dead of the neoliberal revolution," as "the obscene persistence of that which refuses to die" (Calder Williams 2011, 9).

The Strange God

In *The Protestant Ethic and the Spirit of Capitalism*, Max Weber (2001) located the religious origins of the capitalist mode of production in the Calvinist doctrine of predestination and the corresponding pressure for believers to demonstrate through their actions their place among the chosen. Once capitalism had established its dominance, however, Weber (2001) predicted that the faith that had made it possible would be eroded by the instrumental rationality of capitalism itself, resulting in a "disenchanted world" in which the Protestant ethic of abstinence and reinvestment would be reduced to the commonsense attitude of the successful investor. Yet the neoliberal era of triumphant glObal capitalism has seen a resurgence of evangelical Christianity, both in the U.S. heartlands and across the impoverished peripheries of Latin America, Asia, and sub-Saharan Africa. Whereas Calvinism had been committed to frugality and thrift, with the accumulation of wealth legitimated only as a means of demonstrating one's status among the chosen, many of the new evangelical churches directly celebrate the acquisition of worldly riches. The Prosperity Gospel, for example, teaches that "the persistent acquisition of wealth is a divinely endorsed endeavor" (Guest 2010, 257–58), preaching that "God wants everyone to be rich, rich, rich" (Richards 2009, 3) and promising that "the Lord will open up his treasure chest to those who believe" (evangelical pastor, quoted in Comaroff 2009, 27).

This re-enchantment of the world is underpinned by a faith in divine providence, which the new evangelism equates with the abstract gyrations of the self-regulating market. According to Christian doctrine, God's actions are not limited to the Creation but include a ceaseless providential care for the world, operating in ways that do not limit free will but that "weave together even the evil free actions of human beings into a wider, if sometimes indiscernible, greater good" (Richards 2009, 213). The doctrine of divine providence provided the inspiration for Adam Smith's theory of the invisible hand of the market (Oslington 2011) and has since been resurrected as one of the theological pillars of free-market conservatism. This doctrine is expounded by Jay W. Richards, an influential member of the American Enterprise Institute. In *Money, Greed and God: Why Capitalism Is the Solution and Not the Problem*, Richards insists on the compatibility of Christianity and capitalism, arguing that capitalism is premised not on greed but on prudent self-interest and claiming that "Jesus . . . treats risk, investment and interest in a positive light, and trusts his listeners to do the same" (2009, 156). Richards adheres to orthodox neoliberal principles, dismissing moral arguments for fair trade and a minimum wage on the basis that any attempt to organize society in ways that violate the efficient operation of the price mechanism can only lead to catastrophe, as demonstrated by the failure of communism. Rather than attempting to create "an egalitarian utopia" in this world, Richards argues, we must acknowledge that "capitalism is fit for real, fallen, limited human beings" and prepare ourselves for heaven by placing our faith in divine providence, as expressed in the invisible hand of the market (2009, 32, 123):

God . . . can work his will through the free market, which involves countless trillions of individual choices, whether they be good, bad or indifferent. . . . Rather than despising the market order, Christians should see it as God's way of providentially governing the actions of billions of free agents. . . . It is just what we would expect of a God who, even in a fallen world, can still work all things together for good. Seen in its proper light, the market is as awe-inspiring as a sunset or a perfect eclipse. . . . The believer . . . should see in it God's glory." (Richards 2009, 214–15)

Within the symbolic universe of free-market conservatism, the market thus appears as a sublime object, irradiated by a spectral agency that Richards identifies with the will of God. Orthodox ideology critique would dismiss this faith as an ideological representation of market exchange that functions to legitimate and conceal the material reality of inequality and exploitation, as only the latest manifestation of religion as "the opium of the people" (Marx 2009). But we should pause here once again to "look awry" at this anamorphic image in order to glimpse the Real that is disavowed by the fantasy of divine providence. We have already seen that capital is an abstract form of domination, an invisible structuring void at the heart of capitalist society. To this extent, however, the Real of Capital is adequately disavowed by the fetish of the market itself (see chapter 3), as expressed in Friedrich Hayek's atheistic theory of the market as a spontaneously emergent evolutionary mechanism (Centeno 1998, 41–43). Yet in *Money, Greed and God*, Richards insists that Hayek's theory of "market spontaneity" is insufficient in itself and that it "makes a lot more sense in a providential—a purposeful—universe" (2009, 224). This suggests that the Real of Capital exceeds its definition as an abstract form of domination and possesses an additional dimension that is screened by the fantasy of an omniscient and benevolent God. This dimension is embodied in Marx's argument that, through the inexorably expanding circuit of its self-valorization, capital not only emerges as the law of value but becomes an "automatic subject": "Value is here the subject of a process in which . . . it changes its own magnitude, throws off surplus value from itself . . . and thus valorizes itself independently. For the movement in the course of which it adds surplus value is its own movement, its valorization is therefore self-valorization. By virtue of being value it has acquired the occult ability to add value to itself" (Marx 1976, 255).

The spectral autonomous agent that haunts capitalist society, and that is represented by free-market conservatism as a benign and all-powerful God, is thus revealed as the traumatic Real of Capital as Subject. As the emergent subject of glObal capitalism, capital is neither benevolent nor omniscient but is "an alienated, abstract self-moving Other," which is "historically determinate and blind" (Postone 1993, 278, 77). This is "the strange God" described by Marx, the God who "proclaimed the making of profit as the ultimate and sole purpose of mankind" (1976, 918) and who stands behind the fantasy of divine providence. This strange God has less in common with the caring God of the new evangelism than with the wrathful God of the Old Testament, as "a desiring God that demands constant sacrifice, not a homeostatic order but a negativity, whose consequences are devastating" (Tomšič 2015, 98). The doctrine of market providence thus follows traditional Christianity in providing an "imaginary reconciliation between God and humanity in which the anxiety-provoking encounter with the Real is mitigated" (Žižek 2008, lvii), but twists this Christian fantasy into a neoliberal form, in which God Himself is the fantasy and the Real is Capital as Subject.

As Žižek has argued, the experience of the void of the Real "is the original materialist experience, and religion, unable to endure it, fills it in with religious content" (2008, xxix). But to confront the Real of Capital as a secular materialist is not necessarily to be delivered from its religious dimension. As Walter Benjamin claims in his notes on "Capitalism as Religion," Christianity did not merely catalyze capitalism, as Weber suggests, but rather "changed itself into capitalism," which not only continues to be enchanted by religious faiths but is itself "an essentially religious phenomenon" (Benjamin 2005, 261, 259). The religious nature of capitalism is fundamentally located, not in the explicit beliefs of market Christianity, which are limited to a specific sector of capitalist society, but in the fetishistic rituals of commodity production and exchange, which we all perform continuously with unconscious devotional commitment (Lowy 2009, 72). As Pascal long ago observed, religious rituals function to generate a collective faith that can circulate in the symbolic order in the absence of individual belief (Žižek 1989, 49). Regardless of whether we consciously believe in the spectral agency of the market God, we enact this belief in each and every one of the monetary transactions occurring throughout the world market, through which value exerts itself an abstract form of domination. As Žižek argues, "this purely material sincerity of external ideological ritual, not the depth of the subject's inner convictions and desires, is the true locus of the fantasy which sustains an ideological edifice" (1997, 5). Capitalism, as Benjamin concludes, is therefore "a purely cultic religion without dogma . . . [whose] spirit speaks from the ornamentation of banknotes" (2005, 260).

Writing in the 1920s, Benjamin identified capitalism as a cult of guilt: the bourgeois is guilty to the extent that he invests his profits in consumption instead of expanded reproduction, the proletarian is guilty by virtue of his poverty, and everyone is locked into the structural guilt of debt (Lowy 2009, 64–65). This analysis may have been appropriate to an era dominated by the punitive superego of the Protestant ethic and the Fordist production line. But the rise of neoliberalism has been accompanied by a "new spirit of capitalism" (Boltanski and Chiapello 2007), which is ideologically premised on individualistic hedonism and in which Freudian superego guilt has been displaced by the Lacanian superego injunction to enjoy (Žižek 2008). The cult of guilt has therefore been replaced with a cult of *jouissance*, based on the twin imperatives of "shopping and fucking" (Sloterdijk 2013, 214). In contrast to Benjamin's guilt-ridden scenario, the bourgeoisie now perform spectacles of conspicuous consumption for the voyeuristic enjoyment of the proletarians, who wallow in the pittance of surplus *jouissance* that is returned to them via the credit system, through which debt has been ideologically transformed from a burden of guilt into a fountain of purchasing power. The austere rituals of commodity production and exchange are thus augmented by a carnival of enjoyment that transfigures the lack intrinsic to exploitation into a dazzling array of shiny things for sale, before which we perform our unconscious veneration of the "obscene self-reproducing entity" of Capital as Subject (Tomšič 2015, 41, 130).

Conclusion

In the words of the Lacanian analyst Bruce Fink, psychoanalysis aims to invent "new ways to hit the Real, upset the repetition it engenders, dialectize the isolated Thing, and shake up the fundamental fantasy in which the subject constitutes him or herself in relation to the cause" (1995, 92). This chapter has applied this project to the critique of political economy. I

Japhy Wilson

have sought "new ways to hit the Real" by deploying Žižek's methodology of looking awry at certain sociocultural symptoms of the Real of Capital: black holes mirror the paradoxical status of value as "immaterial but objective"; gothic monsters convey the dominance of dead labor over living labor, through which capital emerges as an abstract form of domination; and divine providence provides a phantasmatic representation of the Real of Capital as Subject.

This analysis has aimed to "dialectize the isolated Thing" by bringing these anamorphic stains into focus, in order to drag elements of the Real of Capital into the Symbolic, and has attempted to "disrupt the repetition that it engenders" by exploring how the circuits of capital accumulation and the death drive are materially related through their common embodiment of *jouissance*. The final phase of the analytic process, however, remains to be attempted. This is the disruption of "the fundamental fantasy" through which the subject is related to the Real, the moment that Lacan called "traversing the fantasy" and that Freud sought to capture with the phrase "*Wo es war, soll ich werden*," which Fink translates as "I must come to be where foreign forces . . . once dominated. I must subjectify that otherness" (1995, 68). What might this phrase mean in the context of the Real of Capital, and how might we begin to think about traversing the fantasy in relation to this Real?

In responding to these questions, we must be clear about the status of this relation between fantasy and Real. In *The Capitalist Unconscious*, Samo Tomšič has identified Capital as Subject as the ultimate fantasy to be disrupted, defining "Marx's hypothesis" as the claim that "the individual who is affected by capitalism is the same one who constitutes the subject of value" and arguing that "this clearly inverts the fetishist hypothesis, according to which the subject of capital is capital itself" (Tomšič 2015, 105). As we have seen in the discussion of gothic monsters, Tomšič is correct in his identification of living labor as the producer of the dead labor that comes to dominate it. But this abstract form of domination cannot be dismissed as an "imposed fantasy, according to which capital is the true subject of the valorization process" (Tomšič 2015, 104). What Tomšič identifies here as an "imposed fantasy" is precisely the Real of Capital. We produce capital through our own alienated activity, but we have seen that capital is nevertheless a "real abstraction" that acts with a force that is "immaterial but objective." As Marx himself has argued, "Those who consider the autonomization of value as a mere abstraction forget that the movement of industrial capital is this abstraction in action" (quoted in Harvey 2013, 70).

This is the traumatic Real that fantasy disavows (see chapter 1). More precisely, the ideological fantasies of capitalist society are structured to disavow our relationship to this Real, as both its producers and its slaves. This is the function of divine providence in the symbolic universe of free-market conservatism and of the invisible hand of the market in neoliberal atheism. Both present the Real of Capital as a benign, omnipotent force to which each individual must privately submit and that exists independently of social relations of exploitation. The first step in traversing the fundamental fantasy of capital must be to replace the imaginary independence of Capital as Subject with an understanding of capital as produced and sustained by our own alienated productive activity. In doing so, however, we must resist the temptation to replace this fantasy with a vindication of the proletariat as the true subject of history. This is the fantasy that underpins the orthodox Marxist reading of the gothic monster, according to which capital reduces labor to the status of a zombie by draining it of vitality and depriving it of autonomy. This fantasy rests on a humanist understanding of alienation and a vitalist affirmation of a disalienated humanity, which sees capital as deforming a unified human subject who can be returned to fullness through the abolition of class relations. But as we have seen, zombies are not alienated laborers; they are symptomatic of *undead labor*, the acephalous life force of the drive, which accumulates through our own compulsive repetition of the circuit of capital and in which we are all entangled, not only at the level of production but also at the level of *jouissance*. Alienation is not only *constituted* but is also *constitutive* (Tomšič 2015, 92), inscribed into our identities through the process of castration and producing a relation to *jouissance* that is both alienated and inescapable. In other words, the possibility of an unalienated human

Japhy Wilson

subject is itself a fantasy that conceals our own libidinal investment in the death drive of capital.

Here we confront what is perhaps the sternest lesson that psychoanalysis holds for revolutionary praxis: alienation is not merely imposed by exploitative social relations but is intrinsic to the structure of our being, and the drive cannot be escaped through the abolition of class relations but will pursue us all to the grave. The power of Capital as Subject lies not only in the dull compulsion of economic mechanisms but also in its structural alignment with what I am tempted to call "human nature"—not the utilitarian human nature of liberal fantasy, but the libidinal human nature of *jouissance* and the drive. Unlike previous systems of social domination, neoliberal capitalism does not seek to suppress this nature through moral sanction and religious prohibition but mobilizes it toward the ever-increasing expansion of an abstract form of domination to which the vast majority of proletarian humanity willingly offers its voluntary enslavement. As Tomšič argues, "An important part of the efficiency of global capitalism derives from the fact that . . . its logic of production is coupled to desire and the drive. . . . The capitalist mode of production seems to be the first social and economic system in history [to have] created ideal conditions for their social realization" (2015, 130).

In other words, *we fucking love capitalism*. Indeed, even our resistances bear the trace of this disavowed enjoyment (see chapters 3 and 4). According to Bruno Latour, "If you have failed, it's not capitalism you should revolutionize but rather your ways of thinking. If you keep failing and don't change it does not mean you are facing an invincible monster, it means you like, you enjoy, you love to be *defeated* by a monster" (2014, 9). The acknowledgment of this libidinal attachment, and of the impossibility of adopting a position of external resistance to a system that is all-encompassing, has led certain radical theorists to locate the emancipatory potential of capitalism within the dynamics of capital itself and to advocate the wild embrace of these dynamics, which they claim are "not to be reversed, but accelerated beyond the constraints of the capitalist value form" (Williams and Srnicek 2013). But accelerationism is yet another fantasy, which reproduces the adoration of Capital as Subject contained in the neoliberal fantasy of market providence, while displacing the promise of revolutionary change from the imagined subject of romantic humanism to the equally fantastical "not yet" of an imagined future as "the place of some structural impossibility, while simultaneously disavowing this impossibility" (Žižek 1997, 98).

We are therefore returned to the fundamental deadlock of our complicity in the production of our own domination and to the repetition of Freud's message: *where it was, there I must come to be*. It is precisely the repeated confrontation with this deadlock, however, that can open the possibility of transformation. Fink argues that despite the constitutive alienation of the human condition, Lacanian psychoanalysis does hold out the possibility of a utopian moment beyond castration, but that this can be attained only by going through the fundamental fantasy and confronting our true relation to the Real (Fink 1995, 79). This journey into "the night of the world" (Žižek 1999, 38) has been related to the appearance of the black hole in the discourse of the analysand, which is regarded not as signaling a collapse into psychosis but "as a signifier for an indescribable 'nothing' that, paradoxically . . . can open the space for the emergence of new elements. This experience may precipitate trauma and disruption, but also a 'rearrangement' or 'transformation' of subjectivity" (Hinton 2007, 434, 444). This understanding of the black hole metaphor also resonates with the cutting edge of cosmological theory, according to which black holes not only destroy matter but also release vast quantities of energy, pointing toward "opportunities for stars to be born within the great gathering disk of material accreting into a black hole" and suggesting that "instead of just destroying the arrangement of matter, the black hole environment could conceivably encourage a new start" (Scharf 2012, 212). If there is a way out of here, then the journey toward it must begin by traversing both the fantasy of the providential order of Capital as Subject and the fantasy of the emancipatory destiny of the proletariat and by confronting the black hole of the Real: our profound attachment to the *jouissance* that we derive from the conditions of our own domination and the absence of any inherently utopian dimension within the planetary catastrophe of glObal capitalism.

Japhy Wilson

Works Cited

Arthur, Christopher J. 2004. *The New Dialectic and Marx's Capital*. Boston: Brill.

Bartusiak, Marcia. 2015. *Black Hole: How an Idea Abandoned by Newtonians, Hated by Einstein and Gambled on by Hawking Came to be Loved*. New Haven CT: Yale University Press.

Benjamin, Walter. 2005. "Capitalism as a Religion." In *The Frankfurt School on Religion: Key Writings by the Major Thinkers*, edited by Eduardo Mendieta, 259–62. New York: Routledge.

Boltanski, Luc, and Eve Chiapello. 2007. *The New Spirit of Capitalism*. London: Verso.

Calder Williams, Evan. 2011. *Combined and Uneven Apocalypse*. Ropley, UK: Zero Books.

Centeno, Miguel A. 1998. "The Politics of Knowledge: Hayek and Technocracy." In *The Politics of Expertise in Latin America*, edited by Miguel A. Centeno and Patricio Silva, 36–51. London: MacMillan.

Comaroff, Jean. 2009. "The Politics of Conviction: Faith on the Neoliberal Frontier." *Social Analysis* 53 (1): 17–38.

Crouch, Colin. 2011. *The Strange Non-Death of Neo-Liberalism*. Cambridge: Polity.

Dean, Mitchell. 2014. "Rethinking Neoliberalism." *Journal of Sociology* 50 (2): 150–63.

Dolar, Mladen. 2015. "Anamorphosis." *S: Journal of the Circle for Lacanian Ideology Critique* 8, 125–40.

Featherstone, Mark. 2010. "Event Horizon: Utopia-Dystopia in Bauman's Thought." In *Bauman's Challenge: Sociological Issues for the 21st Century*, edited by Mark Davis and Keith Tester, 127–47. Basingstoke, UK: Palgrave Macmillan.

Fine, Ben. 2008. "Zombieconomics: The Living Death of the Dismal Science in the Age of Neoliberalism." Paper for ESRC Neoliberalism Seminar, School of Oriental and African Studies, London, April 1.

Fink, Bruce. 1995. *The Lacanian Subject: Between Language and Jouissance*. Princeton NJ: Princeton University Press.

Fisher, Mark. 2013. "How to Kill a Zombie: Strategizing the End of Neoliberalism." *Open Democracy*, July 18. https://www.opendemocracy.net/mark-fisher/how-to-kill-zombie-strategizing-end-of-neoliberalism.

Ford, Glen. 2009. "The Great Black Hole of Casino Capitalism." *Black Agenda Report*, September 29. http://www.blackagendareport.com/content/great-black-hole-casino-capitalism.

Guest, Mathew. 2010. "Evangelism and Capitalism in Transnational Context." In "Contemporary British Religion and Politics," special issue, *Politics and Religion* 4 (2): 257–79.

Harvey, David. 2013. *A Companion to Marx's Capital Volume 2*. London: Verso.

Hinton, Ladson. 2007. "Black Holes, Uncanny Spaces, and Radical Shifts in Awareness." *Journal of Analytical Psychology* 52, 433–47.

Jameson, Fredric. 2011. *Representing Capital: A Reading of Volume One.* London: Verso

Kane, Frank. 2012. "Huge Black Hole at Heart of Capitalism." *The National,* August 18. http://www.thenational.ae/business/industry-insights/finance/huge-black-hole-at -heart-of-capitalism.

Kapoor, Ilan. 2015. "What 'Drives' Capitalist Development?" *Human Geography* 8 (3): 66–78.

Latour, Bruno. 2014. "On Some of the Affects of Capitalism." Lecture delivered at the Royal Academy, Copenhagen, February 26.

Lowy, Michael. 2009. "Capitalism as Religion: Walter Benjamin and Max Weber." *Historical Materialism* 17, 60–73.

Marx, Karl. 1973. *Grundrisse.* London: Penguin.

———. 1976. *Capital: A Critique of Political Economy.* Vol. 1, *The Process of Capitalist Production.* Translated by Ben Fowkes. New York: Vintage Books.

———. 2009. *Critique of Hegel's "Philosophy of Right."* Cambridge: Cambridge University Press.

Marx, Karl, and Friedrich Engels. 2002. *The Communist Manifesto.* London: Penguin.

McNally, David. 2012. *Monsters of the Market: Zombies, Vampires and Global Capitalism.* Chicago: Haymarket.

Oslington, Paul. 2011. "Divine Action, Providence and Adam Smith's Invisible Hand." In *Adam Smith as Theologian,* edited by Paul Oslington. London: Routledge.

Peck, Jamie. 2010. "Zombie Neoliberalism and the Ambidextrous State." *Theoretical Criminology* 14, 104–10.

Postone, Moishe. 1993. *Time, Labour, and Social Domination: A Reinterpretation of Marx's Critical Theory.* Cambridge: Cambridge University Press.

Rees, William E. 2012. "Cities as Dissipative Structures: Global Change and the Vulnerability of Urban Civilization." In *Sustainability Science: The Emerging Paradigm and the Urban Environment,* edited by M. P. Weinstein and R. E. Turner, 47–223. New York: Springer.

Richards, Jay W. 2009. *Money, Greed, and God: Why Capitalism Is the Solution and Not the Problem.* New York: Harper Collins.

Santos, Juan. 2010. "The Killing Horizon: Capitalism at the Expense of All Life." *Countercurrents,* October 4. http://www.countercurrents.org/santos041008.htm.

Scharf, Caleb. 2012. *Gravity's Engines: The Other Side of Black Holes.* London: Penguin.

Sloterdijk, Peter. 2013. *In the World Interior of Capital.* Cambridge: Polity.

Smith, Neil. 2012. "Every Revolution Has Its Space." Lecture delivered at the Open Spaces Forum, University of Manchester, April 25.

Smith, Yves. 2012. "Greece's Great Depression: 'Everyone Is Going into a Black Hole.'" *Naked Capitalism*, August 23. http://www.nakedcapitalism.com/2012/08/greeces-great -depression-everyone-is-going-into-a-black-hole.html.

Tomšič, Samo. 2015. *The Capitalist Unconscious: Marx and Lacan*. London: Verso.

Weber, Max. 2001. *The Protestant Ethic and the Spirit of Capitalism*. London: Routledge.

Williams, Alex, and Nick Srnicek. 2013. #ACCELERATE MANIFESTO for an Accelerationist Politics." *Critical Legal Thinking*, May 14. http://criticallegalthinking.com/2013/05/14 /accelerate-manifesto-for-an-accelerationist-politics/.

Žižek, Slavoj. 1989. *The Sublime Object of Ideology*. London: Verso.

———. 1992. *Looking Awry: An Introduction to Jacques Lacan through Popular Culture*. Cambridge MA: MIT Press.

———. 1997. *The Plague of Fantasies*. London: Verso.

———. 1999. *The Ticklish Subject: The Absent Centre of Political Ontology*. London: Verso.

———. 2008. *For They Know Not What They Do: Enjoyment as a Political Factor*. 2nd ed. London: Verso.

PART 3   The Gl*O*bal in the Local

Desire, Resistance, and the City

9 A Feminist Psychoanalytic Perspective on Glass Architecture in Singapore

Nathan F. Bullock

This chapter begins with two questions: How do we bring feminist psychoanalysis to bear on architecture, and how do we expand on previous research in psychoanalytic geography by adding in visual analysis? Psychoanalytic geography has been taken in many directions and explored in the collections *Psychoanalytic Geographies*, edited by Paul Kingsbury and Steve Pile (2014), and *The Geography of Meanings: Psychoanalytic Perspectives on Place, Space, Land, and Dislocation*, published by the International Psychoanalytic Association (Savio Hook and Akhtar 2007). Psychoanalysis has also been employed in the visual analysis of architecture, as in Richard Williams's (2013) *Sex and Buildings*. What this chapter does is cross the fields of geography and architecture, drawing on a theoretical framework of feminist psychoanalysis and a methodology that includes visual analysis by looking simultaneously at actual buildings and urban space, both holistically and theoretically. I apply these perspectives to a specific group of buildings in a particular setting to push further the ways in which feminist psychoanalysis and visual analysis can be used in architecture and the subfield of psychoanalytic geographies.

I have argued elsewhere that "Singapore places itself in the masculine role of a dominant first-world economy in relation to its ASEAN [Association of Southeast Asian Nations] neighbors on whom it can act out its patriarchal fantasy, playing dress up (although in drag), with his mother's clothes" (Bullock 2014, 221). This observation stems from work by Neferti Tadiar (1998) on the sexualized international relations inherent in economic relations from imperialism to the present. To go further, however, requires a deeper analysis of that patriarchal fantasy, the drag performance it engenders, and what the mother's clothes actually look like.

These themes can be best addressed through a feminist psychoanalytic perspective on the critical object of architecture. For the most part, this scholarly work has not been done yet. Indeed, even a 2008 special issue of *Asian Studies Review* on "Heterosexualities and the Global(izing) City in Asia," guest-edited by two Singaporean geographers, included no articles using psychoanalytic methods or frameworks (Huang and Yeoh 2008). I rely most heavily on the works of Judith Butler and Amelia Jones to formulate my own conclusions. As my previous research focused on urban development in Singapore through a case study of the Integrated Resorts (IRS)—Marina Bay Sands and Resorts World Sentosa—it is appropriate to begin there. What was absent from my previous work was a visual analysis of the architecture of these massive urban redevelopment projects as I considered the policy side of urban development and the discourse of the politics behind it. Thus, it is not just the rhetorical language of the public sphere but the visual language of architecture that reveals what Tadiar identifies as "the contradictory symptoms of patriarchy, colonialism, and imperialism" (1998, 229).

Singapore's pre-independence urban past has been defined largely by its weaker position, dependent on the matriarchal metropole of London while it was a British colony (1824–1942, 1945–63), on imperial Tokyo during Japanese occupation (1942–45), and on postcolonial Kuala Lumpur for the period of federation with Malaysia (1963–65). Since independence, Singapore has seen itself as existentially vulnerable and sought to secure itself economically through trade with North America and militarily under the tutelage of Israel. Fast-forwarding to today, Singapore's contemporary urban condition has been celebrated the world over for its safety, infrastructure, and efficiency (BBC News 2013). This overcompensation to be superlative in every area of economic activity is best illustrated in the concept of Total Defence, which defines economic crises as equivalent to military crises and thus of concern to the Ministry of Defence (Government of Singapore 2015). The work of Maureen Sioh (2014) on the libidinal economy of

Nathan F. Bullock

sovereign wealth funds further drives home the point of the psychic drives guiding the elision of economic and military security and the important role this plays in constructing a dominant masculine subject and national identity (see also chapter 2). Turning to the urban built environment as an expression of that libidinal economy, glass architecture is the best critical object of study to reveal the patriarchy, colonialism, and imperialism that continue to guide the values behind Singapore's economic and architectural development.

Why Glass?

Glass as a metaphor for mirror, lens, and window is useful as it ties in the concept of the mirror stage of development propounded by French psychoanalyst Jacques Lacan. The mirror stage is used to explain a process of identification whereby the subject forms its ideal-ego in relation to an Other and constructs its Imaginary. This concept was used in my previous research to frame the discourse of urban development and planning and is alluded to in the following thick descriptions. Glass is the primary building material for the major architectural spaces of central Singapore. Marina Bay Sands, Marina Bay Financial Centre, the Esplanade Theatres by the Bay, and the Singapore Flyer are the four on which I will focus. These four spaces and structures incorporate several major aspects of Singapore's economy: tourism, meetings and events, banking and finance, housing, arts and entertainment, and foreign direct investment. I want to suggest that the mirror stage, like the glass architecture of Singapore analyzed here, reflects a false sense of unity and permanence in the subject's (i.e., Singapore's) identity formation.

The Marina Bay Sands is the landmark IR of Singapore and is set to serve as its global icon for the skyline, making Singapore finally visible and legible on the world urban stage. It incorporates tourism in the hotel, retail, and gambling segments as well as meeting spaces for conferences and conventions. It uses glass as the main element on the front and rear elevations of three bent towers housing the hotel rooms and appearing to hold up the cantilevered floating ship that tops off and connects the entire structure. On this top floor, the Skypark, glass is used as a protective lens through which one can view the panorama of Singapore. While individual hotel rooms are limited to one view of either the sea or the city, the Skypark enables visitors to feel they are gazing more fully on the entirety of Singapore and its environs even though it is neither the tallest building in the city nor the highest observation deck. It is instead the only one that faces the city from the opposite side of Marina Bay and that allows for such views to take place in the luxury of an infinity pool, where glass continues to provide a barrier and a sense of endless reach and knowledge through sight. The glass of the front elevation and the two floating boutiques (one housing a defunct upscale nightclub and the other a Louis Vuitton store) reflect not just the water of the bay but the skyline of the Central Business District (CBD) itself. Marina Bay Sands' glass is a mirror that reflects the values of planning and urban development in Singapore: geared toward foreigners of the tourist and global elite varieties, it is "not for Singaporeans" as one People's Action Party (PAP) activist told me. The only feature that specifically targets local Singaporeans is the theater. The hotel, casino, club, and shops like Louis Vuitton are meant to capture the capital of wealthy outsiders just as the complex is itself the largest foreign direct investment in the country. These mirrors work with the water features and nightly lightshow to deceive (in the sense of "smoke and mirrors"), to act as camouflage of the presence of gambling and money deep at the core of the building and of the government's policies that favor foreign talent in the labor market (even the art installations are all non-Singaporean artists). The exterior glass architecture of Marina Bay Sands works just like the mirrors inside Louis Vuitton—they are used for shopping, putting on clothes, and seeing how you look.

Marina Bay Financial Centre incorporates several tall glass buildings of both private residences and commercial offices. These residential apartments are high-end and, like the front-end offices, command high prestige for their address. Their top location is cemented by the privilege of windows on all sides. The buildings themselves are arranged to maximize the views of Marina Bay and their shade of blue glass is distinct from the other

Nathan F. Bullock

Fig. 8. Marina Bay Sands. Photo by Nathan Bullock, July 2, 2011.

Fig. 9. Marina Bay Financial Centre. Photo by Nathan Bullock, July 2, 2011.

buildings of the CBD. Residents and workers can look out these windows from protected heights, but pedestrians cannot look back in. Still, returning the gaze critically, one can find a window into the chief sector of the Singaporean economy. Marina Bay Financial Center's largest occupants are Development Bank of Singapore (DBS), Standard Chartered, and Oversea-Chinese Banking Corporation (OCBC), and the uniform color scheme of the glass was presumably chosen to separate these new front offices from their previous offices, which are now the middle offices.

The Esplanade Theatres are two oblong glass domes covered in triangular metal shades that jut out in a highly textured way. The structure has been nicknamed "the Durian" because it resembles the thorny contours of the local fruit's exterior. The theater's website is most revealing in its own description: "The final design eventually put Esplanade on the map. Its eye-catching spiky twin-domes became an iconic addition to Marina Bay. This was firmly cemented in 2013, when the centre came to be featured on Singapore's five-cent coins" (Esplanade 2015). Architectural design is the key to being put on the map, to being recognized worldwide, to being iconic—whether for arts, entertainment, or any other aspect of the economy. This iconicity of architectural design completes the logic of the libidinal economy by becoming the signifier of actual currency. The Esplanade Theatres represent the largest government investment in the arts, but it is not the location of the most typical (and critical) local theater productions. These are still performed in community centers and the Drama Center at the National Library. The mention of "final design" is significant because the original design did not include the prickly aluminum sunshades but consisted of just two oblong glass domes unadorned. The original design had to be modified because glass architecture is inherently incompatible with comfortable inhabitation in a tropical climate.

The Singapore Flyer is a standard observation wheel. Its twenty-eight glass capsules rotate at the edge of Marina Bay providing a temporary panoptic experience as one reaches the peak. It faces from a necessary distance the full view of Marina Bay, the CBD, and the skyline—the quintessential tourist gaze. It is, of course, not only taller than the London Eye but was the largest

Fig. 10. Esplanade Theatres. Photo by Nathan Bullock, July 2, 2011.

Ferris wheel in the world until 2014. The familiarity of the Ferris wheel for the tourist in typology and experience make it reproducible in city after city. Every rider knows exactly what she or he will get—a purportedly full view of the city, opportunity for pictures, and the ability to say that one has seen all of Singapore. Given these conditions, the Singapore Flyer's placement is particularly significant as it not only complements the skyline with its easily legible form, but it is also removed enough so that riders can still see and be shown just what the city authorities want them to see and be shown. As magnificent as the view may be from the Marina Bay Skypark, one cannot simultaneously see the entire Marina Bay Sands from that vantage point. Thus, the Flyer is positioned to provide the glass lens that frames the ideal image of the city's architecture and identity.

It follows that the ideal image of Singapore comes from the viewpoint of the tourist. The ideal view of the city is not from the street, the train (or Mass Rapid Transit [MRT]), or even a double-decker bus or the roof of the

Nathan F. Bullock

Fig. 11. Singapore Flyer. Photo by Nathan Bullock, July 2, 2011.

Pinnacle at Duxton, the tallest public housing complex. Instead it is to be had from the pinnacle of a SG$33 (US$23) ride inside an air-conditioned glass capsule (Gallezo-Estuara 2013; Singapore Flyer 2015).[1]

Iconicity

These buildings and their builders have all proudly and uncritically laid claim to their inherent iconicity due to architectural design and geographic placement in the city. The buildings function individually and collectively to create the iconicity of architecture in Singapore at large. As Leslie Sklair notes, "Recognition of the outline of a building, especially in a skyline, is one of the great signifiers of iconicity" (2010, 143). Each of these buildings uses its glass to create an outline that begs to be looked at and recognized (see chapter 7). Sklair recognizes that "the dominant force driving iconic architecture is the transnational capitalist class" (2010, 138). However, using a feminist psychoanalytic perspective, I argue that the drive behind this iconic architecture is not the transnational capitalist class or global elite per se; rather the drive is the desire to be desired by the global elite (Bullock 2014). The spatial symptoms include what Sklair rightly notes: "Much consumerist space operates as restricted public space, that is, restricted to those with the means to buy what is on sale" (2010, 148). But the buildings themselves have more performative agency than they are given credit for. While they are largely funded, used, and promoted by the wealthy, the buildings act on users and viewers to perform a civic (and in this case, national) identity, as well as eliciting a desirous gaze from the Other. That entering and enjoying the interiors of these glass spaces is so restricted by cost and other social barriers makes it clear that the average citizen is not their primary audience. The persistent use of foreign architects—often bemoaned by the Singapore Institute of Architects—is another indicator that these chosen icons must shine in the eyes of foreign observers instead of catering to the (aesthetic) needs of local Singaporeans (Tay 2013, 27).

The Esplanade was built at a time when Singapore's place branding slogan was "Global City for the Arts," and thus the building stands as icon of world-class arts architecture. As T. C. Chang recalls, however, at the time when the plans were revealed it "unleased a flood of criticisms against the state for prioritizing infrastructure over people and foreign over local talent" (2000, 823). The motto at work here is not *ars gratia artis* but building architectural icons that can participate in the semiotics of glObal elitist visions of urbanization (Kong 2012; Yeoh 2005). Similarly, Marina Bay Financial Centre is meant to be the iconic location of front-end and high-end business dealings in all areas of banking, finance, and commerce. It is the closest office building to Marina Bay Sands and mimics an American downtown in density and design, even if not convincingly that of Manhattan. This set of buildings is meant to act as icon of financial control and dominance, particularly in the context of Southeast Asia. In judging its ability to impress viewers and users of its purported iconicity, architectural critic Patrick Bingham-Hall writes, "The only thing that can be said about the completed project is that nobody has really noticed it" (2012, 111). The lack of critical acclaim for what is meant to be the most sought-after business address in Singapore is proof that these foreign building types are the equivalent of an architectural impersonation. Rather than achieving iconicity as the builders promised and the developers intended, the Marina Bay Financial Centre is an architectural performance of style and form sans content.

For the Singapore Flyer, Erica Yap's research shows that the building was one of Singapore's original attempts at iconic architecture meant to visually dominate the world's urban landscapes at the levels of the Empire State Building in New York City and the Eiffel Tower in Paris. She writes, "There has always been a desire for the Singapore Flyer to possess an iconic status similar to the London Eye, an aspiration that can be discerned in Singapore's repeated references to its predecessor" (Yap 2012, 2845). For the Flyer, the idea of a complete copy of pure architectural form was believed to be able to bestow an equal amount of aura and iconicity on the building and the city. This building (like the others outlined here) acted inappropriately in attempting to achieve these ends. These buildings have been rhetorically cast as icons by the architects, developers, and state actors such as the Tourism Board, but in reality they fail to live up to that label in global popular recognition and critical appeal. Thus, they are only performatively iconic—they impersonate the iconic as an architectural ideal without any substance behind the glassy façades.

The subsequent major attempt at iconic architecture came in the form of Marina Bay Sands. Here the building was meant to serve tourism and the conventions and exhibitions sector of the economy. It was to be the final icon of global city status and provide the ultimate symbol of luxury amenities on the level of Monaco. This building's architecture has stood out significantly enough that it has become more well-known abroad, enticing foreigners with a plethora of photographs taken atop its Skypark.[2]

Each of these icons works assiduously to employ its glass structure in a way that allows viewers to see what they want in it. The government sees a set of symbols bestowing the identity of the global city and performing an economic and cultural function. Tourists see an affluent city that makes them feel comfortable, clean, and safe. The foreign investor and global elite professionals see buildings that make them feel familiar, easy to navigate, and in control.

Spectacle

Seeing this architecture as iconic in a way that is active and performative leads to its understanding as spectacle. The specular performance of architecture is representative of the desire to be desired by the (M)Other. Yasser Elsheshtawy writes, "Globalizing cities throughout the world are utilizing spectacular architectural symbols as a way to announce their emergence on the world stage" (2008, 164). This performance of the glObal city uses architecture to attract the global elite as visitors-voyeurs.

But there is a bleaker side to such a spectacle. Peter Eisinger writes, "When local leaders fail to calibrate public expenditures to public returns and speak instead of creating a 'big league' image or a 'world class' city as a way of justifying expenditures on entertainment amenities, then it is fair to conclude that they are offering their constituents not the best basic services that have long been core municipal responsibilities but rather the thin sustenance of bread and circuses" (2000, 331). The spectacle's performance happens even as Singapore's public transportation faces failures and even as a housing bubble exists despite the public sector having trouble meeting demand (Aripin 2013; Channel NewsAsia 2015; Stevenson 2015; Colombo 2014). Looking past the glass façade of Singapore's architecture at the infrastructure and built environment of the local populace reveals the amount of faith the state puts in the ability of these buildings to adequately perform. A glObal city where business and bureaucracy are transparent, efficient, and free of corruption would not have regular breakdowns in public transportation or exorbitant prices and wait times for securing public housing (this is the Real at the heart of the glObal city). The architectural spectacle—its rhetorical language of design—does not reflect the reality of life in the city-state. Thus, a brief look in the reflective mirrors of Singapore's buildings allows for the temporary and illusory belief that the performance of the city's identity is bright, clean, and whole. Singapore's performance is successful only for those who do not stay long enough to pull back the curtain, who mistakenly believe that the performer's outfits are really as fabulous as they appear on stage.

Nathan F. Bullock

Performance

The performance of iconic glass architecture for a foreign audience deserves a deeper analysis than simply concluding that it is a spectacle, that it neglects lOcal citizens' needs, or that it is integral to late capitalist consumerist ideology (see chapter 10). Bringing in a feminist psychoanalytic perspective allows one to see this performance as a specific type of spectacle: drag.

Glass architecture in each of these iconic buildings is an expression of high modernism. It displays the prowess of engineering, using technology and building materials to make glass a viable option in varying shapes, sizes, and heights. This progression of architectural design follows firmly in the Euro-American tradition, as witnessed by the glass and steel skyscrapers designed by the likes of Ludwig Mies van der Rohe in Chicago and New York and Norman Foster in London, New York, Washington DC, and Berlin. Singapore's (drag) performance is not just in its perpetuation of the economic policies of the UK and United States but also in its visual rhetoric in putting on the architectural clothes of its political and economic (M) Other. Singapore's repetition of this foreign architectural language is akin to a novice drag performer putting on the ill-fitting clothing of a (drag) mother. This visual analysis of architecture and space serves to confirm that the physical impersonation of colonial centers is congruous with political, economic, and social policies inherited from colonialism.

The most obvious example comes from the Singapore Flyer—a blatant allusion to the London Eye (aka the Millennium Wheel), which is the largest Ferris wheel in Europe. Similarly, the curved forms of the Esplanade and Marina Bay Sands can be seen as replicating the famous Bilbao effect of Frank Gehry's Guggenheim Museum in Bilbao, Spain, or even the Sydney Opera House. And the blue glass of Marina Bay Financial Centre's tall office buildings is a "perversely neutral . . . tropical tribute to the American downtown skylines of the early 1980s, when clusters of reflective glass towers huddled together to keep themselves warm" as in Minneapolis, for example (Bingham-Hall 2012, 111).

Glass iconic architecture is now the order of the day in London, where besides the London Eye there is the Gherkin by Norman Foster and the tallest building in the European Union—the Shard by Renzo Piano—in Southwark (earning its nickname because it resembles a shard of glass). That Singapore's new architecture imitates foreign design is in large part due to the foreign investment and foreign architects chosen for its building projects. The Singapore Flyer was designed by Japanese architect Kisho Kurokawa and developed by a German project management company. Marina Bay Sands was designed by Israeli-Canadian architect Moshe Safdie and developed by the American Sands Corporation. The Esplanade was designed by UK-based architect Michael Wilford in concert with a large Singaporean firm. And Marina Bay Financial Center was designed by American architectural firm Kohn Pederson Fox and developed by a conglomeration of Hong Kong– and Singapore-based land developers. With these details we can visualize more fully the foreign closets from which Singapore has collected its drag costumes.

Drag

For Judith Butler, in *Bodies That Matter*, "performance, understood as 'acting out,' is significantly related to the problem of unacknowledged loss" (2011, 179). In the case of Singapore's performance, I would like to suggest that this unacknowledged loss is the lack created in identifying with its (matriarchal) metropole, London, leading to the acting out of "the obsession with the idea of the global city—to be cosmopolitan and world class—however it is defined" (Bullock 2014, 218). In drag performance, Butler situates this loss more specifically: "Drag exposes or allegorizes the mundane psychic and performative practices by which hetereosexualized genders form themselves through the renunciation of the possibility of homosexuality, a foreclosure that produces a field of heterosexual objects at the same time that it produces a domain of those whom it would be impossible to love. Drag thus allegorizes heterosexual melancholy, the melancholy by which a masculine gender is formed from the refusal to grieve the masculine as a possibility of love" (2011, 180). This allegory can

Nathan F. Bullock

be seen as how Singapore performs its masculinized persona. Yearning for the big, powerful, and flashy has all the typical markings of heteronormativity. Singapore's glass architecture is acting out a masculinity that is neither vernacular nor indigenous; rather, it is British, but also American, Japanese, Canadian, and Israeli. Singapore does not look to, say, Chiang Mai or Angkor Wat for inspiration, nor does it utilize any architectural typologies native to the Malay Peninsula or maritime Southeast Asia. These glass buildings construct a masculinized and heterosexualized subject. It is in this vein that art historian and performance theorist Amelia Jones's observation ties this performance to architecture: "Architectural spaces represent the civilizing influence—the weight of the law and the structuring force of institutions" (2000, 126).

Jones's use of a feminist psychoanalytic perspective is equally potent here: "For Freud, part of the development of the 'normal' adult subject (a subject who is always implicitly male in his logic) is the fabrication of the ego as a 'façade' of unity, as the putative public identity of the subject" (2000, 125). The glass architecture surrounding Marina Bay provides a uniformity of design against the skyline, and the skyline is constructed to address the wealthy foreign Other. In coffee table books about Singapore, Google Image searches, postcards, websites, tourist advertisements, t-shirts, and posters, Singapore's public identity is presented as successful, unified, and clean through its skyline.

But a feminist psychoanalytic perspective reveals something else: "Masculinity is performed as contingent and hysterical, not transcendent and originary" (Jones 2000, 129). The deconstruction of architectural drag in Singapore shows the masculine to be, paradoxically, a covering up of all that is not "modern": the native, feminine, disordered, chaotic, unclean, corrupt, polluted, traditional. The deployment of glass architecture points instead to notions of Westernization, masculinity, order, purity. The city's mirrored skyline is built to convey transparency and cleanliness and, by association, moral rectitude and lack of corruption. It is name-branded, expensive, and Anglo-American. It is visible and highly legible yet financially inaccessible and exclusive.

Why, then, is this the case? This drag performance is due to the profound paternal lack that exists in the collective psyche of this culture of masculinity. This oppressive culture of masculinity cannot be traced to Confucianism or any of the component parts of Singapore's multicultural background. Rather, this emphasis on a specific form and performance of masculinity is rooted in a culture that has grown out of British colonial control. The leadership of Lee Kuan Yew (Singapore's first and longest serving prime minister) and the bureaucrats, civil servants, and architects in the government who have adopted his party's paradigms exemplifies this culture and makes him an integral part of Singapore as analysand (Bullock 2014). His and his government's obsessive policing of male bodies through forced conscription in the Singapore Armed Forces and the criminalization of men having sex with men are played out in the urban built environment and the attempt through architecture and urban planning to fulfill the insatiable lack of recognition by the glObal (M)Other (Bullock 2014). Furthermore, Singapore's inability to cohere in its multicultural identity drives patriarchal oppression. Demographic fracture lines of ethnicity, religion, and language have led to state-directed attempts to absolve and repress these differences in ways that fail to bring people together (Gwee 2016). These political decisions are directly descended from British colonial legal conceptions of masculinity (Chua 2003). Glass architecture, like the state's control of male bodies, provides the façade of permanence, impenetrability, dominance, and a panoptic view—the key elements of a phallocentric worldview and of a colonial master. What is important to remember, however, is that although drag works to reinforce a patriarchal and heteronormative system, it is a performance that is never secure or permanent.

Searching for Alternatives

This drag performance is not the *condicio sine qua non* of Singaporean identity; it lacks inherency and is, after all, merely an impersonation.

Singapore's drag performance through glass architecture is a donned identity that, as I have tried to show, is alienating and rigid. The drag show is a fantasy that obscures the multiplicity of Singaporean identities.

In Singapore I believe that alternatives can be found in the typologies of the shophouse, the kampong, and the tropical megacity projects proposed by Tay Kheng Soon. Each of these building types has been disregarded in favor of the masculinist glass styles and forms explored in this paper. They also have in common a consideration of a multitude of human senses in their use and design. They pay attention to "life between buildings" and are appropriate for the local tropical climate and environmental concerns (Gehl 2011). These architectures are plural with multiple iterations and an emphasis on touch and experience rather than the ocularcentric use of glass in the designs discussed earlier. While I cannot go into a deep history and visual analysis of these buildings here, a brief sketch will suffice to show the value of this juxtaposition and the need for further research in geography on local building designs and spaces with a feminist psychoanalytic perspective.

The Chinese or Peranakan shophouse is a typically two- or three-story building that provides space for commercial activities on the ground floor and residential space above. They are especially long and narrow so as to facilitate the flow of cooler air in hot and humid weather. This design also allows for greater density in urban environments especially when facing a major road or river for convenient transportation access. The traditional "five-foot way" is a five-foot setback covered by an overhang that protects pedestrians from sun and rain and is conducive to the creation of cooling breezes. The shophouse was extremely common in Singapore but has only been partially preserved in a few select districts and nearly none of them maintain the same function.

The kampong (or compound) house is a building type indigenous to the Malay peninsula and the archipelagoes of Southeast Asia. It is made of natural materials and found in more rural village settings. The steep and wide pitched roof provides shade and waterproofing from the hot sun and heavy downpours of the tropics. The elevated ground level protects from flooding and aids in temperature control (Lim 1987). People living in these types of buildings and communities in Singapore were forcibly removed to live in government-built modernist concrete high-rises (Loh 2013).

Singaporean architect Tay Kheng Soon has actively been involved in promoting a countermodern architecture that is based in the lOcal conditions of environment and design. Through his work with the Singapore Planning and Urban Research (SPUR) Group, the Singapore Institute of Architects (SIA), and his own private practice, Akitek Tenggara, and as a faculty member at the National University of Singapore, he has built and proposed multiple projects, development guides, and master plans that challenge the tenets of state-directed urban development. The most striking example of this work is his development guide plan for Kampong Bugis (a relatively central area of Singapore). The idea behind this proposal was to imitate the rainforest by having multilayered buildings to improve pedestrian circulation and ameliorate the ambient temperature. Additional shading and climate control features included a "canopy" on the tops of tall buildings and vertical landscaping to provide natural protection from the sun and cleaner air. This proposal was rejected by the government in favor of one produced by its own architects in the Urban Redevelopment Authority (Tay 1989).

Glass architecture in Singapore responds to the ocularcentrism of patriarchal systems of economics, politics, and culture that produce it. These spaces of masculine design perform the symbolic order of Singaporean identity as determined by the elites. Like in psychoanalytic practice, further work is necessary to peel back these layers of imaginary identity in search of possible (and latent) alternatives—a worthy task for human geographers and architectural historians.

Notes

1. The amusement ride has been unsuccessful financially and went into receivership in 2013; it also now offers rides including dinner from SG$269 per couple.
2. There was also a limited edition Lego model made for sale in Asian markets only.

Works Cited

Aripin, Nurul A. 2013. "New Downtown Line MRT Service Hit by Second Breakdown within a Week." *Yahoo Newsroom Singapore*, December 27. Accessed March 16, 2016. https://sg.news.yahoo.com/new-downtown-line-mrt-service-hit-by-second-breakdown-within-a-week-183532725.html.

Nathan F. Bullock

BBC News. 2013. "Why Does Singapore Top So Many Tables?" October 24. Accessed December 21, 2015. http://www.bbc.com/news/world-asia-24428567.

Bingham-Hall, Patrick. 2012. *A Guide to 21st Century Singapore Architecture*. Singapore: Pesaro Publishing.

Bullock, Nathan. 2014. "Lacan on Urban Development and National Identity in a Global City: Integrated Resorts in Singapore." *Singapore Journal of Tropical Geography* 35 (2): 213–27.

Butler, Judith. 2011. *Bodies That Matter: On the Discursive Limits of Sex*. New York: Routledge.

Chang, Tou Chuang. 2000. "Renaissance Revisited: Singapore as a 'Global City for the Arts.'" *International Journal of Urban and Regional Research* 24 (4): 818–31.

Channel NewsAsia. 2015. "'Multiple Power Trips' Detected an Hour before MRT Service Disruption: SMRT." July 8. Accessed March 16, 2016. http://www.channelnewsasia.com /news/singapore/multiple-power-trips-detected-an-hour-before-mrt-service-disrupt -8241134.

Chua, Lynette J. 2003. "Saying No: Sections 377 and 377A of the Penal Code." *Singapore Journal of Legal Studies*, July, 209–61.

Colombo, Jesse. 2014. "It's Not a Bubble until It's Officially Denied, Singapore Edition." *Forbes*, January 16. Accessed March 16, 2016. http://www.forbes.com/sites /jessecolombo/2014/01/16/its-not-a-bubble-until-its-officially-denied-singapore-edition /#6b704513393d.

Eisinger, Peter. 2000. "The Politics of Bread and Circuses: Building the City for the Visitor Class." *Urban Affairs Review* 35 (3): 316–33.

Elsheshtawy, Yasser. 2008. "Navigating the Spectacle: Landscapes of Consumption in Dubai." *Architectural Theory Review* 13 (2): 164–78.

Esplanade. 2015. "Architecture and Building Design." Accessed December 22, 2015. https:// www.esplanade.com/about-us/architecture-and-building-design.

Gallezo-Estuara, Krisana. 2013. "Singapore Flyer Placed under Receivership: What Went Wrong?" *Singapore Business Review*, June 5. Accessed December 22, 2015. http:// sbr.com.sg/hotels-tourism/exclusive/singapore-flyer-placed-under-receivership -what-went-wrong.

Gehl, Jan. 2011. *Life between Buildings: Using Public Space*. Washington DC: Island Press.

Government of Singapore. 2015. "What Is Total Defence." Accessed December 21, 2015. http:// www.mindef.gov.sg/imindef/mindef_websites/topics/totaldefence/about_us/what _is_td.html#.VnhhNb__r4l.

Gwee, Li Sui. 2016. "Do You Speak Singlish?" *New York Times*, May 13. Accessed May 14, 2016. http://www.nytimes.com/2016/05/14/opinion/do-you-speak-singlish.html?_r=0.

Huang, Shirlena, and Brenda S. A. Yeoh, eds. 2008. "Heterosexualities and the Global(iz-ing) City in Asia." Special issue, *Asian Studies Review* 32 (1).

Jones, Amelia. 2000. "Paul McCarthy's *Inside Out* Body and the Desublimation of Mascu-linity." In *Paul McCarthy*, edited by Lisa Philips and Dan Cameron, 125–212. Ostfildern, Germany: Hatje Cantz Publishers.

Kingsbury, Paul, and Steve Pile, eds. 2014. *Psychoanalytic Geographies.* Farnham, UK: Ashgate.

Kong, Lily. 2012. "Ambitions of a Global City: Arts, Culture and Creative Economy in 'Post-Crisis' Singapore." *International Journal of Cultural Policy* 18 (3): 279–94.

Lim, Jee Yuan. 1987. *The Malay House: Rediscovering Malaysia's Indigenous Shelter System.* Penang, Malaysia: Institut Masyarakat.

Loh, Kah Seng. 2013. *Squatters into Citizens: The 1961 Bukit Ho Swee Fire and the Making of Modern Singapore.* Singapore: National University of Singapore Press.

Savio Hook, Maria Teresa, and Salman Akhtar, eds. 2007. *The Geography of Meanings: Psychoanalytic Perspectives on Place, Space, Land, and Dislocation.* London: Interna-tional Psychoanalytic Association.

Singapore Flyer. 2015. "Premium Sky Dining Flight." Accessed December 22, 2015. http://www.singaporeflyer.com/unique-experiences/full-butler-sky-dining/.

Sioh, Maureen. 2014. "Manicheism Delirium: Desire and Disavowal in the Libidinal Economy of an Emerging Economy." *Third World Quarterly* 35 (7): 1162–78.

Sklair, Leslie. 2010. "Iconic Architecture and the Culture-Ideology of Consumerism." *Theory, Culture and Society* 27 (5): 135–59.

Stevenson, Alexandra. 2015. "A High-End Property Collapse in Singapore." *New York Times*, February 17. Accessed March 16, 2016. http://www.nytimes.com/2015/02/18/realestate/a-high-end-property-collapse-in-singapore.html?_r=0.

Tadiar, Neferti X. M. 1998. "Sexual Economies in the Asia-Pacific Community." In *What's in a Rim?*, edited by Arif Dirlik, 219–48. 2nd ed. Lanham MD: Rowman & Littlefield.

Tay, Kheng Soon. 1989. *Mega-cities in the Tropics: Towards an Architectural Agenda for the Future.* Singapore: Institute of Southeast Asian Studies.

———. 2013. *Review of Urbanism, Modern Architecture, and Housing: 50 Years of SIA, 1963–2013.* Singapore: Singapore Institute of Architects.

Williams, Richard. 2013. *Sex and Buildings.* London: Reaktion Books.

Yap, Erica X. Y. 2012. "Wheels of Fame and Fortune: The Travels of the Singapore Flyer." *Urban Studies* 49 (13): 2839–52.

Yeoh, Brenda S. A. 2005. "The Global Cultural City? Spatial Imagineering and Politics in the (Multi)cultural Marketplaces of South-east Asia." *Urban Studies* 42 (5–6): 945–58.

Nathan F. Bullock

10 City Life

Glorification, Desire, and the Unconscious Size Fetish

Adam Okulicz-Kozaryn and Rubia R. Valente

In this chapter we conduct a psychoanalysis of the city, analyzing how people, propelled by unconscious size fetish, prefer city life to towns or rural areas, where they may be much happier (Okulicz-Kozaryn 2015).[1] The use of psychoanalysis is appropriate to understanding people's attraction to the metropolis because the city, after all, is a state of mind (Park 1915). When discussing the allure of cities, Park (1915) argued that motives derive from "something more fundamental and primitive" that contributes to attracting people from the security of their homes in small towns into the big, booming confusion and excitement of city life. The importance of understanding this process is even more relevant today as the globe is rapidly urbanizing: its cities are swelling and their buildings are being erected beyond what is imaginable.

The lure to great cities is due in part to people's desire for power and status: people who live in a city often have a feeling of superiority over those relegated to living in the outskirts of town or rural areas. City dwellers desire such elevated status and aspire to work in the tallest towers. An unconscious size fetish is therefore at play: the city is desired because of the power and prestige represented by its size. The city makes urbanites feel more powerful and successful. Concurrently, shame and guilt are also part of the city: glowing towers stand next to working-class row houses; gentrification is pushing out the working class and poor. The city is thus full of inequalities and riven with a range of social desires. The tendency is that the greater the city, the greater the inequality and the size fetish. Size fetish emerges from imbalance—urban-rural and within-urban inequalities among people and the built environment—and it remains largely unconscious. People do not really understand their attraction to the city, which is often attributed to amenities, opportunities, and quality of life. Consumers explain conspicuous consumption in a similar way: it's the craftsmanship, attention to detail, and high quality of the product that makes them buy it. Yet living in the city and buying consumer goods are mostly about dominance-subjugation, demonstrating that by possessing something, one is superior to others.

Another force propelling urbanization is the accumulation drive (see chapters 8 and 11). Different than desire, which is impelled by consumption, drive involves the ultimate compulsion to repeat unceasingly and accumulate for the sake of accumulation (Kapoor 2015). The expansion of capital generated by such drive is often referred to as the "grow or die" (GOD) imperative (Schweickart 2009; Kallis 2011).[2] As people move to the cities and accumulate capital endlessly, they are instrumental in the growth of cities. The bigger the city, the more the average citizen accumulates, produces, and consumes, whether it is goods, resources, or ideas (Bettencourt et al. 2007). Interestingly, when cities grow, they magnify the best and the worst of their residents by a factor of 1.15, that is, when the size of a city doubles, the rate of everything in the city increases by 15 percent. This includes positive indicators such as gross domestic product, wages, patents, and number of educational and research institutions but also negative factors such as crime, diseases, and traffic congestions (Bliss 2014; Bettencourt et al. 2010; Bettencourt and West 2010; Bettencourt et al. 2007).

Urbanization of the world is for the most part a new phenomenon. In 1950 only 30 percent of the world population lived in urban areas, but by 2050 this number is estimated to be 80 percent (Bettencourt and West 2010). Yet most people do not realize why they urbanize—and our contention is that an unconscious size fetish and a city desire and glorification lure people.[3] Academics manifest these phenomena in their writing (Jacobs 1970, 1985, 1993; Glaeser 2011). Jacobs (1970), for instance, glorifies the city and claims that cities play an essential role in the process of economic development.

Adam Okulicz-Kozaryn and Rubia R. Valente

Moreover, she argues that cities ultimately create a healthy global economy. Glaeser's (2011) book title says it all: *Triumph of the City: How Our Greatest Invention Makes Us Richer, Smarter, Greener, Healthier, and Happier*. The "greatest invention" of course is the city. Thus, while scholars write books of worship to glorified cities, common people manifest their unconscious size fetish and desire for cities in their actions through mass urbanization.

In what follows, we start with a brief overview of the notion of freedom as it applies to urbanization and the development of the city. Then, we turn to psychoanalysis and size fetish in the city. Finally, we discuss the implications for specific cities.

The City and Freedom: Illusion of Freedom and Dream Factory

One of the fundamental contrasts between rural, small towns and metropolitan areas relates to the increased perception of freedom experienced in cities (Okulicz-Kozaryn 2015). The small-town sense of community, with intimate face-to-face personal contact and neighborliness, is replaced by impersonal and tenuous ties in the cities (Wirth 1938). Concurrently, the cities' inherent variety of people, occupations, opinions, and interests generates intellectual disputes that lead to broader and freer judgment and a greater inclination to and appreciation of new thoughts, manners, and ideas (Weber 1899). Whereas rural, small towns tend to favor more conservative views, cities favor liberal thinking and tend to be more progressive and accommodating. In recent decades, cities have become an oasis of freedom for people of color, women, LGBTQ people, and any subjugated or nonconformist types (Fischer 1982). An old saying, "City air makes [people] free" (Park, Burgess, and McKenzie 1984, 12), remains relevant today.

The city is also a dream factory, where most dreams emerge from an unconscious size fetish (Pile 2005a). City dreams often capture the imaginary of power, dominance, success, wealth, and social status. Concretely, they manifest as aspirations of having an office space at the Empire State Building or owning an apartment at 432 Park Avenue. Other urban dreams also stem from size fetish—materializing into the pursuit of intellectual superiority, physical perfection, and aesthetic beauty.

These dreams can be achieved, or at least felt, by simply living in a great city, or better yet, experiencing life at its very core. Cities foster dreams and fantasies of status and prestige (see chapter 9). Dreams often boil down to superfluous accumulation of money and goods. A notable example is conspicuous and wasteful acts of consumption, typically exercised to flaunt prosperity and success (Veblen and Banta 2009). Consumption dreams are instigated by pervasive billboards and shopping windows (Pile 2005a), while marketing campaigns incite and commoditize dreams for the masses (Roberts 2011).

The city is also a money-making machine. Modern cities were started by capitalists who were trying to squeeze as many workers as possible near their factories with the purpose of maximizing their profits (Engels 1987). The urbanite is but a tiny cog in the enormous machine called city.[4] Incidentally, the industrialization period that gave rise to the modern city has been labeled the "machine age." Currently, we are witnessing the "second machine age," during which the steam engine is being replaced by the computer (Brynjolfsson and McAfee 2014). Urban sweatshops were moved to Asia and replaced by sanitized towers. The conditions of the working class, however, remain the same: workers are still squeezed in tiny spaces and labor long hours. Psychoanalytically, the contemporary city is a result of the old accumulation drive and new consumerist desire. Many urbanists (Jacobs 1993; Zukin 2009) and psychoanalysts (Pile 2005a) tend to romanticize city life. City dreams are elusive, however. Since most urbanites do not fulfil their ultimate dreams, fantasizing may lead to depression, frustration, and disappointment (Oettingen, Mayer, and Portnow 2016). More fundamentally, city dreaming is an illusion, an escape from the brutal reality of urban life. Urbanites are therefore easy prey to this delusion and do not realize that they are no longer free.

The city is also antithetical to sensuousness or the liberation of senses (Marcuse 2015). Simmel (2005) observed that the city destroys sensuousness by overloading the senses and leading to a blasé attitude. In the city, sensuousness is obliterated by excess information (e.g., advertisements), noise, light, and air pollution. Thus, industrialization and labor specialization

Adam Okulicz-Kozaryn and Rubia R. Valente

exemplified in cities can extinguish spontaneity and joy (Park 1915; Park, Burgess, and McKenzie 1984; in contrast, see chapter 7 in this volume).

Size Fetish

If city life subjugates its people to capitalism, entrapping them in city dreams and in a false sense of freedom, one may ask, "Why are people still attracted to the city?" The lure to great cities is in part a result of unconscious size fetish—an inanimate object of worship. For Sigmund Freud (1927), the fetish is a form of substitution for the male genitalia. Fetishism emerged from *verleugnung*, or "disavowal," a reaction caused by psychological emasculation or castration (Freud 1929). The young male experiences shock upon discovering the differences between male and female genital anatomy and disavows it. Thus, disavowal denotes "a specific mode of defense which consists in the subject's refusing to recognize the reality of a traumatic perception" (Laplanche and Pontalis 1974, 118; see also chapter 3 in this volume). In the city, urbanites (except capitalists) do not have actual power, and hence, they may fetishize the city to disavow their subjugated status.[5] Like Freud's (1927) patients, urbanites seem to be satisfied with their fetish and even praise it. One of Freud's patients had as fetish the luminous shine on a nose; for urbanites, the fetish is often the luminous shine of city towers (see chapter 9).

How does the unconscious size fetish externalize and materialize in the city? A delusional feeling of fulfillment and success can be felt in the city, which is clearly exemplified by powerful people (e.g., Bill Clinton, Oprah, Pope Francis) whose presence resonates across the city space; fulfillment and success is felt just by being spatially close to the powerful.[6] Famous and successful people seem to shine with their power; it feels empowering to be close to them because of the association of oneself with that power. This energy, however, seems to stem from common people in the first place, as powerful people nurture their energy from other people's admiration. Some of this process may be situational. If one meets a person and does not know that person's status or value, there is less allure between them. For instance, in university settings, there is a power distance between professors and students. During lectures, professors shine and glow with charismatic power, but when they leave the classroom to perform ordinary tasks, such as buying coffee at a Starbucks (where students might congregate or work), there may be a lower synergetic difference (although power inequalities still remain). Cities and their towers are less situational; their status and values are fixed in one place; they tend to consistently glow with energy and power. Being spatially close to the city, especially in its core, has a similar effect to meeting a celebrity; it creates feelings of awe, excitement, even ecstasy. Approaching the city—seeing its skyscrapers dominating the horizon and its area spreading as far as the eye can see—one feels an excitement similar to the excitement one feels when approaching a powerful person. There is a (delusional) fulfillment in it.

Size fetish can be experienced as *jouissance*, or enjoyment as excess. There is a certain euphoric joy to be had in being part of an urban behemoth (see chapters 3, 6, 7, and 8). Pleasure stems from the hoarding and profit-making integral to the development of urban capital accumulation. And such enjoyment is materialized in feelings of pride and superiority common to city dwellers (Martinson 2000; Balducci and Checchi 2009). Citizens of New York, Toronto, Milan, and Beijing are consistently proud of their cities, irrespective of their living conditions (in terms of housing, income, education, or health status) or indicators of quality of urban life (Balducci and Checchi 2009). Their perception is arguably shaped by an unconscious size fetish: despite not always satisfactory urban life conditions, they feel proud of living in "their" great cities.

What do urbanites disavow? Their own limitations, notably their lack of power. They deny their smallness and insignificance, and they fetishize city size as a substitute for their own lack of power. A sense of empowerment and an aversion to lack of power coexist in the urbanite's mind, being a tiny cog in the city machine. The problem is that the power derived from the city size is illusory, or rather delusional—just like the power derived from working for a large corporation. City dwellers derive power from the city's size and wealth as a substitute for their own relative insignificance. Part of the illusion is the belief that one will achieve success. This belief is

Adam Okulicz-Kozaryn and Rubia R. Valente

especially vivid in the United States. Americans are famous for disavowing inequalities, believing they will eventually fulfill (the fallacy of) the American Dream (Corak 2013, 2011, 2004).

What do urbanites disavow collectively? City problems, notably poverty (Jargowsky 1997). These problems are hidden in the shadows of glowing city towers. The common imaginary of cities like New York, Tokyo, and London is their spectacular skyscrapers, status, and glamour, and not their social problems, such as inequality or homelessness. If anything, city problems, by means of contrast, may amplify city greatness: towers shine brighter against working slums, while wealth is felt more strongly against the background of poverty (Firebaugh and Schroeder 2009).[7]

Cities attract people, partly because many people strive for power and status. Size fetish is actually similar to Marxian commodity fetishism or domination by things (Marx 2010). It is as if the big size of a city has intrinsic value and bestows its value on urbanites. Big cities have long been centers of broadly understood power (economic, political, and cultural), and if anything, the prominence of cities has been increasing recently (Khanna 2016; Hanson 2015). Therefore, going to the city in search of power seems to make sense. For instance, people often boast about living in Washington DC because they can meet powerful people, and hence feel powerful by association. Most common global power centers are to be found in cities. The fashion center, for example, is in New York or Milan, the second largest city in Italy. The entertainment centers of the world are Los Angeles and Las Vegas (both the largest cities in their respective states). Fundamentally, people seem to embrace large cities in a similar way. They treasure status-conferring or status-signaling things like SUVs, McMansions, and other grandiose material possessions;[8] size often confers or suggests potential power, prestige, strength, success, prosperity. Not surprisingly New Yorkers are proud to be New Yorkers (Balducci and Checchi 2009). Similar pride is found in other countries' largest cities. Countries often compete to boast the world's tallest buildings, while their people compete for space in such buildings. For example, the satisfaction of having an office at the Empire State Building in New York City likely elicits a sense of omnipotence, power, and superiority. Figure 12 better exemplifies this idea. Imagine having an office suite at One World Trade Center, the tallest skyscraper in the Western Hemisphere. This rationale can extend to one's desire to live in cities—isn't it a status symbol to live in Manhattan or in San Francisco?

The tower is, in Freudian terms, a gigantic phallus. In psychoanalysis, the "Phallus" is a symbol of authority and omnipotence (as well as castration; see Kapoor 2014), and arguably, so are city towers.[9] Psychoanalysis sees the unconscious manifested in slippages of language or "bloopers" (Kapoor 2014). For example, in a Republican presidential debate after being challenged by Senator Marco Rubio about the small size of his hands, businessman Donald Trump confidently reassured that the insinuation about the size of his manhood was false: "And he referred to my hand, if they're small, something else must be small, I guarantee you there's no problem." It would certainly be unfitting for the owner and builder of so many great towers to have a small or even average manhood. Although, unconsciously, Trump might indeed be compensating for something he feels insecure about. On September 11, 2001, when the North and South Towers of the World Trade Center came down, Donald Trump was quick to tell a radio interviewer that his seventy-one-story building at 40 Wall Street was now the tallest tower in downtown Manhattan (Trump 2001).

Buildings like One World Trade Center (shown in fig. 12) may make economic sense because people are often willing to pay to have access to its space because of their size fetish. In general, large-scale towers are much more visually impressive than low buildings or underground construction; towers are phallus-like and underground constructions are womb-like. What Thoreau wrote about pyramids, an ancient version of urban towers, is instructive here: "As for the Pyramids, there is nothing to wonder at in them so much as the fact that so many men could be found degraded enough to spend their lives constructing a tomb for some ambitious booby, whom it would have been wiser and manlier to have drowned in the Nile, and then given his body to the dogs . . . whether the building be an Egyptian temple or the United States Bank. It *costs more than it comes to.* The

Adam Okulicz-Kozaryn and Rubia R. Valente

Fig. 12. One World Trade Center, New York. Photo by Rubia R. Valente, July 27, 2015.

mainspring is *vanity*" (Thoreau 1995, 37–38; emphasis added).[10] Human obsession with towers is ancient. The Tower of Babel in the Book of Genesis of the Tanakh (Hebrew Bible) was also about power. Humans tried to organize themselves and become more powerful, so they built a city and erected a tower: "Come, let us build ourselves a city, with a tower that reaches to the heavens, so that we may make a name for ourselves" (Gen. 11; New International Version).

When first meeting people from a big city, one often hears pride in their voices as they announce that they are from London, New York, São Paulo, Shanghai, or some other great city; their face glows and their eyes are wide open. Psychoanalytically, they are experiencing *jouissance*. Conversely, when meeting people from a little town, one may notice an apologetic tone in their voices. To illustrate, imagine a person from New York meeting a person from rural southern New Jersey. Figure 13 shows some possible facial expressions displayed at this hypothetical meeting. On the far left, we see the ecstatic, pleasant, and proud look of a New Yorker, while on the far right, the embarrassed, guilty look of a person from rural southern New Jersey. The urbanite feels in many ways adored and admired by the village dweller, who seems to be enchanted by the urbanite's city glow. Obviously, these illustrations are exaggerations, as most people try to conceal their emotions.

In addition to feeling pride for place of living, urbanites often feel superior to people from smaller areas (Martinson 2000). This phenomenon stems from our human identity formation and stability; we not only form our identity through others but achieve a deluded sense of unity and stability by projecting or displacing our inadequacies onto others. This is exemplified by how some Americans look down on Mexicans, Russians look down on Ukrainians, New Yorkers look down on Kentuckians, Shanghainese look down on Nanjingers, Varsovians look down on Lublinites, and so forth. In addition to the inherent bias that urbanites might feel toward rural folk, urbanites' sense of belonging is usually associated with the city rather than their country of origin, such that a New Yorker would rather ascribe to

Adam Okulicz-Kozaryn and Rubia R. Valente

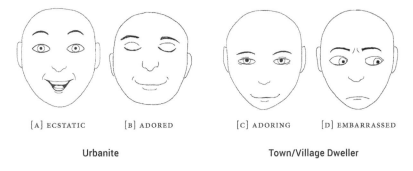

[A] ECSTATIC   [B] ADORED   [C] ADORING   [D] EMBARRASSED

Urbanite   Town/Village Dweller

Fig. 13. Emotional facial expressions of urbanites versus small-town residents. Barry Langdon-Lassagne, Wikimedia Commons.

being from "the Big Apple" than from the United States. Similarly, we've heard several accounts of people who live in Amsterdam (the largest city in the Netherlands) and think that "the Netherlands is Amsterdam" and of people who live in São Paulo (the largest city in Brazil) and often boast that São Paulo is Brazil's beating heart.

In the movie *Gladiator*, the city of Rome is equated with power; it is the seat of the Roman Empire. Rome is large in size with (even in those days) a massive population, an enormous Coliseum, and other grandiose monuments, like the Pantheon, the Roman Forum, and Circus Maximus. The substantial size of these buildings is what makes one feel power in Rome. Incidentally, sizable ancient monuments, like Rome's Coliseum, are in many ways similar to the towers of today, especially the tallest ones, like the Empire State Building or One World Trade Center. Rome was an imperial city, as are today's "greatest" cities, like New York, London, and Shanghai. In addition, Rome was the epicenter of an empire that controlled a lot of land and extracted rents from many workers. Similarly, the great cities of today are the command post of corporate empires that extract rents from their workers, often in a predatory fashion. According to Urry (2007, 137), "The transformation of many cities into places of spectacle is one of the most distinctive features of the contemporary world."

Sanguisuge City

Capital is dead labor, which, vampire-like, lives only by sucking
living labor, and lives the more, the more labor it sucks.

KARL MARX, *Capital*

The unconscious size fetish urbanites have for the city can have serious
implications. The allure of the city and the dreams people have of success or
even glory in the city blindfold urbanites to the reality: the city is actually
draining their lives. Just as in capitalism's spatial materialization, the city
offers an illusion of freedom and justifies its existence with the very idea
of freedom. It offers some freedom but also takes away freedom—just as
capitalists offer some money to their workers in the form of salaries while
keeping millions in profits from their work. People fall prey to the capitalistic profit factory that is the city. Ironically, in the process their lives
seem more exciting and, in a way, fuller. Masochistic city living is exciting
(*jouissance*)—and it is not really, or not only, about the goal or fulfillment
of the desire, but also about the very process of striving.

The city is in a way Machiavellian. It appears welcoming and promising,
but it is deceitful; it absorbs one's psychic and physical energies. Yet most
people do not fight against this paradigm, as if they are hypnotized by the
city. In fact, urbanites do look very much as if they are hypnotized, like
automatons following a daily routine, being sucked in by swelling met-
ros. Urbanites are often worn down, blasé, or Machiavellian themselves—
aggressive mercenaries of the capital that creates and controls the city.

The city has many striking similarities to the folklore character of a vampire. Both are seductive, attractive, exciting. Yet what they offer is merely
a feeling or promise of success and power. They seduce with promise but
rarely confer. Both are doing blood work (sucking up energy) and dream
work (inducing desire; Pile 2005a). What is often overlooked is that the city
is immortal, just like vampires or capital. Nations disappear, companies
disappear, but cities never do (West 2011). They may decline like Detroit,
Michigan, or Camden, New Jersey, but they will never completely die;

Adam Okulicz-Kozaryn and Rubia R. Valente

sooner or later they will be back on top. Yet metaphorically speaking, like vampires, cities are never fully alive; they are full of ghosts of the past that still haunt the present, and when urbanites exit their private lairs and enter the urban social realm, especially at night, they may turn into werewolves (Pile 2005b). In short, the city provides an environment antithetical to life.[11]

It is important to point out the negative side of city life not only because urbanists glorify the city (Glaeser 2011, 2014), but because many scholars, including psychoanalysts, tend to paint an overly positive picture of the city (Meyer 2013; Fischer 1973, 1972; Veenhoven 1994; Pile 2005a, 2005b). Harvey (e.g., 2012) is a notable exception. He argues, as this chapter does, that capital is intrinsically related to urbanization. And we agree with Harvey's call: we need to focus on cities rather than factories as the prime sites of exploitation.

Character Structure

The last two sections address differences across cities. A case is made that while cities can clearly differ in just about anything, they have the same character structure. They all have size fetish and vampire-like qualities, and their negative effects increase proportionally with geographical size and population density.

Many vices are most pronounced in the most urbanized regions, particularly in the coastal United States.[12] It has been long recognized that vice and city are correlated (Park 1915; Park, Burgess, and McKenzie 1984; Wirth 1938). Personality maps from Richard Florida's (2008) Who's Your City? show that the majority of people with neurosis live in and around New York City, the largest American metropolis, and neurosis is also present in much of the Bos-Wash megalopolis (i.e., the urban area from Boston to Washington DC). Neurosis, like the city, isolates. As Henry Thoreau (1995) so well said, "City life is millions of people being lonesome together."

We are strangers to ourselves (Wilson 2009). We do not have direct access to our unconscious and need psychoanalysis to help us understand ourselves. Given the fast pace of city life and the multiplicity of stimuli fighting for attention, urbanites have little chance for introspection. Given the inherent alienation of city life and the importance of deep social ties to understanding ourselves—to help us psychoanalyze ourselves—we are arguably much more strangers to ourselves in the city environment than we are anywhere else.

While each city might have developed its own character organically or spontaneously, today it seems that cities are no longer developing but losing their character. Cities are becoming more alike. Housing and food are good examples. Both are vital to the character of a place but are now largely mass-produced in a few capitalistic profit-seeking factories, in a way that fakes character and essence in order to sell better. For instance, just a few food factories produce most of the meat for the entire United States (Kenner 2008), and this meat, along with other food products, is usually delivered by food distribution giants US Foods and Sysco to a phantasmagoria of "lOcal" and "authentic" restaurants that just name the same food differently to fake unique character. Likewise, housing is mass-produced in the spirit of Le Corbusier and then sprinkled with lOcal elements to forge some idiosyncrasy:

We must create the mass-production spirit.
The spirit of constructing mass-production houses.
The spirit of living in mass-production houses.
The spirit of conceiving mass-production houses. (Le Corbusier 1985, 228)

Mass-production houses are easily seen from an airplane approaching newer cities like Dallas or Las Vegas. Older cities, built during an earlier stage of capitalism, are different. Now, however, even older downtowns are made of mass-production skyscrapers that tend to swallow larger and larger swaths of land. Downtown towers are all essentially the same (if you strip the cookie-cutter design that fakes character). The downtowns of Chicago, London, New York City, and the other largest cities still have some character in the façades of their older buildings. Yet this character

Adam Okulicz-Kozaryn and Rubia R. Valente

is dying with the invasion of Starbucks, H&M, and Apple (Zukin 2009). Increasingly, what remains are precious historic markers that cannot be reproduced anymore. Thus, the city is in many ways a museum of character; its unique identity and charm are relics of the past. Global capitalist accumulation is producing more uniformity, not just through this process of McDonaldization, but also through the production of urban poverty in the form of slums and inner-city ghettos—now a pervasive feature of all large "global" cities.

Dallas, Philadelphia, and New York City

In this section we simply describe cities we know best.

I (AOK) grew up in suburbs and relatively small metropolitan Poznan, Poland, which has a population of about one million. I have spent half of my adult life in the Dallas metropolitan area, which has a population of about six million, with mixed feelings. As in any big city (though Dallas has relatively low density), I felt power, pride, even accomplishment just by being there. I also felt significantly more "free." There was something very attractive about the city; it felt like a better place than Poznan (and other similar, smaller places)—more glObal, more developed, like "progress" or "success." I very much appreciated the diversity and energy that Dallas offered. One great thing about American cities, especially perhaps those more to the West, is that they offer a great deal of freedom, even some kind of lightness, as if less gravity were there. Perhaps, as Pile (2005a, b) argues, there are fewer ghosts of the past haunting the present. Dallas is more modern; it is not under the weight of history; it is younger and more spontaneous. Yet it is fake, as if manufactured by aliens and dumped on the face of earth with its cookie-cutter housing and ocean of concrete and asphalt. Now I live in the Philadelphia metropolitan area, and I see that it is even more "energetic" and "fast-paced" than Dallas. People think and act faster than they do in Dallas. Yet Philadelphia is also dirtier and somewhat sad or even depressing. Perhaps what I feel is the melancholia that old cities carry (Pile 2005b).

I (RRV) have spent half of my life in Dallas and share some of the same positive feeling toward Dallas as Adam does. Being born in an "interior" city named Campinas (with a population of about one million) in the state of São Paulo, Brazil, I remember feeling ecstatic when my family moved to Dallas. I certainly felt pride and had many city dreams. Last year my husband and I were in the academic job market, and combined, we were fortunate to have more than a dozen offers to choose from. We analyzed each of the offers we received, of course, but the cities where these jobs were located played a significant role in our decision. Although the offer we finally accepted included by far the best salary and employer benefits, the job's location in New York City played a significant role in our decision-making process. We chose to live in White Plains, however, a small town in the suburbs, just close enough that we could easily commute and enjoy the city if we wanted to and far enough away to have a better quality of life. All our friends in Dallas were in awe (as visualized in fig. 13) when they learned that we were moving to New York City; it was quite interesting to watch their reactions, as if Dallas became a small town when compared to NYC.

Conclusion

A key human desire, at least in capitalism (Fromm 1992), is to be superior to others. This desire can be stronger than one's desire to be happy. Indeed, both cities and capitalism promise power and success but rarely deliver them; at the same time, they contribute to unhappiness in many ways (Lane 2000; Okulicz-Kozaryn, Holmes, and Avery 2014; Easterlin 2009). Psychoanalytically, cities (like capitalism) are built by an accumulation drive and thrive on consumption desire, leading to *jouissance* rather than (impossible) happiness or human flourishing.

City living can be masochistic in a way; it gives pleasure and pain, and perhaps some of that pleasure comes from pain (i.e., *jouissance*). City living can overload the senses (Simmel 2005; Lederbogen et al. 2011), while providing a certain kind of pleasure or joy, which slowly kills its residents. Approaching a city can be exciting. Seeing towers rising over the horizon, while energizing to some, can also confer the illusion of power and success.

Adam Okulicz-Kozaryn and Rubia R. Valente

Yet the city is always defective: poverty lives alongside gentrification and luxury (this is the Real of the city). Much of urban planning and politics centers on fixing cities, and it is believed that cities can be fixed. But perhaps, like capitalism, cities cannot be fixed, and in the long run they might create more problems than advantages.[13]

As cities continue to grow, these problems will magnify and become even worse. Capitalism, combined with rapid urbanization and commercialization of space, contributes to making the city more defective. In addition, cities are losing their character. They are becoming homogenized just like the food we consume (Kenner 2008). Most downtowns of any large American city look the same: there are towers—some taller, some shorter—often next to old buildings that will be soon replaced by towers without character or commercial malls filled with Apple, H&M, or other giant corporate stores.

Seemingly, city dwellers are happier than small area dwellers—just like the fetishist is happy with her fetish (Freud 1927). Yet city happiness is artificial. An urbanite might display a smile, or even show pride in her face, yet she is typically unhappy; it is *jouissance* she experiences, not human flourishing (Okulicz-Kozaryn 2015). The problem is that a poor rural person may think that the urbanite's happiness is real, and when she migrates to a city searching for that feeling, she will often end up feeling miserable too. In fact, many stories in the daily news, novels, or movies illustrate this scenario. A person is born and raised in a small place but sometime in her teens wants to seek better opportunities and prove herself; she wants to climb up the social ladder. She then moves to a large city. It might be some time before she realizes the city fetish; most will never fully understand that they were driven to the city lights because of the desire for the city (and size fetish).

Cities, like the capitalism that they embody, lure people by exploiting their passions. Cities promise happiness but deliver only momentary enjoyment and pleasure (e.g., shopping). Ironically, the city exudes pride and power. Perhaps the urban promise of success, pride, power, and superiority is the key psychoanalytic explanation of mass urbanization, despite urbanites being unhappy (Okulicz-Kozaryn 2015). When asked whether they would prefer to live in a world where (a) they make $100,000 and others make $50,000 or (b) they make $150,000 and others make $200,000, most people chose option (a). That is, they would prefer to make less money as long as they make more than others around them (Layard 2005; Scitovsky 1976; Frank 2012). There is a saying: "The rich man is the one who makes more than the husband of his wife's sister." We tend to compare ourselves to others all the time, and many people want to be better than (i.e., envy) others.

For Freud (1930), civilization is based on the permanent subjugation of human instincts, and the city is the cradle of civilization.[14] Yet somehow such subjugation goes unnoticed. To be sure, the city frees us in some ways, but it also subjugates us in the form of longer labor, exploitation, and alienation (Rosenthal and Strange 2002, 2003). Consider here some anecdotal evidence: Most people feel genuinely freer and more at ease in a small town, in a village, and especially in the wilderness. Yet somehow the allure and appeal of city affluence and size trap us: "Erotic energy of the Life Instincts cannot be freed under the dehumanizing conditions of profitable affluence" (Marcuse 2015, xxxiii).

Civilization, predominantly through the means of urbanization, has dramatically distorted the relationship between human and nature. The city is a place where dominance and subjugation are greatest. Nowhere else is inequality so pronounced and so spatially close. Millionaires and beggars live next to each other, bump into each other in public spaces, yet live in opposite worlds. Psychoanalytically, they live on the opposite poles of the dominance-subjugation continuum. Cities and their alluring towers provide us with spectacle, yet disavow their patriarchal and imperialistic structures (see chapter 9). Not only is capital centered in the city, but often so is capitalism's most pernicious forms (e.g., monopolistic rent extraction). Land, real estate, and other resources generate much higher rents in cities than they do elsewhere (Harvey 2012). There have certainly been a few urban revolutions around the globe (Harvey 2012), but what is striking is precisely that there have been so few, given the magnificent imbalance and inequality experienced in city life. One explanation is our unconscious size fetish.

Adam Okulicz-Kozaryn and Rubia R. Valente

Notes

Adam Okulicz-Kozaryn thanks the psychoanalysis sessions at the Annual Meeting of the American Association of Geographers (AAG) 2015 in Chicago and the AAG 2016 in San Francisco for inspiration.

1. Latin Americans are unique in this regard. There are no statistically significant differences in the happiness and unhappiness of urban and rural residents. See Valente and Berry (2016).
2. For an overview of the difference between desire and drive, see Kapoor (2015).
3. Marcuse writes, "Western civilization has always glorified the hero, the sacrifice for the city, the state, the nation" (2015, xix).
4. "He [the urbanite] is reduced to a negligible quantity. He becomes a single cog as over against the vast overwhelming organization of things and forces which gradually take out of his hands everything connected with progress spirituality and value" (Simmel 2005, 337).
5. Disavowal is simply turning away from the truth as a way of not coming to terms with loss (see Fletcher 2016, chap. 3).
6. Like religion, at least some aspects of capitalism and urbanization are opium for the masses. They keep people sedated with consumption, money, power, and urban fantasies.
7. On the other hand, there is generally no size fetish in the Kibbutz or the Amish community, for example. Size fetish is most pronounced in the most capitalistic places on Earth: New York City, London, Chicago, Mumbai, Rio, etc. And there can be associated guilt and shame when, for example, approaching and entering the city, the closeness and play of its towers mimic sexual intercourse (see chapter 9).
8. The abbreviation SUV stands for sport utility vehicle, which is typically a large and flashy vehicle. McMansion essentially means cheap, mass-produced mansion, just as McDonald's stands for cheap, mass-produced food.
9. Lacanian scholars (e.g., Slavoj Žižek and Tim Dean) emphasize that the phallus is fallible and signifies castration. We thank the anonymous reviewer for this suggestion.
10. Since Thoreau pointed to the degrading of pyramid builder, and some of the most spectacular contemporary towers, including the tallest one, are in the Middle East, let's point out a similarity in exploitation. For instance, laborers at the New York University campus in Abu Dhabi work and live in poor conditions. See Kaminer and O'Driscoll (2014).
11. Indeed, Fromm writes, "The passion to destroy life and attraction to all that is dead (necrophilia) seem to develop in the new urban civilization" (1992, 165).

12. The maps of vices are available at http://www.nocaptionneeded.com/wp-content /uploads/2009/10/7-sins.png. There are more detailed versions of these maps with descriptions at http://www.upworthy.com/7-deadly-sins-map-how-does-your-state -stack-up.

13. Some aspects of capitalism can be beneficial—to wit, free market and free enterprise. Yet their accompanying negative socio-environmental impacts are not. If some form of capitalism is to stay with us, it is clear that a dramatic redistribution is necessary. Cities may be more difficult to dismantle than capitalism. We simply cannot get rid of cities owing to growing urbanization (see Meyer 2013).

14. We use the term "civilization" following Freud and do not mean that some people are "civilized" and others are not.

Works Cited

Balducci, Alessandro, and Daniele Checchi. 2009. "Happiness and Quality of City Life: The Case of Milan, the Richest Italian City." *International Planning Studies* 14 (1): 25–64.

Bettencourt, Luís M. A., and Geoffrey B. West. 2010. "A Unified Theory of Urban Living." *Nature* 467 (7318): 912–13.

Bettencourt, Luís M. A., José Lobo, D. Helbing, C. Kühnert, and Geoffrey B. West. 2007. "Growth, Innovation, Scaling, and the Pace of Life in Cities." *Proceedings of the National Academy of Sciences* 104 (17): 7301–6.

Bettencourt, Luís M. A., José Lobo, Deborah Strumsky, and Geoffrey B. West. 2010. "Urban Scaling and Its Deviations: Revealing the Structure of Wealth, Innovation and Crime across Cities." *PloS One* 5 (11): e13541. DOI: 10.1371/journal.pone.0013541.

Bliss, Laura. 2014. "Moving toward an Evolutionary Theory of Cities." *CityLab*, November 4. https://www.citylab.com/design/2014/11/moving-toward-an-evolutionary-theory -of-cities/381839/.

Brynjolfsson, Erik, and Andrew McAfee. 2014. *The Second Machine Age: Work, Progress, and Prosperity in a Time of Brilliant Technologies*. New York: Norton.

Corak, Miles. 2004. *Generational Income Mobility in North America and Europe*. Cambridge: Cambridge University Press.

———. 2011. "Inequality from Generation to Generation: The United States in Comparison." In *The Economics of Inequality, Poverty, and Discrimination in the 21st Century*, edited by Robert S. Rycroft, 107–26. Westport CT: Praeger.

———. 2013. "Income Inequality, Equality of Opportunity, and Intergenerational Mobility." *Journal of Economic Perspectives* 23(7): 79–102.

Easterlin, Richard A. 2009. "Lost in Transition: Life Satisfaction on the Road to Capitalism." *Journal of Economic Behavior and Organization* 71 (2): 130–45.

Engels, Friedrich. 1987. *The Condition of the Working Class in England.* New York: Penguin.

Firebaugh, Glenn, and Matthew B. Schroeder. 2009. "Does Your Neighbor's Income Affect Your Happiness?" *American Journal of Sociology* 115 (3): 805–31.

Fischer, Claude S. 1972. "Urbanism as a Way of Life (a Review and an Agenda)." *Sociological Methods and Research* 1 (2): 187–242.

———. 1973. "Urban Malaise." *Social Forces* 52 (2): 221–35.

———. 1982. *To Dwell among Friends: Personal Networks in Town and City.* Chicago: University of Chicago Press.

Fletcher, Robert. 2016. "Beyond the End of the World: Breaking Attachment to a Dying Planet." Presented as the American Association of Geographers, San Francisco, March 31.

Florida, Richard. 2008. "Personality Maps." Who's Your City. http://www.creativeclass .com/_v3/whos_your_city/maps/#Personality_Maps.

Frank, Robert. 2012. *The Darwin Economy: Liberty, Competition, and the Common Good.* Princeton NJ: Princeton University Press.

Freud, Sigmund. 1927. "Fetishism." In *The Complete Works of Sigmund Freud*, edited by James Strachey, 21:147–57. London: Hogarth Press.

———. 1929. "The Infantile Genital Organization." *Psychoanalytic Review (1913–1957)* 16, 72.

———. 1930. *Civilization and Its Discontents.* Translated by Joan Riviere. Edited by James Strachey. London: Hogarth Press.

Fromm, Erich. 1992. *The Anatomy of Human Destructiveness.* New York: Macmillan.

Glaeser, Edward. 2011. *Triumph of the City: How Our Greatest Invention Makes Us Richer, Smarter, Greener, Healthier, and Happier.* New York: Penguin Press.

———. 2014. "Happiness Is Overrated." *Boston Globe*, May 18.

Hanson, Victor Davis. 2015. "The Oldest Divide: With Roots Dating Back to Our Founding, America's Urban-Rural Split Is Wider than Ever." *City Journal*, Autumn. https:// www.city-journal.org/html/oldest-divide-14042.html.

Harvey, David. 2012. *Rebel Cities: From the Right to the City to the Urban Revolution.* New York: Verso.

Jacobs, Jane. 1970. *The Economy of Cities.* New York: Random House.

———. 1985. *Cities and the Wealth of Nations: Principles of Economic Life.* New York: Random House.

———. 1993. *The Death and Life of Great American Cities.* New York: Random House.

Jargowsky, Paul A. 1997. *Poverty and Place: Ghettos, Barrios, and the American City*. New York: Russell Sage Foundation.

Kallis, Giorgos. 2011. "In Defence of Degrowth." *Ecological Economics* 70, no. 5 (2011): 873–80.

Kaminer, Ariel, and Sean O'Driscoll. 2014. "Workers at N.Y.U.'s Abu Dhabi Site Faced Harsh Conditions." *New York Times*, May 18. http://www.nytimes.com/2014/05/19 /nyregion/workers-at-nyus-abu-dhabi-site-face-harsh-conditions.html.

Kapoor, Ilan. 2014. "Psychoanalysis and Development: Contributions, Examples, Limits." *Third World Quarterly* 35 (7): 1120–43.

——. 2015. "What 'Drives' Capitalist Development?" *Human Geography* 8 (3): 66–78.

Kenner, Robert. 2008. *Food, Inc.* DVD. New York: Magnolia Home Entertainment.

Khanna, Parag. 2016. "A New Map for America." *New York Times*, April 15.

Lane, Robert E. 2000. *The Loss of Happiness in Market Democracies*. New Haven CT: Yale University Press.

Laplanche, Jean, and Jean-Bertrand Pontalis. 1974. *The Language of Psycho-Analysis*. Translated by Donald Nicholson-Smith. London: Norton.

Layard, Richard. 2005. *Happiness: Lessons from a New Science*. New York: Penguin.

Le Corbusier. 1985. *Towards a New Architecture*. Mineola NY: Dover Publications.

Lederbogen, Florian, Peter Kirsch, Leila Haddad, Fabian Streit, Heike Tost, Philipp Schuch, Stefan Wust, et al. 2011. "City Living and Urban Upbringing Affect Neural Social Stress Processing in Humans." *Nature* 474 (7352): 498–501.

Marcuse, Herbert. 2015. *Eros and Civilization: A Philosophical Inquiry into Freud*. Boston: Beacon Press.

Martinson, Tom. 2000. *American Dreamscape: The Pursuit of Happiness in Postwar Suburbia*. New York: Carroll & Graf.

Marx, Karl. 2010. *Capital Volume 1*. Seattle: Pacific Publishing.

Meyer, William B. 2013. *The Environmental Advantages of Cities: Countering Commonsense Antiurbanism*. Cambridge MA: MIT Press.

Oettingen, Gabriele, Doris Mayer, and Sam Portnow. 2016. "Pleasure Now, Pain Later: Positive Fantasies about the Future Predict Symptoms of Depression." *Psychological Science* 27 (3): 345–53.

Okulicz-Kozaryn, Adam. 2015. *Happiness and Place: Why Life Is Better Outside of the City*. New York: Palgrave Macmillan.

Okulicz-Kozaryn, Adam, Oscar Holmes IV, and Derek R. Avery. 2014. "The Subjective Well-Being Political Paradox: Happy Welfare States and Unhappy Liberals." *Journal of Applied Psychology* 99 (6): 1300–1308.

Park, Robert E. 1915. "The City: Suggestions for the Investigation of Human Behavior in the City Environment." *American Journal of Sociology* 20 (5): 577–612.

Park, Robert E., Ernest W. Burgess, and Roderick D. McKenzie. 1984. *The City*. Chicago: University of Chicago Press.

Pile, Steve. 2005a. *Real Cities: Modernity, Space and the Phantasmagorias of City Life*. Thousand Oaks CA: Sage.

———. 2005b. "Spectral Cities: Where the Repressed Returns and Other Short Stories." In *Habitus: A Sense of Place*, edited by J. Hillier and E. Rooksby. Farnham, UK: Ashgate Aldershot.

Roberts, James A. 2011. *Shiny Objects: Why We Spend Money We Don't Have in Search of Happiness We Can't Buy*. San Francisco: HarperOne.

Rosenthal, Stuart S., and William C. Strange. 2002. "The Urban Rat Race." Syracuse University Working Paper. http://citeseerx.ist.psu.edu/viewdoc/download?doi =10.1.1.624.4066&rep=rep1&type=pdf.

———. 2003. "Agglomeration, Labor Supply, and the Urban Rat Race." Center for Policy Research Working Paper no. 57, Syracuse University.

Schweickart, David. 2009. "Is Sustainable Capitalism an Oxymoron?" In *The Nation in the Global Era*, edited by J. Harris, 449–70. Leiden, Netherlands: Brill.

Scitovsky, Tibor. 1976. *The Joyless Economy: An Inquiry into Human Satisfaction and Consumer Dissatisfaction*. Oxford: Oxford University Press.

Simmel, Georg. 2005. "The Metropolis and Mental Life." *The Urban Sociology Reader*, 2nd ed., edited by Jan Lin and Christopher Mele, 23–31. London: Routledge.

Thoreau, Henry David. 1995. *Walden*. Mineola NY: Dover Publications.

Trump, Donald. 2001. "America under Attack." *Channel 9 News*, WWOR-TV, September 11. https://youtu.be/PcKIPhFIE7w.

Urry, John. 2007. "Cities of Spectacle." In *International Architecture Biennale Rotterdam*, 131–41. Rotterdam, the Netherlands: NAi Publishers.

Valente, Rubia R., and Brian J. L. Berry. 2016. "Dissatisfaction with City Life? Latin America Revisited." *Cities* 50, 62–67.

Veblen, Thorstein, and Martha Banta. 2009. *The Theory of the Leisure Class*. Oxford: Oxford University Press.

Veenhoven, Ruut. 1994. "How Satisfying Is Rural Life? Fact and Value." In *Changing Values and Attitudes in Family Households with Rural Peer Groups, Social Networks, and Action Spaces: Implications of Institutional Transition in East and West for Value Formation and Transmission*, edited by J. Cecora. Bonn: Society for Agricultural Policy Research and Rural Sociology (FAA).

Weber, Adna F. 1899. *The Growth of Cities in the Nineteenth Century.* New York: Macmillan.

West, Geoffrey. 2011. "The Surprising Math of Cities and Corporations." Filmed July 11, 2011. TED video, 17:33. http://www.ted.com/talks/geoffrey_west_the_surprising_math_of _cities_and_corporations.html.

Wilson, Timothy D. 2009. *Strangers to Ourselves: Discovering the Adaptive Unconscious.* Cambridge MA: Harvard University Press.

Wirth, Louis. 1938. "Urbanism as a Way of Life." *American Journal of Sociology* 44 (1): 1–24.

Zukin, Sharon. 2009. *Naked City: The Death and Life of Authentic Urban Places.* Oxford: Oxford University Press.

Adam Okulicz-Kozaryn and Rubia R. Valente

11 Corruption, Left Castration, and the Decay of an Urban Popular Movement in Brazil
A Melancholy Story

Pieter de Vries

Brazil presently is in disarray. The country is experiencing an economic, political, and moral crisis. President Dilma Rousseff of the Brazilian Workers' Party (Partido dos Trabalhadores, PT) has been accused of having won her reelection thanks to illegal funding. Congress has successfully carried out an impeachment procedure against her. Former president Inácio Lula da Silva has been indicted for accepting illegal payments from Brazilian multinational companies. The gross national product declined in 2015 by 3.9 percent and in 2016 by 3.6 percent (*Wikipedia* 2017), making this crisis the worst in seventy years. Corruption, according to the Brazilian opinion poll company Data-folha (Opinião Pública 2015), has become the most serious preoccupation among the citizenry, even more than traditional topics such as security and the economy. The governing Brazilian Worker's Party is being blamed for this triple crisis. Consequently, the Brazilian Left has lost much of its credibility.

It is remarkable how the image of the PT and the Left in Brazil has changed over the past years. While a couple of years ago the PT was seen as a progressive political movement with a defined Left progressive agenda in a neoliberal world, it is now seen as a party that when in power turned against its own principles and engaged in all the practices—of corruption, favoritism, vote rigging—it used to denounce when it was in the opposition (de Oliveira 2006). As a result, many on the Left in Brazil are in a melancholy mood, nostalgic for the past days of oppositional activism, when the Left was able to mobilize the people on behalf of a program that foregrounded notions of social justice, solidarity, democratic rights, and political integrity. Today, Brazilian social movement leaders are in the difficult position that they have to defend an unpopular government against an emboldened Right that, they fear, is bound to dismantle a series of social conquests that have been achieved over the years. At the same time, there is an awareness that the politics of compromise that the official Left engaged in led to the debilitation of social movements.

In this chapter I reflect on the current situation of disarray within the Left, what I call Left melancholy, or castration, by analyzing first the discourse of corruption in Brazil and second the history of the decay of a popular urban social movement in Recife. The chapter rests on two arguments. First, Left melancholy is a narcissistic sentiment resulting from a feeling of loss the subject experiences when compromising her desire. The loss of the object of desire (that of radical transformation) generates feelings of guilt and disorientation that are sublimated by a never-ending drive to get things done, as manifested in the enjoyment of corruption and engagement in a multitude of dispersed and fragmented developmental activities without a clear goal (see chapter 5). In theoretical terms this is a shift from desire to drive; while in desire the object of desire is (originally) lost, in drive loss itself becomes the object. My second argument is that the disavowal of Left desire—or Left castration—in Brazil expresses itself in a defined biopolitics that emerges as a by-product of the clash between popular participation and neoliberal market forces. The result of this (failed) encounter is the hollowing out of popular sovereignty. This biopolitics, I contend, has the structure of drive.

The chapter is based on field research on urban reform processes in slum areas in Recife over a period of a decade that shows the entanglement, if not growing complicity, of progressive forces with neoliberal urban policies.[1] I draw on previous work (de Vries 2016) to argue that the decay of the popular movement in Recife was caused by the unfolding of a reformist governmental rationality that aimed to reconcile forms of popular participation with neoliberal policies driven by the desire to create a competitive city. This governmentalization of the people—or their capture within the population as an object of biopolitics—in fact, signified a betrayal or taming of the

Pieter de Vries

desire for radical change that animated a powerful popular movement that, with the support of Left activists and community leaders, ensured the right of the poor to the city: first through massive land occupations and later through the constitution of an enduring participatory system. The result was an impasse, a feeling of loss, that manifested itself in a melancholia for the good old days when a united and unified popular movement existed that provided the Left with a mission, a progressive sense of direction. Left melancholy in Recife, thus, is symptomatic for the (un)conscious betrayal of a foundational event staged by the urban poor.

The theoretical analysis is inspired by Lacanian psychoanalysis. I argue that one way to overcome the impasse caused by the unconscious guilt that betrayal carries is by theorizing loss itself, not in a melancholy mood by mourning an object that cannot be recovered, but as a point of departure, a rupture, that may lead to a reinvigoration of Left politics. If, as Lacanian theorists argue, melancholia is characterized by the disavowal of a funda-mental desire, and hence conducive to a state of passivity in which failure itself is suffused with enjoyment, then the question is how to recover the capacity to desire radical transformations that characterizes a Left struc-ture of desire.

The chapter is structured as follows. First, I discuss the present situation of disaffection with, and within, the Left in Brazil and the ideological role the discourse and imagery of corruption plays in revealing and disavowing the loss produced by the betrayal of the desire for radical transformation. In the second section, I provide a glimpse at the present sentiment of Left castration in Recife and discuss the concept of biopolitics as having the structure of drive. In the conclusion, I reflect further about the possibility of a resurgence of a Left structure of desire.

The Current Impasse of the PT, or Compromising the Desire for Radical Transformation

The PT, before the impeachment of President Dilma Rousseff, was in the peculiar situation of having to face the total opposition of the Right while being unwilling to commit itself to the demands of the very social movement whose commitment has been crucial for the electoral successes of the party. Furthermore, the PT was doing everything to accommodate the demands of international financial markets by conducting an economic policy that would not have been much different if the adversaries of the Right would have won the past elections. A couple of years ago the situation was totally different. The economic situation was excellent, people were optimistic, President Inácio Lula da Silva enjoyed high approval rates. Bolsa Familia (a conditional cash-transfer scheme granted to low-income families with children) pulled millions out of extreme poverty. There was much talk about the emergence of a new middle class, denominated "Class C," families earning between three and five minimum salaries, who were buying consumer goods and in this way stimulating economic growth. This new class was seen as the backbone of the ruling Workers' Party.

There has not been a lack of criticism of the PT within the Left—against economic policies aimed at stimulating consumption among the poor and the new middle classes while neglecting to tax the rich so as to improve basic services, such as health and education, and aimed at taking to task multinational and agrarian interests for depleting the ecological resources of the country. In 2004 the Socialism and Liberty Party (PSOL) was founded by former militants who accused the PT leadership of having betrayed the political principles of the party. The new party campaigned for a true socialist program, including land reform, increase of taxation for the rich, defense of workers' rights, strict enforcement of environmental laws, and a serious dialogue with indigenous movements that campaigned against megaprojects such as the Belo Monte Dam. In 2008 Marina Silva, then minister of the environment, resigned after learning that the goals to reduce deforestation were systematically being undermined by the powerful agrarian faction within parliament. The close relationship between the PT government and leadership and Brazilian multinationals (such as Odebrecht, Andrade Gutierrez, and OAS) was widely known. Corruption scandals haunted the PT governments. During the second presidential mandate of Lula, the government was seriously compromised by the *Mensalão* (big monthly allowance) scandal, through which massive bribes were paid to politicians of allied parties by PT leaders in order

Pieter de Vries

to ensure their political compliance. José Dirceu, former minister during the Lula government and one of the founding members of the PT, was declared guilty in 2012 for setting up a criminal scheme aimed at embezzling public money by negotiating bribes with private enterprises in return for public work contracts. The money was used in large part to buy the support of coalition parties in Congress and the Senate so as to ensure a stable government.

At the same time the weakness of political opposition against the PT was noteworthy. The political Right was divided and had no clear agenda that differed significantly from that of the PT. In fact, the Workers' Party had been able to combine the neoliberal economic agenda of the Right with welfare programs that were immensely popular among the poor, such as Bolsa Familia. The PT governance model was based on two legs: social programs for the poor and the new lower middle class and economic policies aimed at ensuring further growth. This was a consumer-based modernization strategy that dismissed the radical language of social movements and critical militants as unrealistic. This model worked for a decade, as long as the glObal context was favorable.

In 2013, on the eve of the 2014 Fédération Internationale de Football Association (FIFA) World Cup, large manifestations erupted. What started as a protest movement against the increase of transport tariffs (the Passe Livre) evolved into a series of massive multi-class demonstrations with diverse and diffuse demands all over the country. Much of the complaints were aimed at the high costs of football stadiums, contrasting with the precarious state of education, health, and basic infrastructure. There was much critique of the gentrification of football, the quintessential Brazilian sports activity. But also other issues, such as taxes and corruption, were taken up, in particular by middle-class demonstrators.

The reaction of the government was quick, with President Rousseff assuming the demands as legitimate and promising to respond to them in an adequate way. While she lacked the personal charisma of former PT president Lula, her predecessor and mentor, she was seen as an able administrator who could operate independently from the old party cadres and was ready to modernize the political system. Significantly, demands by the social movements to hold true to old PT promises of income and resource distribution were dismissed.

Contrary to what many expected, the FIFA World Cup was not disrupted by the manifestations organized to question the event. The situation seemed to be under control. However, the Brazilian national team's loss to Germany in the quarter finals (7–1) was symbolic of the generalized feeling of dissatisfaction that had not yet achieved its apogee. A new scandal involving Petrobras (the national petrol company) and PT politicians was disclosed. Rousseff secured her reelection in 2013 with a small majority. The opposition accused the PT of having financed the elections in an irregular way. It is highly probable that Rousseff won because the popular classes were afraid of losing social benefits, such as Bolsa Familia, if the Right won. Social movements mobilized their constituencies in favor of Rousseff. She, however, did not return the favor and neglected their demands.

The new corruption scandal, named *Petrolão* or *Lavajato* (car wash, which is where the negotiations are alleged to have taken place), was portrayed by the media (in Brazil a monopoly of the Right) as the largest embezzlement operation since the return of democracy. The difference between the *Mensalão* and the *Lavajato* was the involvement of Petrobras, the national petrol company and jewel in the Brazilian crown. The media exploited the fact that Rousseff was the president of Petrobras's executive board at the time that the *Lavajato* scheme was set up.

And yet, as various analysts like to stress, the PT economic model benefitted large sectors of the population: rich and poor, worker and entrepreneur. But not for long, as the model proved to be unfeasible under conditions of glObal capitalism. Yet as long as it lasted, it created the ideological fantasy that it was possible to reconcile the interest of capital with that of the popular classes. Never before was the country so united in the belief that progressive labor policies and welfare programs could be conciliated with neoliberal economic growth. Tellingly, President Lula complained after his first administration that never had private business made such high profits and that he deserved more appreciation for it from the elite (Singer 2014). In psychoanalytic terms, the present crisis signifies the return of the repressed—of the Real of capitalism—and stands as a reminder that the post-political ideological fantasy based on consensus was but a disavowal of the contradictions that divide the country.

So what happened when this fantasy foundered? I argue that the result was resentment and melancholia: resentment among those who benefitted without being committed to leftist desire and melancholia by those who resent the times that the PT was still a truly radical party. My point is to show such Left resentment as an ideological reaction.

All this critique of the PT is utterly hypocritical. Everyone knew about the scale of corruption, and everyone participated and benefitted from it, all state institutions, private enterprise, labor unions. Their complaints are not concerned with corruption, but with a loss that they cannot assimilate. The point is that they were deprived of the Big Tit, the source of wealth that made everybody happy. We live in a state of complicity. All these middle-class people, enacting this false moralism, complaining that they were cheated by the PT, are secretly hoping that the old state of things will be restored. The anti-PT, anticorruption movement is driven exclusively by nostalgia for the good times when everybody was free to indulge in corruption. (Rosângela Sabino da Silva, pers. comm., January 2015)

This statement is a good reminder of the Lacanian assertion that there is no Other of the Other; there is no Master, state, or center that pulls the string. In effect, the Big Tit in this statement stands for the nostalgia for a corrupt master who guarantees happiness for all, a master who enjoins his or her subjects to enjoy. Further, the Big Tit stands for the belief—propagated by the PT electoral machine—in the possibility of a nonantagonistic economic model that could guarantee justice and prosperity for all. The moment that the unsustainability of this model was revealed, the belief in the master that pulls the strings and enables us to enjoy became a farce.

Arguably, corruption within this ideological edifice operates as a fetish that both reveals and disavows the Real of antagonism. Here we see the typical ideological position of fetishistic disavowal so well described by Slavoj

Žižek (1989) in his formula: "they know very well what they are doing, but still, they are doing it" (see also chapters 3 and 12 in this volume). Which in this case can be phrased as, "I know very well that we all are benefitting from the Big Tit and that this will lead to a big crisis but still I connive in the everyday practice of corruption for the reason that this is the way things function." This, in effect, was the position of many of those who criticize the PT while having been aware—and part—of the networks of complicity hidden behind the workings of the model. The fact is that corruption was a public secret and so many—in particular the elite—benefitted from it (see Fletcher [2013] on the concept of public secret). But the reaction of this group to the foundering of the fantasy is resentment, caused by the end of the benefits and the enjoyment these entailed.

Melancholy as a symptom deriving from compromising Left desire is illustrated by this statement by a PT member who comments on the *Lava-jato* corruption scandal:

We live in a deficient democracy. You need massive sums of money to win elections, and the only way of getting that money is by negotiating contracts with private businesses. The Right always did it, and we could not escape from incurring in the same practices. This is the obscene, hidden underside of electoral politics. PT politicians such as Dirceu understood very well that the only way of carrying out the political program of the PT was by engaging in these practices. Dirceu didn't do it for his personal benefit, he did it for the party, so it is unjust that now he is being sacrificed. (Anonymous politician, pers. comm., January 2015)

Although there may be a grain of truth and even pathos in this statement, it is indicative of a Left structure of desire that is betrayed. The fetishistic formula of ideology manifests itself as follows: "I know very well that in indulging in illegal funding practices we are betraying the leftist promises of putting an end to the corruption of democracy by capital, and yet, that is the only way in which the Left can pursue a political project on behalf of the popular classes in a capitalist world." This is a way of compromising the desire for radical transformation that produces the feelings of guilt and disorientation so characteristic of Left melancholy. Corruption, accordingly, does not reside in the practice of illegal negotiations but in the betrayal of a promise as manifested in connivance with, and surrender to, a logic of complicity for the sake of attaining practical and temporary gains aimed at political survival.

Corruption, as a form of fetishistic disavowal, thus is symptomatic of a Left structure of desire that bemoans a loss of innocence as manifested in the imagery of a Left that had to betray its principles in order to serve the country. The point, however, is that this Left was always ruptured, contested, and conflicted and that it has sublimated its goals and responsibilities into a quest for the pleasures of consumption that served both the interests of capital accumulation and a sense of prosperity among an emergent middle class. In a Lacanian framework, capitalism produces desiring subjects who "engage in endless shopping, moving from one commodity to the next, forever searching for the 'real thing,' which always proves elusive" (Kapoor 2015, 69). The fantasy of consumption—as a uniting principle for the emergent middle classes—produces an enjoyment of its own, a *jouissance*, that can never be satisfied and that serves to disavow leftist promises—of better health, education, social security, etc., expressly to be funded through policies of income and resources distribution.

But as argued, the ideological fantasy of post-political consensual politics renders possible another way to enjoy, as exemplified in the case of the enjoyment that derives from playing the corrupt game for the sake of the party. This is the enjoyment of the melancholic who maintains that he is sacrificing himself for the party and thereby sublimates the betrayal of the desire for transformation with a drive characterized by incessant activity, inhabiting a continuous state of agitation. This is how, in the context of corruption, enjoyment captures the subject (Dean 2009). Here we see the shift from desire to drive, from the enjoyment derived from the inability to obtain satisfaction to drive's inability "not to enjoy." Paraphrasing the Rolling Stones, the shift is from "I can't get no satisfaction" to "I cannot escape satisfaction." As intimated earlier, this shift from desire to drive is homologous to different ways of dealing with loss. In Left desire, the object is (originally lost), and this feeling of loss expresses itself in a longing for fullness as imagined in an unadulterated, uncorrupted, and unified Left. In drive, in contrast, loss itself becomes the object, as manifested in the fragmentation and demobilization of the Left. Isn't the enjoyment that iconic leftist militants derive from engaging in, and performing, corruption not a good example of Left castration, brought about by the feelings of guilt and disorientation caused by the betrayal of Left desire, whereby loss itself becomes an object of agitated, corrupt activity, and enjoyment attaches to the repeated failure to hold true to the principles of Left desire?

In the next section I show how this structure of drive informing Left melancholy gives way to a biopolitics characterized by incessant developmental activity in the slums of Recife, Brazil.

Biopolitics as Having the Structure of Drive

Recife is known as the city of slums, or *favelas*. Less known, however, is that Recife was also the scenery of a powerful popular movement that struggled for the right to the city. It was one of the most penalized cities during the military dictatorship (1964–86) on account of its reputation for strong leftist movements and charismatic politicians. After the military coup, a wave of popular struggles for the right to the city took place under the leadership of Dom Hélder Câmara, a Roman Catholic archbishop. The scale of popular mobilization was unparalleled: as many as 250,000 people were involved in eighty invasions from 1978 to 1981 (Assies 1994, 122). Because of these mobilizations, a coalition of progressive policymakers and nongovernmental organizations (NGOs) constructed a veritable apparatus of social protection, reflected in programs such as participatory budgeting and the PREZEIS, a highly advertised slum governance system that grants residents of informal settlements tenure, security, and financial provisions for improving urban infrastructure (de Vries 2016). A fact that cannot be stressed enough, however, is that this social protection system was the outcome of an alliance between *favelados*, civil society organizations, and the Catholic Church. This was a truly political event in the sense that it exposed the existence of a wrong by people who demanded their right to

Pieter de Vries

equality in the city. As Swyngedouw puts it, "A demand that calls the political into being, renders visible what is invisible, and exposes the 'wrongs' in the present order" (2010, 302).

Twenty years later and after three successive PT municipal administrations, the political mood within the Left is one of disarray and disorientation. Such a mood is well represented by Eufrasio, a well-known political activist in Mustardinha, Recife, and prominent member of the Communist Party of Brazil (PCdoB). As he puts it,

> The crisis did not start in Brazil but in the USA and then spread over to Europe and the periphery. This is a typical capitalist crisis. In this sense the criticism against the government is unjustified. At the same time, we must admit that the coming to power of the PT at the national level and municipal level has not been good for the popular movements. When the Right was in government, we were able to mobilize the people for all kinds of struggles: for land, for decent housing, etc. Yet when the PT was in power, it was difficult to continue with these mobilizations since we were not anymore in the opposition. We have accomplished much for the working classes over the past years. However, I must admit that we have neglected the hard work of educating the people to fight for their rights. The Right has now found a way to take revenge, to rewind the clock. Of course there was corruption. The PT is a very complicated party, and of course many took advantage of the privileges of power. But corruption was not invented by the PT; it has always been part a country that is profoundly unjust and has always benefitted the rich. (Eufrasio, pers. comm., July 2015)

Eufrasio is a highly respected leftist political leader who teamed up with Catholic Church and NGO activists in the struggle for the right to live in the city. He has been involved for thirty years in local and city politics, as president of the housing association of Mustardinha (for ten years) and as a municipal employee in different positions (but always linked to the party). The PCdoB has been a loyal ally of the PT-led municipal government in Recife from 2001 to 2012. Currently, the Community Party forms part of

Fig. 14. Political activist Eufrásio Elias de Oliveira (*center*) with the author (*right*) and Rosângela Sabino da Silva (*left*). Photo by Pieter de Vries, August 11, 2015.

the municipal government headed by the Brazilian Socialist Party (PSB), a former ally of the PT that now is part of the rightist anti-Dilma/PT bloc. As Eufrasio himself admits, even for communists who have been in power it has been difficult to avoid the lures of office. The following excerpt of our conversation is revealing:

> PDV: What do you think about the growing polarization in Recife between a modern city characterized by high-rises and gated communities and a popular city with large deficiencies in terms of basic urban infrastructure?

Pieter de Vries

E: We live in a capitalist world; we cannot deny it. Of course we had to compromise with economic forces intent on making as much profit as possible. Still, through participatory budgeting and social programs such as Bolsa Familia, we were able to improve the life conditions of the population at large. What you say concerning the growing polarization of the city may be true. I don't have the figures. However, this is an objective fact of capitalist development. We as leftists should work together with the people, by supporting their demands and instilling a class consciousness. Of course, developers have always been powerful in the city. The difference with previous administrations is that we were better in negotiating with them on behalf of the popular classes.

PDV: At the level of the communities, how has this improvement in life conditions influenced leftist political activity?

E: It is sad, but since I left the housing association, there has been very little political activity in Mustardinha. Political vices such as buying votes have never been so strong as now. In the last elections, ten reais [two and a half U.S. dollars] was paid for a vote at the electoral booth.

PDV: Our research in slum neighborhoods such as Mustardinha shows that community leaders play an important role in local politics and that they combine all kinds of developmental activity with electoral work for politics of different sorts. How do you explain this phenomenon?

E: There are indeed many community leaders around, and some are very committed to the people. Some of them have been members of our party but left because some politician offered them an allowance in return for campaigning. They may struggle for the reparation of a couple of roads or the rights of some people who have been removed, but the truth is that they achieve very little. They are easy preys of political and economic actors who use them to promote small projects—cultural, environmental—in return for political support. When elections come, they campaign for their patrons. They really enjoy doing small projects and believe they are achieving a lot. I know that very well because one of my sons is such a community leader. I tell them that development must always be grounded in a larger political project of emancipation.

PDV: What solution do you see then for this dispersal of energy among so many community leaders?

E: Now that I'm retired, I'll dedicate myself again to the organizing activities in the neighborhood. We will hold meetings and invite residents and community leaders to join forces.

From this excerpt we can observe three states of mind: first, a nostalgic attitude concerning the times when oppositional mobilization was possible and the people could be educated to fight for their rights; second, a realistic stance concerning the need to compromise with the demands of the market as expressed in the emphasis on the improvement of life conditions through (bio)political programs; and third, a preoccupation with the fragmentation of politics due to the proliferation of political brokers who engage in all kinds of projects that have no effects in terms of political emancipation.

The same points were the subject of another interview with Flavio, a community leader from the same *favela*, who specialized in working with the youth on cultural and environmental issues. Flavio used to work with the son of Eufrasio as a political campaigner for a candidate of the Right before the PT came to power in 2001. Thereafter he became involved in leftist politics—first for the PT and later for the PCdoB—but never received the financial support he expected. In the elections of 2004 and 2012 he campaigned for an oppositional candidate of the Right. He always combined his activities as a community leader with small jobs for the municipality and support for politicians in electoral times. The following dialogue is illuminating.

PDV: What do you think about Eufrasio's critique of community leaders concerning their lack of political consciousness?

F: Eufrasio has been an important reference for all of us here, together with the Catholic Church. They have accomplished important things. However, things are complicated for us community leaders. There are about a dozen here in Mustardinha, and we play an important role as representatives of the community. You know me, I like working with young people, raising their consciousness regarding the environment, organizing cultural activities so as to prevent them from getting into drugs or prostitution. There is much poverty here, and the kids need these activities. I'm not a political activist like

Pieter de Vries

Eufrasio. I have been influenced by his ideas, and I even was a member of the party for a short time, but I do not have that kind of political ambition. Other community leaders like to work closely with municipal programs at the City Hall, or with the PREZEIS. I do not like that work of political articulation. Neither do I like electoral politics, but I do have to earn an income, and as a community leader I'm approached by politicians to campaign for them. In the last presidential elections, I voted for Dilma [the PT], but campaigned for a senate candidate of the PSDB [Social Democratic Party of Brazil, a center-right party]. That's the way it works. Now I am working for this construction company that obtained a concession to build a park nearby. They pay me 450 reais [120 dollars]. I'm also working as a delegate for the new participatory program Recife Participa. It's a little money, but I have to survive.

PDV: And what do you think about Eufrasio's critique of the lack of efficacy of the work of community leaders? Have you thought of coordinating your activities?

F: He may be right. It would be nice to change the world. I liked these big plenaries of participatory budgeting when we thought about the problems of the city as a whole. We were involved in choosing our development priorities. I participated in the cultural thematic plenaries. With Recife Participa [the participatory program introduced by the PSB major after participatory budgeting], we are asked to provide inputs in the design of policies in various participatory councils. But this is not real participation. Actual activities are mostly funded by private companies that work for the municipality. Our work as community leaders may not be very effective, but then the overall context is not very supportive. It would be nice to work in an integrated way, wouldn't it? But the truth is that it's all so fragmented. Every secretariat has its own programs, and they work all according to different rules. There is no coordination between them. Here in Mustardinha we community leaders get along well with each other. If it seems all fragmented, it is because the situation is imposed on us.

PDV: So what alternative do you see?

F: The point is that PT really fucked up. All these accusations of corruption. The PT claimed to do politics for the poor, but apparently it received kickbacks from big construction companies in return for concessions. Of course I know that the new park they are making here is meant to benefit

Fig. 15. Community leader Flavio Reis. Photo by Pieter de Vries, August 8, 2015.

the companies by building apartments for the rich in gated communities. We are very disappointed, we feel betrayed by the politicians we voted for. For my part, I do enjoy the work I do with the youth. Whether it has an impact at a higher level, that of the city, is not something that bothers me at this point (Flavio, pers. comm., January 2015).

Interestingly, Flavio does not disagree with Eufrasio regarding the lack of effectivity in the work of community leaders, as expressed in the fragmentation and dispersion of their developmental and political activities. However, he lays the blame elsewhere, not on their lack of political consciousness, but on the political context. The critical point he makes is that unlike professional politicians, such as Eufrasio, who have access to governmental positions, he cannot afford being ideologically correct. Community leaders are always compelled to offer their services as political brokers to politicians of different stripes in order to make a living. This puts them in the odd situation that they often campaign for political patrons espousing political positions they do not agree with. Neither does Flavio exhibit a certain nostalgic attitude regarding "the good old times" of oppositional politics. On the contrary, he blames the Left for having betrayed the expectations of the people. Furthermore, he is very much aware that the compromises between the political Left and private business interests have led to a hollowing out of the promises of political emancipation.

What kind of politics is this in which community leaders who in the past were representatives of a powerful popular movement become complicit in a structure that leads to passivity, demobilization, and division? It is important to note that there are many such community leaders in Recife, and they used to play important roles in social protection structures such as the PREZEIS and participatory budgeting. From 2001 to 2011 the PT held municipal power in Recife and used its own brand of participatory budgeting to capture and discipline community leaders through a kind of progressive governmentality that aimed to conciliate neoliberal aspirations to create a competitive city with a participatory tradition (de Vries 2016). Finally, in 2014 the PSB gained power and discontinued the participatory projects of the PT while continuing its neoliberal policies. The PSB introduced its own participatory program, Recife Participa, which operates as a consultative forum for the design of sectoral policies (health, education, security) with the participation of the private sector under public-private arrangements. The result of the PT's twelve years of hegemony has been political division and the gentrification of *favelas* located in strategic points in the city.

The fragmentation of political activity, as manifested in the pervasiveness of community leaders and political brokers, is indicative of a politics characterized by an incessant drive to engage in developmental activity characterized by dispersion and demobilization, leading to the creation of a passive population. This, I argue, is a biopolitics of improvement that goes along with a form of enjoyment deriving from "repeating failure—from never reaching [one's] goal despite obstinately trying" (Kapoor 2015, 68; see also chapter 6 in this volume). Such is the case of community leaders' engagement in a multitude of dispersed activities, small projects funded by political patrons and business interests that conduce to political division in the community. Community leaders, in fact, know that these small projects only distract from larger issues concerning public services for the poor and the right to housing and that by engaging in them they become complicit with the aspirations of capitalist developers to expand their operations in strategically located slums in the city. Drawing on Lacanian theory I will now argue that this is a biopolitics that has the structure of drive.

Let me spell out further this notion of a biopolitics that has the structure of drive.[2] Biopolitics, according to Michel Foucault (2008), is a politics that takes life itself as its target and "man" as a species-being, as reflected in the dictum of "make live and let die." It entails paying attention to the overall characteristics of a population, such as rates of reproduction, fertility, medical health, and security. Students of Foucault, such as Giorgio Agamben and Antonio Negri, have further analyzed the concept of biopolitics in radically contrasting ways. Agamben (1998, 96) argues that biopolitics is about the indistinction between life and politics, operative in the capture of the population through governmental technologies that cancel out the distinction between qualified political life and bare (biological) life. This threshold—or indistinction—of life and politics, he argues, is the hidden foundation of the Western political tradition as witnessed by the concentration camp (not the polis). Negri, alternatively, sees biopolitics in an affirmative way, exceeding or overflowing sovereign power (what he calls Empire) as expressed in the creativity of the multitude (Hardt and Negri 2009, 58–59). Biopolitics, on this understanding, is not based on a power over life but is the power of life itself, based on the capacity of a multiplicity of singular beings to cooperate and the inability of government to capture or co-opt it. When applied to the urban situation in Recife, Agamben's view on biopolitics helps us attend to the various ways in which the state deals with slums through programs of securitization, eradication, and slum upgrading (de Vries 2016). In contrast, Negri's affirmative understanding of biopolitics enables us to focus on the creativity of slum dwellers as manifested in their production of lively informal economies. This would be the case, for instance, of Carnival in Recife, considered to be—and marketed by the municipality as—the most multicultural in Brazil.

Here, however, I draw on Jodi Dean's Lacanian theorization of biopolitics to theorize a politics of life in Recife that manifests itself in the existence of large number of programs that target slums with a view to improving life conditions, alleviating poverty, and dealing with the supposed security threat that a large contingent of poor *favelados* (especially young, black, and male) constitutes to society. This, in contrast with Agamben's essentialist thesis, is a biopolitics with a history. To be precise, it is that of the decay of a strong popular movement that once stood for popular desires for justice and egalitarianism but that increasingly resigned itself to the realpolitik of neoliberalism. Furthermore—and in contrast to Negri's affirmative thesis—this is a biopolitics that emerges from defeat, the hollowing out of a participatory governance system by market forces. In effect, this is a biopolitics of improvement that achieves its aims by betraying the desires for social transformation that motivated the popular mobilizations for the right to the city and that led to the establishment of a powerful protection system for the urban poor.

By drawing parallels between Foucauldian and Freudian theory, Dean argues that biopolitics is not a primary force; it is not a biopower invented by experts aimed at managing populations. Rather, it is the by-product of the clash between popular sovereignty and the market. In psychoanalytic terms, it is the by-product of a shift from desire to drive. As she puts it,

> In drive, one doesn't have to reach the goal to enjoy. The activities one undertakes to achieve a goal become satisfying on their own. Because they provide a little kick of enjoyment, they come themselves to take the place of the goal. Attaching to the process, enjoyment captures the subject. . . . So, drives don't circulate around a space that was once occupied by an ideal, impossible object. Rather, drive is the sublimation of desire as it

turns back in on itself, this turning thereby producing the loop of drive and providing its own special charge. (Dean 2009, 12).

Conclusion: New Beginnings and the Subjectivity of the Gap

I have argued that leftist melancholia, or castration, is characterized by the disavowal of a fundamental desire conducive to a state of passivity in which failure itself is suffused with enjoyment. I drew on psychoanalytical theory to show that the compromise or betrayal of Left desire in Brazil is conducive to a politics that is driven by corruption, dispersion, and fragmentation—in short a biopolitics that has the structure of drive. My point of departure was that the challenge for a Left politics is that of recovering the will to struggle for radical transformations, hence reconstituting a Left structure of desire. In what follows, I argue that such a reconstitution of Left desire requires the cultivation of a drive that is no less obdurate than that of the capitalist developers who are set to destroy the social protection system that emerged from the popular movements against the dictatorship. The case of Recife, I think, is symptomatic for the Brazilian situation at large.

Lacanian theorists hold that drive is more radical than desire in its capacity to destabilize the situation and hence create opportunities for radical change, since the creative destruction of drive can herald a "will to create from zero a will to begin again" (Lacan, cited in Dean 2009, 4). Kapoor (2015, 76) speaks about an ethics of anticapitalist struggle, arguing that we need to cultivate a drive that "would need to be nothing less than uncompromising in the face of the capitalist drive's dogged persistence; [for, without] an obdurate spirit, without inhabiting drive's derailed excess, it is hard to see how a broad global coalition could persist energetically or indeed adequately oppose the power of capital."

The question is, How do we theorize a new beginning, capable of inhabiting drive's derailed excess and reconstituting a Left structure of desire? How do we conceive of a will to create from zero that ensues from defeat and failure without falling into the trap of Left melancholia? How do we harness the excessive side of *jouissance* to the will to begin again?

Pieter de Vries

To begin to answer these questions, it is important to rethink the relationship between the excessive enjoyment of desire and that of drive with regard to the object or goal of radical social transformation. As Žižek puts it,

in both cases, the link between object and loss is crucial, in the case of *objet a* as the object-cause of desire, we have an object which is originally lost, which coincides with its own loss, which emerges as lost, while, in the case of *objet a* as the object of drive, the "object" is directly the loss itself—in the shift from desire to drive, we pass from the lost object to loss itself as an object. That is to say, the weird movement called "drive" is not driven by the "impossible" quest for the lost object; it is a push to directly enact the "loss"—the gap, cut, distance—itself. (2008, 328)

As I read this passage, the dialectic of desire and drive is both destructive and affirmative, as it contains the possibility of a new beginning. While both desire and drive arise as a result of an impossible striving for fullness (the recovery of lost *jouissance*), desire is a futile attempt to fill the void with particular objects that never satisfy. Drive, in contrast, is a constant circulation around objects that provide immediate satisfaction, detaching enjoyment from a quest to a larger goal. The circulation of drive around the object, therefore, performs the contrary of the formula of fetishistic disavowal: from "they do not know it, but they still are doing it" to "they know it very well and keep on doing it." Drive feeds on and reveals the betrayal of desire. Rather than bemoaning the loss drive enacts it, hence liberating the subject from the grips of leftist melancholy.

Applying these insight to the case of Recife, we can conclude that the enactment of the "loss" gave rise to a biopolitics of improvement characterized by the dispersion of politics over a social terrain in which community leaders act as political brokers for patrons who represent the interests of developers. This is a biopolitics of improvement that emerged as a by-product of the clash between popular sovereignty and the market; in psychoanalytic terms, the by-product of a shift from the desire for egalitarianism as embodied in the rights of the poor to the city to the incessant drive for profit of neoliberal capitalism. The point is that the same actors that constituted the backbone of the popular movement in Recife, the community leaders who in the past voiced the demands and expectations of the poor, have become the agents of political dissolution and fragmentation in the slums. Community leaders, as argued, are aware of the perverse consequences of such a biopolitics in a non-melancholic mood.

Does this mean that everything is lost? Is a new beginning possible? And if yes, who are the agents embodying the needed drive to enact such a new beginning? What kind of politics can ensure the militancy and obdurate spirit that can harness the excess of drive to counter the onslaught of neoliberal development and reconstitute a true leftist structure of desire?

To answer these questions, it is important to go back in time. Before the military takeover in 1964, Recife was known for its strong popular movements, led by strong and charismatic leaders, struggling for land reform in the countryside and for better housing and living conditions for the urban poor. The military putsch was a serious blow to the progressive movements. The repression was fierce; political parties were forbidden; leftist politicians were jailed or had to go into exile; housing associations in slum areas were closed—that of Mustardinha, for instance, at gunpoint by the military. Decades of struggle seemed to be lost.

And yet the acknowledgment of defeat gradually led to a grassroots popular movement after a series of floods in the city that endangered the subsistence of poor slum dwellers. An alliance of activists and community leaders, protected by the Catholic Church, created the conditions for the poor, the part of no part, to voice its demands. This was a truly political event setting forth a political sequence by rendering visible what was invisible.

The magnitude and significance of the subsequent squatter invasions cannot be underestimated. They made up a true event accompanied by the eruption of a new kind of subjectivity, that of the poor as the Children of God. This event was the product of a drive as obdurate and uncompromising as that of the capitalist interests that were bent on displacing the poor from the city. This was an event that lingers on in the collective unconscious of the city.

Pieter de Vries

Fig. 16. Slums at the Capibaribe River targeted for redevelopment. Photo by Pieter de Vries, August 10, 2015.

Is it possible then to see a new beginning, a return to the principles of this event, giving birth to a new subjectivity emerging from the gap between the neoliberal fantasy of beautifying the city and the lives of those who have no place in it? This is the question with which I wish to end this chapter.

Notes

1. I have conducted longitudinal research on slum-upgrading projects and partici-patory planning in Recife since 2010 (see Koster and de Vries 2012; de Vries 2016). Interviews for this article were held in January–February and July–August 2015.

2. Here I draw heavily on Dean (2009).

Works Cited

Agamben, Giorgio. 1998. *Homo Sacer*. Translated by Daniel Heller-Roazen. Stanford CA: Stanford University Press.

Assies, Willem. 1994. "Reconstructing the Meaning of Urban Land in Brazil: The Case of Recife." In *Methodology for Land and Housing Market Analysis*, edited by A. Gareth Jones and P. M. Ward. London: University College London Press.

Dean, Jodi. 2009. "Drive as the Structure of Biopolitics." Research paper, Hobart-William Smith Colleges. SSRN (1460759). https://ssrn.com/abstract=1460759.

De Oliveira, Francisco. 2006. "Lula in the Labyrinth." *New Left Review* 42, 5–22.

De Vries, Pieter. 2016. "The Inconsistent City, Participatory Planning, and the Part of No Part in Recife, Brazil." *Antipode* 48 (3): 790–808.

Fletcher, Robert. 2013. "How I Learned to Stop Worrying and Love the Market: Virtualism, Disavowal, and Public Secrecy in Neoliberal Environmental Conservation." *Environment and Planning D: Society and Space* 31 (5): 796–812.

Foucault, Michel. 2008. *The Birth of Biopolitics*. Translated by G. Burchell. New York: Palgrave Macmillan.

Hardt, Michael, and Antonio Negri. 2009. *Commonwealth*. Cambridge MA: Belknap Press of Harvard University Press.

Kapoor, Ilan. 2015. "What 'Drives' Capitalist Development?" *Human Geography* 8 (3): 66–78.

Koster, Martijn, and Pieter de Vries. 2012. "Slum Politics: Community Leaders, Everyday Needs, and Utopian Aspirations in Recife, Brazil." *Focaal* (62): 83–98.

Opinião Pública. 2015. "Corrupção lidera pela primeira vez pauta de problemas do país." Datafolha. http://datafolha.folha.uol.com.br.

Singer, André. 2014. "Rebellion in Brazil: Social and Political Complexion of the June Events." *New Left Review* 85, 19–38.

Swyngedouw, Erik. 2010. "The Communist Hypothesis and Revolutionary Capitalisms: Exploring the Idea of Communist Geographies for the Twenty-First Century." *Antipode* 41 (s1): 298–319.

Wikipedia. 2017. S.v. "2015–2017 Brazilian Economic Crisis." Last modified November 10. https://en.wikipedia.org/wiki/2015-2017_Brazilian_economic_crisis.

Žižek, Slavoj. 1989. *The Sublime Object of Ideology*. New York: Verso.

———. 2008. *In Defense of Lost Causes*. New York: Verso.

12 The Pervert versus the Hysteric
Politics at Tahrir Square

Ilan Kapoor

The pervert in Lacanian psychoanalytic thought is one who appears to be violating the Law but is in fact simply being incited by it: what looks like a challenge to the status quo is, in this sense, merely a guilt-ridden yet pleasurable acting out of it. The hysteric, on the other hand, is one who is much more deviant and out of joint: he/she gets off on doubting and questioning the prevailing hegemony, thereby posing a threat to it. This chapter examines the recent politics at Tahrir Square in this light: the politics of the perverts (the Muslim Brotherhood, standing for a communitarian religious fundamentalism, and the Egyptian Army, upholding a secular authoritarianism that entails further integration into global capitalism) versus the politics of the hysterics (engaged citizens demanding democracy and economic justice). The chapter also reflects on the broader psychoanalytic potentialities and pitfalls of popular uprisings, including the danger that a politics of hysteria can all too easily morph into a politics of perversion.

Perversion and Hysteria

Let me begin by tracing the meanings of perversion and hysteria in Sigmund Freud, Jacques Lacan, and Slavoj Žižek, each of whom underlines different yet related psychoanalytic dimensions, with Žižek infusing the terms with a distinctly political bent.

The concept of perversion was popularized by nineteenth-century European psychiatry. Freud, in particular, argued for a "polymorphous perversion," which according to him predisposes human infants to an open and ambiguous sexuality. But he also saw perversion as sexual behavior that falls outside the heterosexual norm—homosexuality, for example (Freud 2000, 15). For him, infants derive sexual gratification indiscriminately (i.e., from any part of the body), although this polymorphousness is later constrained by social norms. Sexual perversion is thus the result of our entry into the social, which acculturates us to what is "normal" and "perverted."

The concept of hysteria, for its part, has its origins in ancient Greek medicine, denoting a female disease of the womb (*hysteron*) (Evans 1996, 79). Once again, nineteenth-century psychiatry revived and recast the term, with Freud in particular developing his psychoanalytic method through his treatment of "hysterical" women, notably in the case of Dora.[1] Accordingly, for Freud, hysteria is an anxious reaction to trauma, a kind of perplexed fascination in the face of paternal authority; Dora is precisely someone who complains about being the object of her father's and Mr. K's affective and sexual machinations (see Findlay 1994).

LACAN

Lacan differs from Freud in detaching both perversion and hysteria from their sexual stereotypes, making them technical rather than moral concepts. Eschewing Freud's ambiguity, he defines both terms in relation to social norms, not natural aberration or biology (Lacan 1988, 221; Kotsko 2008, 46). Thus, perversion and hysteria are not to be restricted to the subject's identity or behavior (e.g., as queers or women); they are character structures describing how the subject relates to the Law (or what Lacan calls the "big Other," the realm of social and institutional authority). As a consequence, anyone can be a pervert or a hysteric.

Of primary importance to Lacan is the dialectical relationship between Law and desire. As human animals, we enter into the Symbolic (qua Law) with the purpose of regulating access to our unlimited biological drives.

For Lacan (1977, 697–98; 1991, 84), the function of the Law is not to prohibit but regulate our *jouissance*, that is, to protect the subject from unbridled and unbearable enjoyment (see chapter 7). In this sense, Law manages pleasure, stabilizing and reassuring the subject, enabling her to desire within the ambit of its prescriptions: "The subject gives up the dream of unlimited enjoyment and in return gets desire within the pleasure principle" (Aristodemou 2015, 19; see also Kapoor 2014). In contradistinction, desire "is the reverse of the law" (Lacan 1977, 787): it only emerges through the possibilities offered by the Law, in response to the establishment of limits and restrictions. As Evans puts it, "Desire is essentially the desire to transgress, and for there to be transgression it is first necessary for there to be prohibition" (1996, 102).

Lacan (1993) posits three main character structures—perversion, neurosis (subdivided into hysteria and obsessionality), and psychosis—which are all failed attempts at resolving the impasse between desire and Law.[2] Perversion for him describes a way of desiring that infringes the Law (e.g., the normative requirements of the Oedipus complex). In a way, simply to desire is to defy the Law, and in that sense, everyone is a pervert. We seek enjoyment, but the Law stands in our way, so we transgress it. Yet the problem with perversion is that it is characterized by disavowal: perverts, according to Lacan, are aware that the mother lacks a phallus but nonetheless deny it. In fact, they often resort to the use of a fetish (e.g., a shoe, underwear) as a substitute for the lack, to soothe and cover over the trauma of castration. In other words, perverts know well that the Law stands in the way, but when it comes down to it—orienting their desire toward challenging the Law—they opt for a reflective and distant position. Their knowledge becomes extraneous and inoperative when they act.

The upshot is that the pervert seeks enjoyment by trying to cross the Law but ends up siding with the very Law that he purportedly seeks to overcome. He may well outwardly criticize and expose the power games of the master, but by not carrying through with his desire to transgress, he effectively becomes a complicit partner in the master's fantasy. In fact, according to Lacan, he makes himself the instrument of the master's pleasure, enjoying such self-instrumentalization (1977, 320). His propensity toward disavowal allows him to evacuate any nagging questions, to relish assuming the position of the object, and to find in that a relief to his torment: "The pervert has no doubt that his acts serve the *jouissance* of the Other" (Evans 1996, 142).

If perversion is ultimately about refraining from challenging the Law, hysteria is about constantly questioning it. For Lacan, hysteria is a form of neurosis, wherein the subject struggles against being integrated into the symbolic order or Law. Commenting on the case of Dora, for example, he seizes on one of her key questions—"Am I a man or a woman?" For him, not only does Dora question her gender identity, she also probes why the authority figures around her (her father, Mr. K, Freud / her analyst) insist on wanting to pin her down (Lacan 1993, 170–78). The Other may well be issuing orders or symbolic mandates, but Dora the hysteric contests them, doubts them, interrogates them. Unlike the pervert, she dreads rather than relishes becoming the tool of the Other. And the more she resists and dreads, the more she gleans that the Other is an impostor with no legitimate authority over her. Lacan champions such a questioning attitude, seeing it not as a neurosis to be cured (à la Freud) but as a subject position to come to terms with.

ŽIŽEK

Žižek, for his part, follows in Lacan's footsteps in viewing the pervert as false transgressor and the hysteric as questioner. For Žižek, by treating the Law as a screen preventing unlimited *jouissance*, the pervert ends up confirming the status of the Law. So the irony is that the pervert-as-putative-transgressor actually longs for the rule of Law (Žižek 2008, 17). He is certain he knows what the Other wants and proceeds to try and deliver it: "[The pervert] is the instrument of the Other's enjoyment. A simple, but nonetheless poignant, expression of this perverse attitude is found in Hugh Hudson's *Chariots of Fire*, when the devout Eric Liddel explains his fast running which brought him a gold medal at the 1924 Paris Olympics: 'God made me for a purpose, but He also made me fast. And when I run,

Ilan Kapoor

I feel His pleasure'" (Žižek 2004, 103). The pervert thus lives his own secret fantasy by acting out that of the Other. But his acting out, his conviction about what brings enjoyment, only covers over the deadlock inherent in the Other's—and his own—fantasy (the traumas of life and the world that, in this example, religion helps soothe).

But Žižek's most original and important contribution to this discussion is his notion of the "obscene superego supplement." Like Lacan, he underlines that the Law doesn't only generate transgression but *needs* transgression to assert itself as Law (Žižek 1999, 46). And he points out that perversion fits well into this schema since the pervert's (false) transgression serves as the condition of the Law's operation, with the Law requiring such transgression to establish itself. His crucial insight, though, is that the Law is split between the "public letter and its obscene superego supplement" (Dean 2006, 135). This is evident in the way that, for example, the global North's industrial might is enabled by (neo)colonial plunder, a regime's stability is secured by emergency laws, or a new political regime is inaugurated by violent revolution: in each case, for the Law to be instituted, its defenders must disavow its dirty underside (i.e., its violent, racist, or criminal founding).

There is, moreover, a crucial enjoyment factor to add here, and this is where the superego comes in: the superego for Žižek (as for Lacan) is not the Freudian moral conscience that keeps the ego in check but the unconscious command to enjoy that accompanies the Law (Žižek 2006, 80–81). It is the "obscene supplement" to the Law that enjoins the subject (or pervert) to take pleasure in trespassing or complying with the Law. The superego helps mitigate the anxiety or guilt the subject may experience through his/her compliance or challenge by inciting the subject to desire, thereby increasing the Law's hold over the him/her. So the Law may well allow a degree of deviation and defiance, but submission is ensured through its libidinal complement (compliment?).

There are many ways of illustrating this process. Take, for example, the case of conventional mores and rules, which we may outwardly criticize but secretly enjoy (see Žižek 2006, 22ff.): the ascetic who renounces worldly desires but engages in strict ritual practices that themselves become a source of pleasure; the civil servant who publicly scorns red tape but covertly revels in it, delighting in his/her power to apply rules and procedures; or the academic pressure to "publish or perish" that many of us dislike and forever feel guilty about but that thereby libidinally binds us to the university and the (corporate) academic publishing machine. To be sure, not only is doing one's duty or complying with the Law pleasurable, but even resisting or perverting the Law brings feelings of enjoyment and guilt that oblige the subject to the Law.

Then there is the shadowy underside of the Law, also a source of *jouissance*—deviant rules, rituals, behaviors that are unofficially tolerated but must remain unwritten and unspoken (Žižek 2008, 73). Žižek has in mind here such varying social practices as speeding, petty corruption and tax evasion, the use of sexist and ableist jokes in private, or homophobic or racist initiation rituals in frat houses and the armed forces. These are all gray areas in public law and civility, institutional dirty secrets, which far from undermining the social system, serve as its inherent support. The rule of law is asserted and maintained through both quasi-transgressions (including deceit, lies, jokes, and prejudice) *and* people's secret enjoyment of them. As McMillan puts it, "The dominant law of a discourse does not function through repression but is infused with *jouissance* produced through the unconscious acknowledgement of sanctioned violations of the law" (2015, 63).

So we glean, once again, the complicity between the explicit Law and its unconscious superegoic supplement. But we need to note, too, the important implication that follows—when we comply with the Law, it is not necessarily because this Law is morally right and good but because it is libidinally charged: "The moral Law is obscene in so far as it is its form itself which functions as a motivating force driving us to obey its command—that is, in so far as we obey moral Law because it is law and not because of a set of positive reasons: the obscenity of moral Law is the obverse of its formal character" (Žižek 1989, 81). This is why Žižek stresses the importance of the "fetishistic disavowal" (Žižek 1989, 18, 32–33); we may be aware that the Law is problematic, that it has a dirty underside, but we go ahead and

Ilan Kapoor

submit to it anyway, so libidinally alluring are its superegoic commands and charms (see chapters 3 and 11).

In this scheme of things, the pervert for Žižek turns out to be a status quo, political conservative. This is because she/he can only enjoy within the purview of the Law. She/he may well critique the status quo, but this is merely an ironic acting out that ultimately sides, and takes enjoyment in siding, with the Law (Žižek 1999, 247ff.). Through processes of pleasure and guilt, the Law's obscene superego supplement may well incite her or him to transgress, but it does so only within the political and libidinal limits prescribed by the Law, that is, "in a completely non-dangerous way" (Kotsko 2008, 49).

Now to turn to the issue of hysteria: Like Lacan, Žižek valorizes hysteria because it is "much more subversive and threatening to the predominant hegemony" (1999, 247). The hysteric approaches and responds to authority with radical doubt and uncertainty, yielding a more provocative, albeit unrehearsed and unpredictable, politics. She/he is out of joint in the face of the Law: "What is hysteria if not precisely the effect . . . of a failed interpellation; what is the hysterical question if not the articulation of the incapacity of the subject to fulfill the symbolic identification, to assume fully and without restraint the symbolic mandate?" (Žižek 1989, 113; see also Dolar 1993, 78). The hysteric recognizes the hail or call of the master but is not sure it is meant for her. "What does he want from me? Who is he to hail me? And why is he hailing *me*?" she asks. A kind of dialogue of the deaf ensues, with the hysteric resisting and challenging her putative master (Kay 2003, 164; Cixous and Clément 1986, 148). She may provisionally accept his role as master but may just as quickly decide that he is neither appealing nor masterful enough for her. She is, in a way, in search of a master, secretly wishing he will help unlock the deadlock of her desire, yet ultimately finding it impossible to locate anyone who quite fits the bill.

The hysteric's questioning attitude means that she is constantly trying to find out what the Other wants, yet she never identifies with the Other's desire, always aspiring to something different (Žižek 2008, xvi, 44). In this sense, she resists the superego supplement, forever postponing satisfaction and refusing to be the object of the Other's enjoyment. This postponement, this constantly unsatisfied desire, translates into a demand for something else, outside the bounds of what is on offer by the Law. Hence the possibility of a deviant politics.

Thus, in contrast to the pervert, the false transgressor who refrains from making any threatening demands, the hysteric is the perpetual doubter who bombards the master with questions and impossible demands. The pervert protests, cynically resigned to the fact that only that change will happen that is tolerated by the Law, while the hysteric insists on change that exceeds the limits of the Law. The pervert knows what the master wants and enjoys delivering it; the hysteric questions the master's desires, postponing enjoyment in favor of other possibilities. The pervert is, in this sense, confident and ready to act but more unconscious of the deadlock of desire, whereas the hysteric is circumspect but more psychoanalytically aware of the ultimate impossibility of enjoyment.

The problem, though, is that the hysteric can so easily succumb to the trap of perversion. Žižek therefore asks, "How can I break out of [the] vicious cycle of the Law and desire, of Prohibition and its transgression?" (1999, 149). Rather than opting for an alternate politics, the hysteric may snugly give in to the superego command to enjoy, seduced by what the Law has to offer (e.g., capitalist consumerism, liberal democracy). Perversion after all is much easier—you get to cut to the chase by adopting the master at hand and promptly enjoying. While hysteria is comparatively much harder: you have to postpone your enjoyment and bear the burden of being your own master. Hysterical politics can thus all too frequently get diverted, stopped in its tracks by the lure, comfort, and authority of the status quo. Hence today, Žižek ponders, "the question of how we are to hystericize the subject caught in the closed loop of perversion (how we are to inculcate the dimension of lack and questioning in him) becomes [all the] more urgent" (1999, 248).

The properly (meaningfully?) hystericized subject, then, is not one who is just questioning, but one more conscious of the machinations of *jouissance*. Unlike perversion, hysteria *does* offer a way into the unconscious

Ilan Kapoor

(Žižek 1999, 247), and so the challenge is to take advantage of this opportunity to resist the seductions of Law and desire. It is the realization that *jouissance* is in fact not possible, that there is no enjoyment beyond the Law, that enables the hysteric to see that mere transgression or perversion of the Law is not necessarily a path to liberation (Wells 2014, 28). Hence understanding that what is on offer by the master is suspect and fraudulent, that his authority is incomplete and illegitimate, is what makes the obscene superego supplement obsolete and inoperative.

Wells stresses the important point that, ultimately, the hysteric needs to grasp that the "obstacle to the realization of desire is not beyond the Law, but internal to desire itself. The obstacle to desire's fulfillment beyond the Law is precisely its secret reliance on the Law to sustain itself" (2014, 29). So it seems, as a consequence, that only after being able to suspend the obscene libidinal attachments to the Law, to make the "radically negative gesture of 'unplugging' from the symbolic order" (Kotsko 2008, 47), can one begin transforming into a self-legislating subject.

Politics at Tahrir Square

Let us now examine how the notions of perversion and hysteria apply to the 2011 popular uprising at Tahrir Square. Before looking at the uprising itself, I will briefly consider the main factors leading up to it. I will then contrast the politics of hysteria advocated by the demonstrators with the politics of perversion espoused by the army and the Muslim Brotherhood during and after the revolution. I will end by reflecting on the pitfalls of Egypt's Arab Spring, that is, how hysteria has effectively morphed into perversion.

PRECURSORS TO THE REVOLUTION

The 2011 revolution was not, of course, a spontaneous political act but the result of a cumulative sociopolitical process. The Mubarak regime had been in power for almost three decades. Apart from a brief interlude in 1980–81, it had maintained a permanent state of emergency (in effect since 1967), giving it the powers to suspend the rule of law, prohibit public gatherings, punish political opponents, and suppress dissent. Meanwhile, the state party, the National Democratic Party, monopolized the political process. It controlled state institutions and decision making, repressed or co-opted civil society organizations, and harassed or banned political parties and movements, including the Muslim Brotherhood. It also dominated local and national elections (largely seen as rigged), periodically winning them with overwhelming majorities. It had won the 2010 national parliamentary elections, for instance, with a 97 percent majority.

The state maintained friendly ties with the Egyptian army (Hosni Mubarak was himself an officer in the air force), although the army enjoyed a relatively high degree of autonomy from the regime. This was in large part due to the army's strong economic clout: it is estimated that it controls some 30 to 40 percent of the Egyptian economy, with a stake in a wide range of agricultural and industrial activities (e.g., arms production, real estate and construction, food and consumer goods production, hotels; Bhuiyan 2015, 502; Salem 2013).

In the wake of the debt crisis in the late 1980s, the Mubarak regime was driven to negotiate stabilization and structural adjustment programs with the International Monetary Fund (IMF) and World Bank. As a result, two major waves of neoliberal reform were instituted (in 1991–97 and 2003–8), involving a panoply of economic liberalization policies. Although an outward success—gross national product (GNP) rose fourfold between 1981 and 2006 and grew by an average of 6 percent annually in 2007–11—such policies were also accompanied by historic rising levels of inequality: for example, real wages actually declined during this period despite massive wealth accumulation (Shahin 2012, 50; Maher 2011, 35). The one to two years before the revolution saw soaring inflation, including a 30 percent rise in food prices, and increasing unemployment, reaching 40 percent among young people and university graduates (Shahin 2012, 50). Obviously blind to such hardships, the IMF released a glowing 2010 economic report just days before the revolution, praising the government for its "careful fiscal management" (cited in Maher 2011, 37).

Egypt's wealth accumulation from the 1990s onward translated into the spectacular rise in wealth and power of a small elite coalescing around

Mubarak's son, Gamal, widely seen as Mubarak's "natural" successor. Through cronyism and corruption, Gamal and his associates handsomely profited from the government's neoliberal policies (e.g., privatization of health care and state-owned enterprises, government subsidies and tax breaks, favorable bank loans). So powerful did this group become, in fact, that its economic and political ambitions increasingly came to threaten those of the army. This almost certainly prepared the ground for the army's impending support for the revolution (Roccu 2013, 432; Shahin 2012, 59).

The rise of the Gamal-led oligarchy saw the concomitant rise of the impoverishment and proletarianization of large sections of the country's lower and middle classes. Privatization and price liberalization policies meant increasingly squeezed public-sector workers (including judges, tax collectors, teachers) and dispossession and unemployment among small farmers and factory workers, with many having to take on additional jobs in the informal economy to make ends meet (Roccu 2013, 434). From 2004 onward, despite state repression, labor unions organized a series of protests and strikes against privatization, low wages, and high inflation. In fact, between 2004 and 2010 more than three thousand labor actions happened across the country (Shahin 2012, 58; Maher 2011, 36). This period also saw notable protests by youth groups (Kefaya, the youth wing of the April 6 Movement) against unemployment, rises in food prices, and police brutality.

THE REVOLUTION

Popular opposition to the Mubarak regime gained momentum after the Tunisian Revolution in December 2010. Demonstrations took place across Egypt through January 2011, peaking on the Day of Rage on January 25. Eighteen days of mass protests followed in Cairo and other key cities, involving some fifteen million protestors, about four million of whom congregated at Tahrir Square (Elzoughby 2011; Shahin 2012, 48). The protests were accompanied by a quasi-economic shutdown of the country, with most factories, banks, and shops closed (Maher 2011, 40). The revolution culminated on February 11, when Mubarak finally resigned.

Fig. 17. Tahrir Square, February 9, 2011. Photo by Jonathan Rashad, Wikimedia Commons.

The mass demonstrations were mostly leaderless, in the sense that no single participant or party commanded broad-based support. This was very much a "networked revolution," bringing together a wide array of groups and relying heavily on the Internet and social media for organization and mobilization (e.g., Twitter, Facebook, YouTube, sms, email; Telmissany 2014, 40). Youth groups played a key organizing role (e.g., the Youth of Tomorrow, Kefaya, the Youth of Justice and Freedom, the Young People of the Muslim Brotherhood), supported by labor (e.g., trade unions, the April 6 Movement) and other sociopolitical organizations (e.g., the Campaign for the Support of ElBaradei, We Are All Khalid Said, National Association for Change; Shahin 2012, 55). While the youth wing of the Muslim Brotherhood took an active role from the start, the main organization did not, joining the mass demonstrations only later in the process.

The protests reportedly gathered a broad range of people from varying socioeconomic backgrounds (Goes 2105, 59; Shahin 2012, 48). These included men and women, young and old; workers and middle-class people;

Ilan Kapoor

housewives and trade unionists; civil servants, journalists and independent judges; secular and religious people (Muslims, Copts); urban and rural residents; and the unemployed, the disaffected, and the dispossessed.

The demonstrations at Tahrir Square, as well as in other parts of the country, were largely peaceful, avoiding clashes with the dreaded state security forces and instead inviting the latter to join in. Tahrir Square was turned into a kind of "'mini state' that provided food and supplies, health services, defense and security, media and communications, and entertainment for the millions of participating protestors" (Shahin 2012, 48). People took part not just in protest, but in song and collective prayers, as well as in public debate on an assortment of issues ranging from the type of state they desired and the virtues of democracy to the improvement of living standards and the role religion should have in public life (Telmissany 2014, 40; Goes 2015, 59–60).

What united protesters was an uncompromising political demand: the end of the Mubarak regime. Mubarak initially responded with violence, relying on state security forces for "riot control" and intimidation and trying (mostly unsuccessfully) to shut down communications and the Internet. Then, as the army's sympathies turned in favor of the protestors, Mubarak offered concessions (political reform, fresh elections, the promise not to rerun as president). But the protestors would have none of it. There was no desire to enter into dialogue with the regime for risk of legitimizing it. The protestors insisted on nothing less than for Mubarak and his cronies to step down. The youth group Kefaya's slogan, for example, was "No extension for Mubarak. No hereditary succession."

In contrast to the increasing desperation of the regime, the protestors refrained from violence or provocation. Quite the contrary, as mentioned earlier, they explicitly called on the security forces and army to join the struggle. For Žižek (2011b), this feature "clearly distinguishes an emancipatory demonstration from a right-wing populist one: although the [R]ight's mobilisation proclaims the organic unity of the people, it is a unity sustained by a call to annihilate [a] designated enemy" (e.g., outsiders, traitors), wholly absent in this case.

The protestors' demand for the end of the regime was complemented by a secular-political call—for "freedom," "democracy," and "social justice." Several participating groups used those three terms in their platforms and outreach materials, with *Horreya* (freedom) and *dimuqratya* (democracy) as the most highly visible placards in Tahrir Square and chants of *adala igtimaya* (social justice) as the most audible (Roccu 2013, 437; see also Shahin 2012, 62). The revolution needs to be seen therefore neither as a pro-Western protest nor as some inward-looking religious movement; in fact, even the Muslim Brotherhood, which eventually joined the revolution, ended up adopting the "language of secular demands" (Žižek 2011b; Telmissany 2014, 39, 41). (Cleavages between the Brotherhood and other groups developed in the days and months following.)

The outcome, on February 11, 2011, was that Mubarak stepped down. He had few other options, especially after the army sided with the protestors. Power was transferred to the Supreme Council of the Armed Forces (SCAF), which dissolved parliament, suspended the constitution, and organized the country's transition to democracy.

THE HYSTERICS

One can see why the protestors can be considered hysterics. They had had enough with years of authoritarian rule, police repression, and socioeconomic deprivation, and so began to doubt, interrogate, and increasingly contest the Mubarak regime, culminating in the demonstrations at Tahrir Square. As the revolution progressed, they steadfastly stood their ground. It would have been easier for them to give in to the obscene superego supplement to the Law, to secretly take comfort in what the status quo putatively offered them, but they resisted. Even as Mubarak subsequently relented by offering concessions, they decided to postpone immediate gratification for other political possibilities. In this sense, they refused to become the tool of the Mubarak regime (as the pervert would), realizing that the more they resisted, the more the Master stood as an increasingly desperate impostor with no legitimate authority.

Ilan Kapoor

The demonstrators' postponement of enjoyment, their unsatisfied desire, translated into a refusal not only to dialogue or compromise with the Law but to make demands that fell outside the limits of the Law. As hysterics, they bombarded the master with impossible demands (freedom, democracy, social justice) as if to say, "Prove your worth to us!" In effect they were demanding a "true" master, one that the Mubarak regime did not, and could not, measure up to.

But unfortunately the revolution was not over on February 11. Once victory had been achieved and the master deposed, significant dangers loomed. The demonstrators' hysterical politics, their political and psychoanalytic resolve, was to be further challenged and tested by new putative masters.

THE POLITICAL AFTERMATH

In June 2012, sixteen months after the February 2011 revolution, Mohamed Morsi, a former leader of the Muslim Brotherhood, became Egypt's first democratically elected president. But his regime was short-lived. Rather than addressing the key socioeconomic concerns raised at Tahrir Square and by the population at large, he focused on fulfilling the Muslim Brotherhood's platform, namely, the implementation of Sharia law and the Islamization of the state. He clamped down on public protests and appointed mostly Islamists to the constituent assembly (charged with drafting a new constitution).

But his Islamization agenda received little support from the civil service, increasingly causing him to isolate himself by relying exclusively on his party and ruling by presidential decree. In the wake of worsening economic conditions and growing public dissatisfaction, Tahrir Square once again became the site of massive protests in June 2013. Protestors demanded Morsi's resignation, opposing his Islamization campaign and tacitly endorsing what looked like an impending military takeover. In July Morsi was ousted by a bloody (Abdel Fattah el-Sisi–led) military coup that saw Morsi arrested, the Muslim Brotherhood banned, and its assets seized. The SCAF dissolved the newly elected parliament, suspended the constitution, and announced new elections. In May 2014 (former) army general el-Sisi was elected president, gaining some 93 percent of the votes (albeit with low voter turnout and a boycott by most political parties).

Let us now consider ways in which the army and the Muslim Brotherhood are perverts. Neither is straightforwardly a pervert, as we'll see, and each engages in the politics of perversion differently.

Before proceeding, though, let me clarify what I specifically take to be the Law (qua symbolic authority or "big Other"), since perversion, and for that matter hysteria, only make sense in relation to a given Law. In the Egyptian case, I mean by Law the authority of both the Egyptian state (its institutional/discursive, political, and economic power) and the broader cultural and political economy (e.g., global capitalism, the forces of Westernization, other powerful actors/states, such as the United States or the IMF and World Bank).

The Army

The army might well have had reasonably close ties to the Mubarak regime, but as pointed out earlier, it also enjoyed relative autonomy given its significant stakes in the Egyptian economy. Moreover, its ties to the regime had considerably strained and weakened by the time of the 2011 revolution, as it was faced with the growing threat of the Gamal-led oligarchy. So when it broke with its political master (Mubarak) and sided with the protestors in early 2011, it was perverting or transgressing the Law. The state had become an obstacle to its enjoyment (of its political-economic power and autonomy), hence the superegoic incitement to violate the Law.

But after the revolution, the army has increasingly *become* the master and Law. It organized the transition to "democracy" (twice), instigated the coup against Morsi, and now stands as key support for el-Sisi's regime. Since coming to power in 2014, el-Sisi has gradually suffocated the emancipatory potential of Tahrir Square, reinstituting restrictions on civil society groups and more recently imposing draconian decrees

Ilan Kapoor

that restrict freedom of expression, association, and assembly (Kingsley 2014; Goes 2015).

Yet in relation to the (global) capitalist political economy, the army/el-Sisi regime is indeed a pervert (in the same way that the Mubarak regime can also be considered to have been on this issue while it was in power). It may well have explicitly identified with, and supported, the Tahrir Square protestors, including their demands for alleviating poverty and improving social justice (Bhuiyan 2015; Goes 2015; Salem 2013), but to date it has done little to address these problems, preferring instead to advance the country's integration into the global economy. In this regard, el-Sisi has flatly stated that "democratic aspirations are hindering much needed economic reforms" (quoted in Goes 2015, 65). His government has proceeded, accordingly, to institute labor laws that restrict the right to strike. And it has helped consolidate the army's sizable stake in the economy, for example, awarding it state building contracts worth a billion dollars (Kingsley 2014). The latter move, it must be pointed out, is evidence of the increasingly symbiotic relationship between the army and the el-Sisi regime.

As a consequence, Egypt is being ruled by an authoritarian capitalist state, not unlike that of contemporary Russia and China. It is hard not to see el Sisi's clampdown on labor and freedom of expression and assembly as anything but a way of ensuring law and order for the sake of the smooth functioning of the neoliberal economy (i.e., attempting to cover over the Real of Capital). No wonder that global financial institutions like the IMF have been eager to extend further loans to the el-Sisi government, with the Obama administration announcing a billion-dollar debt swap that reduces Egypt's debt burden as long as the funds are used in accordance with neoliberal conditionalities (e.g., market liberalization). As Maher argues, Egypt's massive debt is a sure-fire way of guaranteeing continued neoliberalization of the economy and a self-reinforcing cycle of dependency (2011, 1).[3] For its part, the new Trump regime has cozied up to el-Sisi, choosing to validate rather than turn a blind eye to the latter's political repression and strongman tactics, while also reconsidering whether to reinstate a military financing deal suspended under Barack Obama (Baker and Walsh 2017).

The army has thus engaged in a politics of perversion. This is certainly true in its relationship to the Mubarak regime during the revolution and in its relationship to the global political economy since accession to political power after the revolution. Typical of the pervert-fetishist, it has made itself the instrument of glObal capital (and Egyptian ruling elites), helping to create a stable political environment and an open and safe economy for trade and investment. It has forsaken the goals of social justice and inequality in favor of continuing global capitalist integration. Such fetishistic disavowal, to be sure, is the stamp of perversion ("I know well that something is bad, but I do it anyway"). The army's recent trajectory—from violating the Law and supporting revolution to becoming a status quo, authoritarian capitalist—underlines once again Lacan and Žižek's important point that the pervert's (false) transgression becomes the very condition of the Law's operation. In a sense, then, Egypt's political-economic status quo *needed* the army's perversion or violation to move beyond the dead-end created by the Mubarak regime, and the army, it seems, was only too willing to oblige.

The Muslim Brotherhood

Relative to the army, the Muslim Brotherhood at first sight appears more transgressive: it deviated from the Law by joining the revolution *and* trying to Islamize the state. Yet appearances deceive. I want to suggest that the Brotherhood's transgressions ultimately reinforced the Law, although not in the same way as the army's did.

It is true that, like the army, the Brotherhood challenged the master (the Mubarak regime), thereby violating the state's authority. It may not have instigated the revolution, but it did end up participating in it from the Day of Rage onward and in that sense helped transgress the Law. It is also true that, in contrast to the army's secular vision and integration into global capitalism, the Brotherhood endeavored to impose religious rule on the state. Once Morsi came to power, he and the Brotherhood focused on Islamizing the state and instituting Sharia law.

But what looks like a seeming break from the status quo isn't. Even if the Islamization program had been realized (it was aborted by the military

Ilan Kapoor

coup), it would still have been only falsely transgressive. This is because contemporary religious resurgence is a reaction to, not a departure from, global (capitalist) modernity. Several analysts have made this point (Ali 2003; Bayat 2007; Mamdani 2004), arguing that Muslim "fundamentalism" (or for that matter, Christian, Hindu, Buddhist, or Jewish fundamentalism) is not a regressive, antimodern movement but a thoroughly modern response to globalization and (Western) neo-imperialism. In this sense, the Brotherhood's assertion of "tradition" and religious identity is integral to the ideological universe of neoliberal globalization; it is proof that imperialism has worked (at least to some extent), successfully deracinating communities and threatening their cultural identities.

The Brotherhood's return to its roots, to some "pure" Islam, is thus an unthreatening, idiosyncratic search for a path to *jouissance*. It may well be transgressing the Law by seeking out a particular identity, but it does so without really making any menacing demands on the global order. Its Islamic program fits nicely in the existing glObal multicultural capitalist constellation, which encourages and accommodates new perversions (e.g., extreme sports, strict diets; Žižek 1999, 251).

This argument is further buttressed by the Brotherhood's economic position. Indeed, the movement may well stand against poverty and unemployment or criticize greed and "corruption" (Wickham 2013, 301–3; Osman 2013), but it has no critique of capitalism per se. The "true enemy is not Western economic neocolonialism . . . but its 'immoral' culture" (Žižek 2015). The Brotherhood's socioeconomic commentary remains mostly at the level of religious rhetoric and proselytizing. Furthermore, its popularity across Egypt derives mainly from its vast social service network (educational, health, and job-training programs, mostly in poor neighborhoods), but these have remained largely apolitical. In many ways, in fact, these charitable social services help legitimize the ills of the market, letting the state off the hook by filling gaps in its welfare responsibilities (see Kapoor 2013, 65–66).

Now the el-Sisi regime, like the preceding Mubarak regime, does see the Brotherhood as a threat, to the point of not only banning it and imprisoning Morsi but also trying to dismantle its social services network. But this is a (ruthless) political ploy aimed less at any fear of genuine sociopolitical revolution by the Brotherhood and more at eliminating a successful electoral competitor that would likely have unseated el-Sisi and his military allies (as did Morsi in the 2012 elections).

The Muslim Brotherhood therefore also engages in a perverse politics. It implicitly recognizes and rebels against the deracinating and neocolonial ills of modernity but disavows these through a knee-jerk and reactionary socioreligious program. It fails to carry through on its political desires, choosing by default to be the instrument of the master's pleasure. Or more precisely, in serving the *jouissance* of God, it ends up serving the *jouissance* of neoliberal globalization. In this sense, unlike the perversion of the army, which more straightforwardly becomes the object of capitalism's desires, the Brotherhood's perversion is so-to-speak displaced: in obliging the one (God) it is also obliging the other (capitalist globalization). Once again, this confirms, not weakens, the master's authority. One can indeed transgress globalization, but only within certain limits, that is, in a relatively safe and unthreatening way. And the consequence is that one's unconscious desire to obey has strengthened, not diminished.

EGYPT'S UNREALIZED REVOLUTION: HYSTERIA TRANSFORMS INTO PERVERSION

But then, one might ask, what about the protestors? Aren't they perverts too, since they have failed to follow through on their revolution? Ultimately (or at least to this point in time), I would have to say yes. They *did* carry through on their initial desire for political change, successfully toppling Mubarak. This was an important milestone in Egypt's political landscape. But then, equally crucial, they compromised their desire, settling for a master in the person of the army. One master replaced (and was allowed to replace) another, with el-Sisi turning out to be equally (if not more) authoritarian as Mubarak, failing once again to deliver on meaningful democratic change and social justice.[4] The protestors' acquiescence resulted in the army's using its iron fist to keep dissent tightly in check so as to be able to impose further neoliberalization of the economy.

Ilan Kapoor

In retrospect, the much lauded "diversity" and "leaderlessness" of the revolution likely turned out to be its Achilles' heel. More detailed research is required on the social composition of the protest movements across the country to determine whether they were indeed broad-based: Did they perhaps suffer from inadequate participation by disenfranchised peasants and workers? Or were they dominated by bourgeois educated young people? A narrower social base of the uprisings would certainly help explain their lack of adequate political resolve and their willingness to compromise on such key goals as social justice. In any event, the secular Left appears to have lacked adequate leadership and organization to unite disparate groups and mobilize and direct people's energy and rage (Goes 2015, 62). This allowed the army to divide and conquer, standing first with all the protestors against Mubarak and then with the secular Left against the Islamization program to isolate and topple the Muslim Brotherhood.

Knowing well that the Egyptian army brass is (and since the 1950s, has always been) part of country's ruling elite, the protestors appear to have engaged in a double disavowal: wanting revolution, yet supporting the military coup against Morsi; and calling for change ("freedom," "democracy," "social justice"), yet settling on a master most unlikely to bring it about. The protestors' revolutionary fervor was thus perverted when it allowed itself to be seduced by what the Law seemingly had to offer (the promise of secularism and stability, as opposed to Islamization). So rather than postponing their enjoyment and bearing the burden of searching for a worthy master, the protestors settled for the master at hand and the prospect of imminent *jouissance*.[5]

But in addition to this libidinal trap, the Left's failure to adequately mobilize and tap into people's revolutionary potential has meant that the comfort and authority of the status quo won over a more unpredictable and out-of-joint hysterical politics. As mentioned earlier, revolutionary zeal is not enough; it must be mobilized, articulated, and deftly deployed to have lasting impact. Hence Žižek states, "This is the fatal weakness of recent protests: they express an authentic rage which is not able to transform into a positive programme for sociopolitical change. They express a spirit of revolt without revolution" (2011c; see also Žižek, 2013, 2012, 63ff., 2011a).

Conclusion: Hystericizing Politics?

I have tried in this chapter to highlight the libidinal underpinnings of popular uprisings. What Lacan and Žižek emphasize is that critiquing or challenging the Law is only seemingly rebellious. By way of the obscene superego supplement to the Law, not only is our violation needed for the Law to function, but such violation binds us to the Law, keeping our rebellion within the (unthreatening) bounds that the Law itself defines and tolerates. "Perversion" is the name given to such quiescent defiance, and "hysteria" to a more thoroughgoing transgression that enables the rebel to uncompromisingly hold on to his or her desire for radical change.[6]

What the Egyptian case underlines is not only how perversion and hysteria can play out (and have played out) in a specific power constellation, but also how hysteria can mutate into perversion. Doubting authority, always maintaining a questioning attitude toward it, is so very difficult when the stability of the status quo and the prospect of immediate *jouissance* seem comparatively easier and more compelling. In the Egyptian case, a hysterical politics would have required not just a more effective political mobilization and articulation by the Left (no easy task), but also tremendous psychoanalytic resources, it seems.

The revolutionary subject would need, then, to be able to stick obstinately to his/her desire (see chapter 11), to be so attuned to the machinations of *jouissance* as to suspend the commands of the obscene superego supplement. Žižek calls this the "ethical Act": "'Falling into some kind of death.' . . . There is no ethical act proper without taking the risk of such a momentary suspension of the big Other" (1999, 263). This means not just violating the Law but reconstituting its parameters, not just refusing to play the master's game, but restructuring the nature of the game itself and one's position within it.

And in Egypt, who knows? Despite what may now look like a failed revolution, such an ethical Act might yet be in the works.

Ilan Kapoor

Notes

1. The case of Dora (Freud's pseudonym for a female patient he treated for hysteria; see Freud 1997) is about Dora's suspicion that her father, involved in an unhappy marriage with her mother, is underhandedly trying to palm her off to his friend, Herr K, in return for having an illicit affair with Frau K, Herr K's wife. Dora ends up abruptly terminating her psychoanalytic treatment, with Freud seeing the case largely as a therapeutic failure, although a pioneering one he learned from (he blames himself for, among other things, not adequately considering Dora's attachment to Frau K).

2. I will only focus on perversion and hysteria here, but in short, perversion is about being aware of the machinations of Law or authority but ultimately failing to transgress them (through processes of disavowal). Hysteria and obsession are both about questioning the Law, although in the former case, it implies a demand for knowledge about oneself and the Other ("Who/what am I?" "What am I to you?" "What do you want from me?"), and in the latter, it is about an uncomfortable ignorance, that is, engaging in never-ending questions or talk to avoid confronting trauma (one's own or that engendered by the Law). Finally, psychosis is about having no awareness of the Law qua symbolic order and hence never being able to submit to any Law (including one's own).

3. Between 2006 and 2009, Egypt's net transfers/outflows (the difference between received loans and debt payments) reached $3.4 billion, with its debt growing by 15 percent during that period (Maher 2011, p. 42). Such debt has ensured that the economy is kept open to foreign investors, with loans only being given subject to neoliberal conditionalities and structural adjustment programs.

4. This points up Walter Benjamin's famous statement that "every rise of Fascism bears witness to a failed revolution" (quoted in Žižek 2013).

5. The only worthy master would presumably be the self-legislating subject.

6. I see Left reformism (as opposed to Left radicalism) as a form of perversion. It compromises its desire for meaningful change by settling for patchwork reforms (e.g., liberal human rights, welfare/charity for the poor and marginalized) that are unthreatening to, and in fact supportive of, liberal democratic capitalism. This stands in contrast to today's notable *hysterical* Right radicalism (e.g., the politics of Donald Trump, Narendra Modi, or Silvio Berlusconi), which refuses to compromise its desires (e.g., for a flourishing capitalism) in the face of what it sees as a threatening Left secularism/multiculturalism—to the point of unapologetic racism, xenophobia, and sexism that targets Muslims, Latinos, immigrants, women, etc. (see epilogue). I thank Eleanor MacDonald for suggesting clarification of this point.

Works Cited

Ali, Tariq. 2003. *The Class of Fundamentalisms: Crusades, Jihads and Modernity*. London: Verso.

Aristodemou, Maria. 2015. "The Pervert's Guide to the Law: Clinical Vignettes from *Breaking Bad* to Breaking Free." In *Žižek and Law*, edited by L. de Sutter, 13–30. London: Routledge.

Baker, Peter, and Declan Walsh. 2017. "Trump Shifts Course on Egypt, Praising Its Authoritarian Leader." *New York Times*, April 3. https://www.nytimes.com/2017/04/03/world/middleeast/-egypt-sisi-trump-white-house.html.

Bayat, Asef. 2007. *Making Islam Democratic: Social Movements and the Post-Islamist Turn*. Stanford CA: Stanford University Press.

Bhuiyan, Shahjahan H. 2015. "Can Democratic Governance Be Achieved in Egypt?" *International Journal of Public Administration* 38, 496–509.

Cixous, Hélène, and Catherine Clément. 1986. *The Newly Born Woman*. Translated by Betsy Wing. Minneapolis: University of Minnesota Press.

Dean, Jodi. 2006. *Žižek's Politics*. New York: Routledge.

Dolar, Mladen. 1993. "Beyond Interpellation." *Qui Parle* 6 (2): 75–96.

Elzoughby, Moaaz. 2011. "The Dynamics of Egypt's Protest: An Inside View." Arab Reform Brief 46. http://www.arab-reform.net/en/node/423.

Evans, Dylan. 1996. *Dictionary of Lacanian Psychoanalysis*. London: Routledge.

Findlay, Heather. 1994. "Queer Dora: Hysteria, Sexual Politics, and Lacan's 'Intervention on Transference.'" GLQ 1 (3): 323–47.

Freud, Sigmund. 1997. *Dora: An Analysis of a Case of Hysteria*. New York: Touchstone.

———. 2000. *Three Essays on the Theory of Sexuality*. Translated by James Strachey. New York: Basic Books.

Goes, Eunice. 2015. "Power and the Public Sphere: Lessons from Tahrir Square." *Portuguese Journal of Social Science* 14 (1): 57–70.

Kapoor, Ilan. 2013. *Celebrity Humanitarianism: The Ideology of Global Charity*. London: Routledge.

———. 2014. "Psychoanalysis and Development: Contributions, Examples, Limits." *Third World Quarterly* 35 (7): 1120–43.

Kay, Sarah. 2003. *Žižek: A Critical Introduction*. Cambridge: Polity.

Kingsley, Patrick. 2014. "Worse than the Dictators: Egypt's Leaders Bring Pillars of Freedom Crashing Down." *Guardian*, December 26. http://www.theguardian.com/world/2014/dec/26/sp-egypt-pillars-of-freedom-crashing-down.

Kotsko, Adam. 2008. "Politics and Perversion: Situating Žižek's Paul." *Journal for Cultural and Religious Theory* 9 (2): 43–52.

Lacan, Jacques. 1977. *Écrits: A Selection*. Translated by A. Sheridan. New York: Norton.

———. 1988. *The Seminar, Book I: Freud's Papers on Technique, 1953–54*. Edited by Jacques-Alain Miller. Translated by J. Forrester. Cambridge: Cambridge University Press.

———. 1991. *The Seminar, Book II: The Ego in Freud's Theory and in the Technique of Psychoanalysis, 1954–55*. Edited by Jacques-Alain Miller. Translated by S. Tomaselli and J. Forrester. New York: Norton.

———. 1993. *The Seminar, Book III: The Psychoses, 1955–56*. Translated by Russell Grigg. London: Routledge.

Maher, Stephen. 2011. "The Political Economy of the Egyptian Revolution." *Monthly Review* 63 (6): 32–45.

Mamdani, Mahmood. 2004. *Good Muslim, Bad Muslim: America, the Cold War, and the Roots of Terror*. New York: Doubleday.

McMillan, Chris. 2015. "Changing Fantasies: Žižek and the Limits of Democracy." In *Žižek and Law*, edited by L. de Sutter, 60–79. London: Routledge.

Osman, Tarek. 2013. *Egypt on the Brink: From Nasser to the Muslim Brotherhood*. New Haven CT: Yale University Press.

Roccu, Roberto. 2013. "David Harvey in Tahrir Square: The Dispossessed, the Discontented and the Egyptian Revolution." *Third World Quarterly* 34 (3): 423–40.

Salem, Sara. 2013. "The Egyptian Military and the 2011 Revolution." *Jadaliyya*, September 6. http://www.jadaliyya.com/pages/index/14023/the-egyptian-military-and-the-2011 -revolution.

Shahin, Emad El-Din. 2012. "The Egyptian Revolution: The Power of Mass Mobilization and the Spirit of Tahrir Square." *Journal of the Middle East and Africa* 3, 46–69.

Telmissany, May. 2014. "The Utopian and Dystopian Functions of Tahrir Square." *Postcolonial Studies* 17 (1): 36–46.

Wells, Charles. 2014. *The Subject of Liberation: Žižek, Politics, Psychoanalysis*. London: Bloomsbury.

Wickham, Carrie R. 2013. *The Muslim Brotherhood: Evolution of an Islamist Movement*. Princeton NJ: Princeton University Press.

Žižek, Slavoj. 1989. *The Sublime Object of Ideology*. London: Verso.

———. 1999. *The Ticklish Subject: The Absent Centre of Political Ontology*. London: Verso.

———. 2004. *The Abyss of Freedom / Ages of the World*. Ann Arbor: University of Michigan Press.

———. 2006. *How to Read Lacan*. London: Granta.

———. 2008. *The Plague of Fantasies*. London: Verso.

———. 2011a. "Democracy Is the Enemy." *London Review of Books*, October 28. http://www.lrb.co.uk/blog/2011/10/28/slavoj-zizek/democracy-is-the-enemy/.

———. 2011b. "For Egypt, This Is the Miracle of Tahrir Square." *Guardian*, February 11. http://www.theguardian.com/global/2011/feb/10/egypt-miracle-tahrir-square.

———. 2011c. "Shoplifters of the World Unite." *London Review of Books*, August 19. http://www.lrb.co.uk/2011/08/19/slavoj-zizek/shoplifters-of-the-world-unite.

———. 2012. *The Year of Dreaming Dangerously*. London: Verso.

———. 2013. "Deaths on the Nile." *In These Times*, August 23. http://inthesetimes.com/article/15508/deaths_on_the_nile.

———. 2015. "The Need to Traverse the Fantasy." *In These Times*, December 28. http://inthesetimes.com/article/18722/Slavoj-Zizek-on-Syria-refugees-Eurocentrism-Western-Values-Lacan-Islam.

Epilogue
Affect and the Gl0bal Rise of Populism

Ilan Kapoor

The contributors and I were in the process of finishing the first drafts of our chapters for this book when two unexpected world events happened: Brexit and the election of Donald Trump. Pollsters, political elites, and the media had counted on "rational" voter behavior in each instance, predicting that most Britishers would see through the demagoguery of the "Leave" campaign and most Americans the vulgarity of Trump. Instead, the opposite happened: voting in both situations was marked by an "irrational," affective wave that pushed the Brexit and Trump campaigns over the edge. In the case of Trump, liberal Americans were shocked at his overt racism and misogyny, perceiving in his uncouth behavior (e.g., disrespect for the parents of a Muslim war hero, boasting about grabbing women's genitals) a fatal flaw that would cost him the election. But rather than hurting Trump, these may well have boosted his popularity. Žižek (2017) puts it this way: "[Liberals] missed how identification works: we as a rule identify with the other's weaknesses, not only or even not principally with the strengths, so the more Trump's limitations were mocked, the more ordinary people identified with him and perceived attacks on him as condescending attacks on themselves. The subliminal message of Trump's vulgarities to ordinary people was: "I am one of you!", while ordinary Trump supporters felt constantly humiliated by the liberal elite's patronizing attitude towards them." What political pundits and prognosticators ignored, in other words, is the dimension of the unconscious, which, as this book has shown, psychoanalysis is unique in being able to help decipher. For once again, it is affect—the deployment of unconscious desire and enjoyment—that is key to understanding the recent glObal rise of populist politics, of which the Brexit and Trump campaigns are the latest manifestations.

Indeed, the last decades have witnessed a populist wave across the world, from a surge in street protests in Venezuela, Greece, and Spain against neoliberalism to the rise of conservative populism (mostly anti-minority/immigrant) in the United States, Europe (Poland, Hungary, France, Holland, Austria, the UK), Turkey, and Asia (Narendra Modi's India, Rodrigo Duterte's Philippines). There are several structural factors explaining such a wave, principal among them the political economy factors described in many of the previous chapters (chapters 1, 2, 8, 11, 12): rising income and wealth inequalities within and among countries (which has led, at least in part, to increasing flows of migrant labor and refugees), growing state and personal debt, shrinking welfare safety nets, neoliberal austerity and privatization measures, the decline of organized labor, etc. These late global capitalist crises and contradictions have been accompanied by what some have called a "post-politics" (Rancière 1999, 108–10; Žižek 1999, 198–205): the waning of traditional party politics in favor of a mass-mediated politics of enlightened "experts" (pollsters, scientists, economists, celebrities, corporate billionaires). States have been increasingly subjected to neoliberal economic policymaking and the demands of the corporate sector, with a diminished say in socioeconomic matters, but an increasing presence in questions of security, surveillance, and control. The result is the rise of a depoliticized expert administration, a politics without politics.

While taking on distinctive forms in different parts of the world, the socioeconomic antagonisms of the late global capitalist order—rising economic insecurity, dispossession, social deprivation—have fueled alienation, anger, and resentment among people in many countries. This is particularly true for the likes of slum dwellers, migrants, poor inner-city neighborhoods, public housing residents, low-wage workers, unskilled/non-college-educated workers, the long-term unemployed, single-parent families, dispossessed farmers, marginalized immigrants—all of whom have experienced acute forms of socioeconomic insecurity and shrinking welfare benefits (Mishra

Ilan Kapoor

2017, 36ff.; Inglehart and Norris 2016). Their disaffection is rendered all the more intense in the face of the aforementioned growing institutionalized post-politics and lack of meaningful political debate, making it difficult to find avenues to articulate political demands. The overall result has been a breakdown of political consensus—the rise of antiestablishment rage, mistrust of political and economic elites, and suspicion of the media (yielding to rumormongering and alternative and "fake" news). The time has thus become ripe for the emergence of demagogues and political opportunists— Chávez, Trump, Farage, Modi, Erdogan, Duterte, Le Pen, Wilders, Golden Dawn, the Kaczyński brothers, etc. Each has successfully tapped into the generalized malaise, introducing political passion into an alienating and stale post-politics through paranoia, fear, xenophobia, racism, misogyny.

A Psychoanalysis of Populism

Populism is not, then, the antithesis of democracy as some liberals like to claim (e.g., Sartori 1962, 72–128; Lipset 1994, 97–130),[1] but its political symptom; it is a "shadow cast by democracy itself," as Canovan (1999, 3) argues or the "inherent shadowy double of institutionalized postpolitics," as Žižek (2006, 567) suggests. It is, in this sense, revealing of the underlying socioeconomic contradictions of liberal democratic capitalism, a kind of "return of the repressed." Populism may well be antiestablishment, aiming to disrupt the "normal" democratic order, but it is the product of the inherent processes of alienation, inequality, and insecurity wrought by this very order (Arditi 2005, 88).

But what precisely is populism? Ernesto Laclau sees it as the rhetorical act of naming "the people" over and against the establishment (e.g., economic and political elites, the mainstream media; Laclau 2005a, 73–74; see also Canovan 1999, 3). That is, in summoning or appealing to the demos, the signifier "people" serves as an affective bond, helping to rally the populace against an antagonistic frontier (i.e., politics as usual). The populist leader is able to successfully link what were previously disparate unsatisfied social demands into broader popular demands, thus effectively producing "the people." Often this is done with the help of slogans: Trump's "Make America

Great Again," Farage's "Take Our Country Back," Modi's "Good Days Are Coming," Erdogan's "Bring Strength to Turkey," Iglesias's "Yes, We Can," Duterte's "Change Is Coming," Chávez's "Fatherland, Socialism or Death." The slogans become master signifiers, broad enough to encapsulate a range of social demands, and ambiguous enough for a sweep of people to identify with them and become emotionally attached to them.

When the populist leader summons "the people," he is conjuring a fantasy that promises the "absent fullness of society" (Laclau 2005b, 226). Since the subjects of post-political society are marked by loss (social alienation, insecurity), he is pledging to recapture people's bygone enjoyment (*jouissance*) through an imagined fiction in which social antagonisms (allegedly) disappear. A political community is thus constituted libidinally as people identify with their leader's promise of social harmony (i.e., the prospect of greatness, strength, prosperity, autonomy, real change, etc.).

But as Glynos and Stavrakakis (2008, 262) emphasize, the populist fantasy not only attempts to cover over social antagonisms through the promise of fullness; it also identifies obstacles preventing the attainment of such fullness.[2] A populist discourse notably displaces people's sense of frustration and loss onto an external enemy and intruder (Muslims, Jews, terrorists, European Union bureaucrats, refugees, immigrants, international bankers, American imperialists) or a perverse and parasitic social element (single mothers, gays, drug dealers, welfare bums, inner-city African Americans, Gülenists, federal bureaucrats). Often, it is not about the Other preventing one from enjoying, but the Other stealing one's enjoyment (Žižek 1993, 203–6): immigrants who take away our jobs, refugees who harass our women, single mothers who abuse our welfare system, bureaucrats who claw back our freedoms. Populist discourse is therefore founded on stark us/them distinctions that exalt community pride and togetherness and revile betrayal, intrusion, and theft (of enjoyment). In attempting to create a unified "people," populist leaders prey on people's fears and paranoia, most frequently ceding to racism, homophobia, misogyny, xenophobia, and ethno-religious nationalism. Here, the tendency is to rely on rhetorical intemperance, invoking dangerous ideas (e.g., registries for Muslims,

Ilan Kapoor

expulsion of immigrants), inventing or exaggerating claims ("alternative facts"), resorting to censorship (e.g., blocking social media), or threatening dissenting journalists or academics. The character of debate thus frequently becomes one of increasing excess and hostility.

A notable feature of populist ideology is its ability to hold together a number of contradictions and ambiguities. For example, while the Other-as-enemy must be destroyed in order to restore social harmony, it can never really be annihilated since without an enemy, populism loses its force. It is not just that the "outside" or Other is constitutive of the "inside" or Self so that the production of an enemy is necessary to preserve the sanctity of "the people"; it is also that the construction and identification of an enemy is required to produce the people's affective bond (*jouissance*). Populism's enjoyment results, then, not from reaching, consuming, or in this case, eliminating the object, but from a constantly receding and ungraspable object—despite the outward vilification of the Other, there is an unfulfilled and unfulfillable desire for the Other. The same applies to populist ideology's often incongruous characterization of the Other: refugees are lazy, but they steal our jobs; Asians are workaholics, but they drain the welfare state; terrorists are wily and calculating, but they are also brainwashed religious fanatics. Again, these contradictions are evidence that *jouissance* is very much at work in populist fantasy: it is enjoyment that ensures that people can relish the fantasy while ignoring its contradictions. Absent such enjoyment, the contradictions would more easily stand out, weakening the hold and credibility of the fantasy.

It should also be noted that, for the most part, populism tends to be associated with the Right (e.g., Albertazzi and McDonnell 2008; Ionescu and Gellner 1970). This is likely because, since the early 1930s at least, it is the Right, more than the Left, that has been successful in mobilizing political passions and constructing collective forms of identification (e.g., right-wing nationalism in Hitler's Germany, Mussolini's Italy, Orbán's Hungary, Modi's India, Erdogan's Turkey). But Laclau, in particular, has been adamant in claiming that, because identification is a highly open process, populism is ideologically open-ended (2005b, 34). Popular rage is free-floating and can be redirected to the Left as much as to the Right. This is borne out in recent Left politics across the globe (e.g., Chávez's Venezuela, Spain's Podemos, Greece's Syriza) and is perhaps most striking in the recent U.S. elections, with both the Right (Trump) and the Left (Bernie Sanders) tapping into the same well of popular frustration.

Laclau tends to celebrate neo-populism (of the Left), believing it can help instill new passion into our increasingly fossilized post-political democracies. For his part, Žižek (2008, 264–333) is more circumspect and critical. It is not just that populist discourse, according to him, tends toward the excessive and can thus all too easily morph into authoritarianism and a cult of personality (e.g., Trump and Erdogan as much as Chávez or Perón); it is, more important, that such a discourse tends to be ideologically mystifying, refusing to confront social antagonisms directly: "for a populist, the cause of the troubles is ultimately never the system as such but the intruder who corrupted it . . . not a fatal flaw inscribed into the structure as such but an element that doesn't play its role within the structure" (Žižek 2006, 555). In other words, populist rage, while symptomatic of fundamental systemic problems in the global capitalist order, tends to be displaced onto the wrong targets—the big bad Brussels bureaucrats, refugees, immigrants, terrorism, U.S. imperialists, etc.— that is, symptoms, singular agents, and contingent enemies rather than structural contradictions (post-politics, inequalities wrought by capitalism, etc.).[3]

It is thus because populism veers toward ideological mystification and disavowal that Žižek argues against the populist temptation, even in its Left incarnations. The challenge, for him, is for the Left to tap into people's passions like populism does, but to transform people's fears, usually (mis) directed toward an external threat or enemy, into a more productive anxiety (see Žižek 2017). For unlike fear, anxiety makes us more aware of our own limitations, forcing us to confront not the symptoms but the causes of the problems we face.

Why Psychoanalysis Matters

The advent of neo-populism is thus further evidence of the need for psychoanalysis to better understand the contemporary glObal. To the extent

Ilan Kapoor

that the unconscious is integral to our symbolic world, as all the chapters in this book have claimed, then affect plays a primary role in the discursive construction of the glObal; socioeconomic, cultural, environmental, and political links are at the same time libidinal. And since the unconscious is the realm of excess and unpredictability, then the rational subject, the "objective" scientist, or "neutral" policymaking process is always guided by whimsical desire or irrational identification. This is why this book's contributors have claimed that the politics of debt and finance, while purporting to be based on technical and economic reasoning, are replete with extra-economic dimensions (racialized hierarchy, envy, humiliation); that addressing global warming has less to do with putting better environmental policies into place than confronting our unconscious attachments to the capitalist order; that varied global cultural phenomena—from the representations of war, women, and zombies to the architecture of the city—are never as straightforward as they seem but have to be looked at "awry" to glimpse their accompanying global circuits of anxiety and enjoyment; that far from being affect-free, Left or popular alternatives to neoliberalism and authoritarianism can often fail to face the Real of their own desire; and of course, that the advent of Trump or Modi is not simply about democracy gone wrong but about the manipulation of genuine popular loss and the displacement of socioeconomic frustration onto an external object.

The implication, therefore, is that the ideology of globalization today—whether it takes the form of neoliberal economic policy, media representation, or neo-populist politics—has to be prosecuted not just at the level of intellectual critique: it is not enough to deconstruct discourse, that is, identify its gaps, elisions, and exclusions. No, ideology critique has to happen at the level of affect as well (and perhaps especially). And here there are many questions to ask: What is the (or our) libidinal investment in capitalist globalization? How is one (or are we) seduced by such things as advertising, consumer goods, media images, urban architecture, political rhetoric, or charismatic leadership? To what extent are we projecting our desires, or displacing our own limitations, onto others? Is the problem being raised tackling the symptom or the cause? These are some of the key questions the contributors of this book have tried to answer, homing in on the unconscious desires around which ideology both coheres and stumbles. They are the type of questions that psychoanalysis is best equipped to tackle, since it alone is able to probe the Real of desire—the desire nested in ideology, but perhaps most important, our own desire, since it is easier to analyze the Other and so much more difficult to face up to our own complicities, excesses, contradictions, limitations. A psychoanalysis, like the ideology critique that it has inspired in this book, is made all the more arduous precisely by the psychic effort required to come to terms with our own libidinal investment and implication in the (glObal) ideological nexus.

Notes

1. Liberals such as Sartori and Lipset (see also Riker 2008) usually see populism as antithetical to (liberal) democracy because, according to them, the latter protects pluralism and individual rights, whereas the former sees the people as a homogenous whole. Yet they conveniently disregard how the market undermines socioeconomic rights and in so doing creates precisely the grounds for populism.

2. Glynos and Stavrakakis (2004; see also Stavrakakis 2007, 82ff.) take Laclau to task for inadequately spelling out the affective nature of populism, especially the dimensions of fantasy and enjoyment.

3. For Žižek (2006, 566), the ultimate problem with Laclau's championing of neo-populism is that it brackets the question of capital: the global capitalist system is accepted as a background to the emergence of populist movements. Capital, in this sense, determines the political options available. Thus, not only does populism tend to misdirect its rage by targeting symptoms and pseudo-concrete enemies, but the political options made available to it tend to exclude ones truly threatening to the System. Here, Žižek's critique rejoins the classical Marxist critique of populism (e.g., Lenin 2004) that populism may well be antiestablishment, but it does not address the key dimension of class exploitation.

Works Cited

Albertazzi, Daniele, and Duncan McDonnell. 2008. *Twenty-First Century Populism: The Spectre of Western European Democracy*. Basingstoke, UK: Palgrave Macmillan.

Arditi, Benjamin. 2005. "Populism as an Internal Periphery of Democratic Politics." In *Populism and the Mirror of Democracy*, edited by F. Panizza, 32–49. London: Verso.

Ilan Kapoor

Canovan, Margaret. 1999. "Trust the People! Populism and the Two Faces of Democracy." *Political Studies* 47 (1): 2–16.

Glynos, Jason, and Yannis Stavrakakis. 2004. "Encounters of the Real Kind: Sussing Out the Limits of Laclau's Embrace of Lacan." In *Laclau: A Critical Reader*, edited by Simon Critchley and Oliver Marchart, 201–16. London: Routledge.

———. 2008. "Lacan and Political Subjectivity: Fantasy and Enjoyment in Psychoanalysis and Political Theory." *Subjectivity* 24 (1): 256–74. DOI:10.1057/sub.2008.23.

Inglehart, Ronald, and Pippa Norris. 2016. "Trump, Brexit, and the Rise of Populism: Economic Have-Nots and Cultural Backlash." HKS Working Paper No. RWP16-026. SSRN (2818659). https://papers.ssrn.com/abstract=2818659.

Ionescu, Ghiţa, and Ernest Gellner, eds. 1970. *Populism: Its Meanings and National Characteristics*. London: Weidenfeld & Nicolson.

Laclau, Ernesto. 2005a. *On Populist Reason*. London: Verso.

———. 2005b. "Populism: What's in a Name?" In *Populism and the Mirror of Democracy*, edited by F. Panizza, 32–49. London: Verso. https://www.scribd.com/document/39427519/Populism-What-s-in-a-Name-Ernesto-Laclau-2005.

Lenin, Vladimir I. 2004. *The Development of Capitalism in Russia*. Honolulu: University Press of the Pacific.

Lipset, Seymour Martin. 1994. *Political Man: The Social Bases of Politics*. Baltimore: Johns Hopkins University Press.

Mishra, Pankaj. 2017. *Age of Anger: A History of the Present*. New York: Farrar, Straus and Giroux.

Rancière, Jacques. 1999. *Disagreement: Politics and Philosophy*. Minneapolis: University of Minnesota Press.

Riker, William Harrison. 2008. *Liberalism against Populism: A Confrontation between the Theory of Democracy and the Theory of Social Choice*. Long Grove IL: Waveland Press.

Sartori, Giovanni. 1962. *Democratic Theory*. Detroit: Wayne State University Press.

Stavrakakis, Yannis. 2007. *The Lacanian Left: Essays on Psychoanalysis and Politics*. Albany NY: SUNY Press.

Žižek, Slavoj. 1993. *Tarrying with the Negative: Kant, Hegel, and the Critique of Ideology*. Durham NC: Duke University Press.

———. 1999. *The Ticklish Subject: The Absent Centre of Political Ontology*. London: Verso.

———. 2006. "Against the Populist Temptation." *Critical Inquiry* 32 (3): 551–74. DOI: 10.1086/505378.

———. 2008. *In Defense of Lost Causes*. London: Verso.

———. 2017. "Donald Trump's Topsy-Turvy World." *Philosophical Salon*, January 16. http://thephilosophicalsalon.com/donald-trumps-topsy-turvy-world/.

Contributors

Dan Bousfield researches social movements, political protest, and critical political economy, with an emphasis on psychoanalysis, gender, technology, pedagogy, and resistance. He received his PhD from McMaster University in Hamilton, Ontario, in 2009. His current research deals with intersections between cybersecurity and indigeneity in Canadian Arctic security; queer sensibilities in Canadian foreign policy and practice; and the implications of speculative realism on framing contemporary critiques of capitalism. He has published articles in *American Review of Canadian Studies, International Studies Perspectives*, and *Historical Materialism*.

Nathan F. Bullock is a PhD candidate at Duke University in the Department of Art, Art History, and Visual Studies. His concentration is in the history and theory of architecture and urbanism. His dissertation and research focus on contemporary Singapore, the performance of citizenship, and feminist critiques of identity politics. He has spent time in Singapore as a Fulbright fellow and made subsequent trips for fieldwork.

Pieter de Vries is assistant professor at the Sociology of Change group at Wageningen University in the Netherlands. He has conducted research in Costa Rica (on state-peasant relations), Mexico (on local power), French Polynesia (on the socio-medical consequences of nuclear testing), Peru (on the cultural construction of community), and Brazil (on slum politics). His latest article on participatory planning in Recife, Brazil, was published in *Antipode* in 2016.

Robert Fletcher is associate professor in the Sociology of Development and Change group at Wageningen University in the Netherlands. He is the author of *Romancing the Wild: Cultural Dimensions of Ecotourism* (Duke University Press, 2014) and coeditor of *Nature™ Inc: Environmental Conservation in the Neoliberal Age* (University of Arizona Press, 2014).

Ilan Kapoor is a professor of critical development studies at the Faculty of Environmental Studies, York University, Toronto. He teaches in the area of global development and environmental politics, and his research focuses on postcolonial theory and politics, participatory development and democracy, and ideology critique (drawing on psychoanalytic Marxism). He is the author of *The Postcolonial Politics of Development* (Routledge, 2008) and *Celebrity Humanitarianism: The Ideology of Global Charity* (Routledge, 2013). He is currently writing a book on *Psychoanalysis and International Development*. In 2014 he edited a subtheme of *Third World Quarterly* on "Psychoanalysis and Development."

Eleanor MacDonald is associate professor, Department of Political Studies, Queen's University at Kingston, Ontario. She is cross-appointed to the Department of Gender Studies and the Graduate Program in Cultural Studies. Her teaching and research are in the field of contemporary political theory, and she is working on themes of property and identity using the analytical tools of feminist, psychoanalytic, critical, and Marxist theories.

Adam Okulicz-Kozaryn, born in Poland in 1979, is assistant professor of public policy at Rutgers University, Camden Campus. He earned his PhD from the University of Texas at Dallas in 2008. His work has covered a variety of topics: income inequality, consumption, preferences for redistribution, urban and rural issues, cultural economics, values, religion, and especially happiness. One of his favorite topics is psychoanalysis.

Lucas Pohl is a PhD candidate at the Department of Human Geography in Frankfurt. His PhD project is on vacancy and abandonment of *Ghost-scrapers*, focusing on the consequences of urban vertical ruins. He is interested in post-Marxist, post-structuralist, and psychoanalytic theories for the study of urban politics. His recent work relating to psychoanalytic thought includes "Imaginary Politics of the Branded City: Right-Wing Terrorism as a Mediated Object of Stigmatization," in *Negative Neighbourhood Reputation and Place Attachment: The Production and Contestation of Territorial Stigma*, edited by Paul Kirkness and Andreas Tijé-Dra (Routledge, forthcoming).

Chizu Sato is lecturer and researcher in Sociology of Consumption and Households at Wageningen University in the Netherlands. She received her doctorate and completed a graduate certificate in advanced feminist studies from the University of Massachusetts Amherst. Her research interests lie in the areas of transnational feminist studies, Marxian theory, and international development studies with a focus on the intersections of women, empowerment, and development. Her recent work has appeared in *Rethinking Marxism, International Political Sociology, Gender, Place and Culture*, and *Women's Studies International Forum*.

Anna J. Secor is professor of geography and the Hajja Razia Sharif Sheikh Islamic Studies Professor at the University of Kentucky. Her research focuses on theories of space, politics, and subjectivity and has been funded by the National Science Foundation and the National Geographic Society. She is author of over thirty articles and book chapters, an editor of the *Wiley-Blackwell Companion to Political Geography* (2015), and an editor of the journal *Cultural Geographies* (Sage).

Maureen Sioh is associate professor in the Department of Geography at DePaul University. She trained as a hydrologist and worked in East Asia and with First Nations communities in Canada on erosion and pollution before she returned to academia. She currently works on anxiety and financial decision making in emerging economies.

Rubia R. Valente, born in Brazil in 1985, is a research associate at the University of Texas at Dallas, where she obtained her master's (2009) and PhD (2013). Some of her research interests include social and economic development; race relations; the education system; affirmative action; inequalities due to race, class, and gender; urban versus rural development; poverty; human rights; religion; and life satisfaction.

Japhy Wilson is lecturer in International Political Economy at the University of Manchester. His research concerns the intertwining of space, power, and ideology in the political economy of capitalist development. He has published in journals in the fields of human geography, political economy, and development studies. He is the author of *Jeffrey Sachs: The Strange Case of Dr Shock and Mr Aid* (Verso, 2014) and coeditor with Erik Swyngedouw of *The Post-Political and Its Discontents: Spaces of Depoliticization, Spectres of Radical Politics* (Edinburgh University Press, 2014).

Index

Adorno, Theodor, 70–71, 87–88, 90

affect, xvi, 283

Agamben, Giorgio, 158, 250

anamorphosis, xiv, 164–66

anxiety, x, xii, xx, xxv, xxx, 30, 32–35, 37, 41, 57–58, 97–99, 103–6, 111–13, 125, 177, 261, 288–89

architecture, xiii–xiv, xx–xxi, xxiii, xxx, 142, 144–46, 152–60, 161nn7–8, 161n10, 189–206, 289

Arthur, Chris, 168

Asian values, x, 26–27, 29–33, 40–42

Badiou, Alain, xxxin2

Ballard, J. G., xiii, 144, 149–51, 155–56; *High-Rise*, 158, 161n10

Barad, Karen, 98–99

Benjamin, Walter, 92n8, 102, 113, 177–78, 279n2

Bersani, Leo, 82

Bichler, Shimshon, 16–17

Bingham-Hall, Patrick, 198

biopolitics, xv, 234–35, 242, 250–54

Blum, Virginia, 98

Bollas, Christopher, 27, 32, 34, 36, 38, 40

Bononno, Robert, 145

Brazil, xv, xxv, xxix, 129, 134, 219, 233–38, 242–43, 251–52

Brearley, Michael, 63

Brexit, xvi, xx, xxv, 283–84

Butler, Judith, 190, 202

Cairo, xxxi, 267

Calder Williams, Evan, 170–71

Canclini, Néstor, xxiii

capitalism, ix–xii, xiv–xvi, xx–xxi, xxiii, xxv–xxxvi, xxxin1, 3, 5–9, 12–14, 16–22; "black hole," 166–69; Cambridge controversy and, 3, 7–8, 21; capital and, ix–x, xiv, xxii, xxiv–xxv, 4–8, 14–21; differential accumulation and, 17; faith and, 3–4, 6–9, 12–16, 18, 20–22, 174–77; fantasy and, 3–4, 9–13, 18–22; Real of Capital and, xiv, xxiii, xxxi, 12, 63, 65, 171–72, 174, 176–77, 179–80, 239, 273; transnational capitalist class and, xiv, 197

Carter, Kevin, 101–2

castration, xv, xxix, 82, 104, 180, 182, 213, 216, 227n9, 233–35, 242, 252, 259

Chang, T. C., 198

city, the, xiv–xv, xxi, xxiii, xxx, 63, 142, 149–50, 158, 190, 192, 196–200, 202, 209–26, 234–35, 242–52, 289; as "dream factory," 211–13

climate change, xi, xx, xxix, 49–65; "magical thinking" and, 49, 53–54, 59, 63

Coleman, Nathaniel, 152

environment, x–xi, xii, xxiv, xix, xxii, 17, 48–65, 70, 72–73, 79, 82, 122, 155, 160n1, 191, 200, 204–6, 228n13, 236, 245–46, 289; psychoanalysis and, 56–59, 70–73

Erdogan, Recep Tayyip, xvi, xx, 99, 285–88

Europe, ix, xxiv–xxv, xxvii, 3–22, 65, 99–100, 111–12, 142, 201, 243, 284, 286; debt crisis, xxiv, 6, 11, 13; Eurozone and, 6, 9, 21; financial crisis and, xxiv, 3–22; southern European countries and, xxiv, 10

European Central Bank (ECB), ix, 9, 10–11, 13, 15, 20–21, 25

Evans, Dylan, 259

Fanon, Frantz, xxvii

fantasy, ix, xii–xiii, xiii–xiv, xx, xxiv, xxvi, xxx, 3–8, 10–11, 18–22, 50, 54, 56–57, 59, 60, 63–64, 82, 86, 97–98, 106–7, 111, 119, 124–26, 148, 154, 174, 176, 178–82, 189–90, 204, 212, 227n6, 238–41, 255, 259, 261, 286–87, 290n2; capitalism and, 3–4, 9–13, 18–22, 178–82; traversing the, 50, 63–64, 179–80, 182. See also ideology

Fassin, Didier, 103

feminist literacy practices, xiii, xxx, 117–19, 134–36

Ferguson, Charles, 8

fetish/ism, xiv, xx, xxiii, 131, 133, 176, 213–14, 225, 239–40, 259; commodity, 5, 177, 179, 215; fetishistic disavowal and, 239–41, 253, 262–63, 274; size, xiv, 209–26, 213–16, 225–26, 227n7

Fine, Bernard, 79, 91n4, 169

Foucault, Michel, 54, 136n1, 250

Frankfurt, xiii, xxix, xxxi, 142–43, 158

Frankfurt School, 70, 88, 142

Freud, Sigmund, xx–xxi, xxvii–xxviii, 25, 29–31, 37, 40, 43, 72–81, 97–98, 147, 164, 173, 179, 182, 203, 213, 226, 228n14, 257–58, 260, 279n1

Fromm, Erich, 227n11

Fukuyama, Francis, 12, 40

Gay, Peter, 30–31, 40

Germany, 9, 11, 15, 17, 111, 142, 238, 287

Gibson-Graham, J. K., 130, 136n3

Gill, Stephen, 14–15

Glaeser, Edward, 211

glObal, ix, xvi, xix–xxvii, xxix–xxxi, 21, 28, 42, 48, 52, 63, 70, 72, 73, 81, 91, 97–100, 106, 112–13, 131, 135, 157, 158, 168–69, 173–74, 176, 182, 198, 200, 204, 223, 237–38, 274–75, 283–84, 288–90; versus globalization, xix, xxii; hole and, xix, xxii–xxvii; Real and, xix–xx, xxii. See also globalization

global capitalism. See capitalism

globalization, ix–x, xix–xx, xxii–xxvi, xxviii, xxix–xxx, xxxin1, 25, 27–28, 33–35, 37, 40, 89, 275–76, 289; borderless world and, xxii; colonial history and, xxiv; discourse of, xxii, xxiv; free trade and, xxii; Hyperglobalist theory of, xxii; ideology critique and, xxvi, 289; imperialism and, xxiv; Marxist versus psychoanalytic approach to, xxxin1; Real and, xix–xx; resistance to, xxx; skeptics and, xxiv; transformationalists and, xxiv. See also glObal

global South, xxv, 116–17, 120–21, 123, 128, 136n7

Malaysia, 25, 29, 36–37, 39, 41–42, 190
Mamdani, Mahmood, 37
Marcuse, Herbert, 227n3
Marx, Karl, 4–6, 19, 70–71, 90, 157, 168, 171–73, 177–78, 220; commodity fetishism and, 5, 177, 179, 215; primitive accumulation and, 5, 14, 19
masculinity, 14, 74–75, 203–4
masochism, xii, xxx, 97, 106, 111, 113, 220, 224
Massumi, Brian, 102, 112
McGowan, Todd, xxviii
McNally, David, 170–72
melancholia, xv, 50, 59–60, 73, 83, 202, 223, 233–35, 239–42, 252–54; as castration, 234, 242, 252
migration, xxii–xxiii, xxiv–xxv, 99, 101; obscene enjoyment and, xxv, 97. See also refugees
mirror stage, xiv, 191–92
Mishan, Joseph, 56, 63
Modi, Narendra, xvi, 279n6, 285, 289
Mohamed, Batool, xii, 97, 107–11
Mohammad, Mahathir, 37
Moore, Burness, 79, 91n4
Moore, Sarah, 57
Moser, Caroline, 120
Mouffe, Chantal, 118
mourning, 49–50, 59–60, 63–65
Muslim Brotherhood, xvi, 257, 265–66, 268, 270–72, 274–77

Nandy, Ashis, xxviii
narcissism, xi, xv, 29–30, 40, 73, 77–81, 85, 89, 91n3; narcissistic injury and, x, 27–29, 31–35, 42. See also desire: narcissistic; rage: narcissistic

nationalism, xxii, 30, 286–87. See also populism
Negri, Antonio, 250
neoliberalism, xv, xx, xxii, xxiv, xxvi, xxxin1, 14, 20, 28, 34, 36, 49, 52–56, 116–17, 132, 134, 165, 169–75, 177–78, 180–82, 233–34, 238, 249, 251, 254, 255, 266–67, 273–74, 276, 279n3, 284, 289; "neoliberal gothic" and, 169–74. See also capitalism
neo-populism. See populism
Nitzan, Jonathan, 8, 16–17

O'Connor, Brian, 88
Oedipus complex, xxvii, 74, 76–77, 80, 82, 85, 259
oil, xi, 53, 57, 61–62, 64
O'Neill, Brendan, 101, 103

Papandreou, George, 13
Park, Robert E., 209
Peck, Jamie, 169
perversion, xv–xvi, xx, xxix, 58, 60–61, 63, 78–79, 131; politics of, xvi, 257–78
Phillips, Adam, 82
Pile, Steve, 189, 223
political economy, xi–xii, xvi, xx, xxvi, xxx–xxxi, xxxin1, 4, 6, 70, 170, 178, 272–74, 284; alternative, xi–xii, xxvi, xxx, 70–91
popular movements, xv–xvi, xx–xxi, xxv, xxvii, xxix, xxxi, 54, 65, 257–78; in Brazil, xv, xxix, 233–55; in Egypt, xvi, xxvii, xxix
populism, xvi, xx, 6, 269, 283–88
Postone, Moishe, 171
Proudfoot, Jesse, 144, 161n6

Syria, xii, xxv, 97–113; war and, xii, xxv, 100, 104

Tadiar, Neferti, 189–90
Tahrir Square, xv–xvi, 257, 265–78
Thoreau, Henry David, 216, 218, 221
Ticktin, Miriam, 103
Tomšič, Samo, 179, 181
transnational corporations, xxii, 18, 61, 195, 202, 214
trauma, xxi, xxviii–xxix, 34–35, 182, 258–59, 279n2
Trump, Donald, xvi, xx, xxv, 35, 216, 273, 279n6, 283–85, 288–89
Tyler, Imogen, 82

unconscious, the, ix–xii, xiv, xix–xxi, xxiii, xxvi–xxvii, xxix–xxxi, xxxin1, 28, 34, 42, 48, 50, 55, 58, 60, 64–65, 72–73, 83–84, 86, 91, 92n5, 113n1, 133, 146, 166, 177–79, 209–26, 235, 254, 261–62, 264, 276, 283–84, 289–90; externalization and materialization of, xx–xxi, xxix–xx; Real and xix–xxi. *See also* Real
United States, xxv, 35, 41–42, 53, 136n6, 201, 215, 219, 221–22, 272, 284
universalism, xxviii–xxix; negative universalism and, xxviii–xxix; Real and, xxviii–xxix

urbanization, xv, xxix, 166, 198, 210–11, 221, 225–26, 227n6, 228n13
Ut, Nick, 100–101

Varoufakis, Yanis, 25, 166
Vucetic, Srdjan, 6–7

Walmart, 122–23, 126–27, 129
Weber, Max, 174, 177
Weintrobe, Sally, 57–58, 61
Wei Wei, Ai, 104–5
Wells, Charles, 265
women, xii–xiii, xxii, xxv, xxvii, 75–76, 78, 85, 89, 112, 116–36, 211, 258, 268, 279n6, 283, 286, 289; gender politics and, xx–xxi, 122, 132, 202, 260; patriarchy and, xxix, 189–91, 204, 226
World Bank, 25–26, 36, 38, 42, 120–21, 126, 129, 266, 272; James Wolfensohn and, 121; Robert B. Zoellick and, 120–21, 132

Yap, Erica, 199

Žižek, Slavoj, xi, xx, xxv–xxvi, xxix, xxxin2, 6, 10, 18, 48, 56, 59–60, 62, 64, 147, 149, 158, 164–65, 168, 171, 173, 177, 179, 227n9, 240, 253, 257, 260–65, 269, 274, 277–78, 283, 285, 288, 290n3

In the Cultural Geographies + Rewriting the Earth series

Topoi/Graphein: Mapping the Middle in Spatial Thought
Christian Abrahamsson
Foreword by Gunnar Olsson

Psychoanalysis and the GlObal
Edited and with an introduction by Ilan Kapoor

To order or obtain more information on these or other
University of Nebraska Press titles, visit nebraskapress.unl.edu.

Lightning Source UK Ltd.
Milton Keynes UK
UKHW01n0035260718
326317UK00007B/270/P